The Sea Survivors

THE SEA SURVIVORS

Edited by
Denys Val Baker

A COMET BOOK

A Comet Book
Published in 1986
by the Paperback Division of
W.H. Allen & Co. PLC
44 Hill Street, London W1X 8LB

First published in Great Britain by W.H. Allen, 1979

Printed and bound in Great Britain by
Biddles Ltd, Guildford and King's Lynn

ISBN 0 86379 101 8

CONTENTS

ACKNOWLEDGEMENTS

'All The Lies About Cape Horn Are True' by Rosie Swale is from *Children of Cape Horn* (Elek Books, 1974); 'Pitchpoled' by Miles Smeeton is from *Once Is Enough* (Hart-Davis, 1966); 'Hurricane Alma' by John Ridgway is from *A Fighting Chance* (Hamlyn, 1966); 'Last Voyage' by Ann Davison is from *Last Voyage* (Peter Davies, 1951); 'Knockdown' by Sir Francis Chichester is from *The Romantic Challenge* (Cassell, 1971); 'Force Nine! – What Will It Be Like?' by Frank Dye is from *Ocean Cruising Wayfarer* (David and Charles, 1977); 'Dismasted' by Hammond Innes is from *Seas and Islands* (Collins, 1966); 'Beset By Ice' by David Lewis is from *Ice Bird* (Collins, 1975); 'The Homecoming' by Robin Knox-Johnston is from *A World of My Own* (Cassell, 1969); 'Come Hell or High Water' by Clare Francis is from *Come Hell or High Water* (Pelham, 1977); 'The View From Seaward Was Unsettling' by John Riding is from *Sea Egg Again* (Pelham, 1972); and 'Rescued!' by Dougal Robertson is from *Survive The Savage Sea* (Elek Books, 1973).

PREFACE

To compile a collection of true exploits, to select particular men and women who have risked everything against the sea and its moods is a formidable task.

It is not so much a question of whom to include, but which story must be laid aside. For the oceans of the world are as varied as the men and women, who from choice or necessity pit their resources against them: the ordinary merchant seaman, the deep-sea fisherman, salvage-masters, and the crews of a hundred classes of vessel from lifeboat to herring drifter. Each seafarer has a story to tell, if you can drag it from him, and nobody but a fool can fail to be impressed by their ally and enemy, the ocean.

It has been said, often enough, that we in the British Isles have the sea in our blood. Perhaps not surprising when you consider it is impossible to be born more than eighty miles from salt water. But our links are far stronger than that.

Down through the years, men have left harbours for countless reasons. To face an Armada, to follow Nelson to the Nile. To fish or extend trade and keep commerce flowing in every direction.

Unlike some nations we have often accepted the sea as a friend rather than a barrier of final defeat. The exhausted British 'Tommy', slogging through France, alone or with a handful of bewildered companions, kept the name of Dunkirk fixed firmly in his mind. *Just get me to Dunkirk and somehow I'll get home.* It seemed the only natural thing to do. In the Second World War there were too many times when men were forced to trust their fate and their lives to the mercy of the sea.

The sea is rarely absent from our daily way of life. The nautical and sailing terms of the old square-riggers are part of our language, and our heritage. So too, the same sense of risk and daring is very much alive today.

It is hard to pin-point the actual moment when a man or a woman decides to take up the challenge. *Because it was there* is too trite, too simple. Perhaps it is desperation, the need to be completely free and self-dependent, if only for a small proportion of a lifetime. To escape.

It is also part of a dream. We are so used to seeing television films of brave young men in their space capsules or treading gingerly on the moon. More to the point we have seen the vast armies of experts and technicians who are required to keep them up there and later to land them safely. But it is all too overwhelming, too remote for the average person to digest. There seems to be no one person's decision, no precious moment when an ordinary man or woman can assess the margin between survival or death. If you ask someone the name of every man who has perhaps walked in space, or the order in which the various capsules landed on the moon, you will very likely receive a blank stare.

But mention names like Chichester or Knox-Johnston, Davison or Swale, and within seconds you see the eyes come alight. In harbours or at the various boat shows you can see that same, dreamy, faraway look. *One day I shall get a boat for myself and sail around the world. Or somewhere.* It is very reassuring to read of the people who have actually done it, and have provided more dreams for the rest of us.

What I find particularly interesting is the way in which seafaring people, and especially the lone-sailors, describe *their* ocean, its characteristics and passions. There is always something fresh and new, and despite the fact that you may have sailed across the same areas several times yourself, you will find novelty in each description.

A mild, empty morning, the sea stretching away to nowhere on every hand. Perhaps an early mist which leaves no division between sea and sky. An unexpected chill in the bones which can tell the experienced seaman, better than any glass, that hell is about to break loose around him. When you try to think back, to reassemble the order of events in a storm, *your* storm, you recall mostly a sense of hopelessness, but also of the need to be doing something. You were dazed and breathless. The world went mad about you, there was momentary darkness as a wave reared higher and higher beneath the stern so that you felt that the hull must be driven helplessly into the depths.

There were curling crests, some pure white, others jagged and yellow like the jaws they really were.

And finally, when the storm cleared, what did you feel? If you are a fool you would have felt a sense of victory, that you had won and would never be afraid again.

If you are wise, you would have accepted your survival as a truce, the ocean's act of charity, and no more.

Even after reading this collection of exploits, I am still undecided as to which one holds the greatest challenge. The lone-sailor, with only his courage and skill to sustain him? Or the one who takes his whole family with him? The latter must have the greater responsibility, but nevertheless must find comfort in their companionship no matter how hard the conditions.

And what of the oarsmen? Surely to row an open boat across the Atlantic, an ocean well known and feared for its conquests and savagery must be the greatest challenge of all. The strength of a man's arms and an iron self-discipline are vital: it is no game for amateurs.

When you stop to think of all the vessels large and small which have fallen victim to the Atlantic, from clipper to ocean liner, from trawler to nuclear submarine you must marvel at the odds.

John Ridgway with his companion Chay Blyth, had a soldier's discipline, and with it an additional strength of coolness, the ability to assess each threatening situation when most people would have lost their heads. But all these stories are moulded into one lasting adventure, the start of which is not known, and which has no end in sight.

John Paul Jones summed it up very well when he wrote, 'It seems to be a law inflexible and inexorable that he who will not risk cannot win.' With such men and women as described here, I think we have little to fear on that score.

Douglas Reeman

EDITOR'S INTRODUCTION

The sea is both a great leveller and a formidable summit: it can appal and yet it can inspire. In a world of increasing standardisation and mediocrity the sea remains one of the world's great imponderables – untamed, unpredictable, unknown. Perhaps it is hardly surprising that so many yachtsmen and women have been drawn to face what the late Sir Francis Chichester called 'the romantic challenge' – nor that in most cases they have chosen to do so alone, entirely dependent on their own initiative. The sea then becomes, indeed, the moment of truth:

'The *Äg* had now no sails up and was alternatively wallowing and being suddenly smashed in smothering rushes between waves which spent their energy in furious broadsides and quartering explosions of fearful wildness. Visibility was mainly limited to a few yards with intermittent glimpses of bewildering confusion. Hovering between black and grey, large tumbling monsters thundered towards *Äg* from all directions, their crumbling, livid crests whipped mercilessly into shattered spray needles with the impact of bullets. These incredible leaping mountains of watery destruction had several times tried their damndest to obliterate my tiny craft. All orientation was lost as the stupendous power, speed and impact of the massive careering seas found obstruction in their path, and after the first stunning smash and roll as wave met hull the indescribable thrust and carry forward until the monster collapsed, sank ... then with renewed energy heaved itself aloft for a further terrible surge. *Äg* was at times completely submerged and on her side, at others she was pounded clear of the sea to land with a heart-stopping plunge, her mast smacking the writhing grey ocean – then the sickeningly slow rise to a more preferable angle. Master of this turmoil was the impersonal black wind screaming through the rigging....'

That seemingly somewhat lurid description by John Riding, author of *The Voyage of the Sea Egg*, is in fact no exaggeration at all, as anyone who has ventured across the world's great oceans will readily agree. Each of our other contributors has written of similar alarming experiences when encountering rough seas, perhaps gales and storms or even hurricanes. But there are many other kinds of confrontation to be faced as well:

'I had just dozed off when I heard shouts from Chay. "Get up quickly and put your harness on. We could be overturned . . ." I crawled out and asked him what was the matter.

' "Look at these," he said, pointing to two huge whales in the water outlined by the moonlight. They were just about the biggest we had seen since we started, and were a magnificent, frightening sight as they cruised first one way and then the other. Suddenly one of them came towards us like a submarine just below the surface. You could see the top of his huge black head and his massive tail swishing about forty feet behind. It came closer to us, and we both just sat there, watching them, patiently waiting for our boat to rise and – we hoped – slide off its massive back. But twenty feet away it turned swiftly and joined its partner, which was blowing like a steam gusher a couple of hundred yards away. . . . It was an unnerving ordeal.'

That is from among the many dramatic memories of John Ridgway, who with Chay Blyth rowed *English Rose III* across the Atlantic – an example of a handful of sailors who *chose* life in an open boat on a great ocean. Sometimes, alas, the sea does the choosing for you, as Dougal Robertson found when he and his family were sunk in the Pacific and had to exist for many weeks in a small inflatable. Under such conditions there are yet different problems to be faced:

'We had decided to use the sail to collect water instead of the rubber sheet, to see if we could collect a supply of water that didn't taste of rubber. The sail was not exactly impervious to water but it held it long enough to allow it to be collected. The raindrops grew in size and intensity and the main curtain of rain now almost upon us, and we eagerly sipped at the puddles gathering in the sail to test for salinity. The sail was clear first and as the main weight of rain started to cross us, the welcome sound of water pouring into tins was music to our ears. I reached for the second can and Robin was filling the jar when, as suddenly as it had started, the heavy downpour fell to a sparse patter of drops; we gazed blankly at the retreating curtain of rain, churning the water only a few hundred yards distant, but moving faster away from us than we could ever hope to chase it. Desperately we scooped the remaining drops into the cans, nearly three pints gathered but one of these, from the rubber bow canopy, brackish and unpalatable. After half an hour we silently folded the sail into the stern and slumped back into our places.'

Fortunately life at sea is not all melodramatics. There are sunny times, calm times, indeed times of near ecstasy – as Dr David Lewis, making the first single-handed voyage to Antarctica in his sloop *Ice Bird*, discovered:

'Now I really did appreciate the magnificent panorama – sixty miles of ice cap and glacier topped by serrated summits two miles high . . . The Anvers snowfields appeared, for all the world like level sheetings of fog, filling and hiding the valleys, above which soared the lofty summits, culminating in 9,000 foot Mount Français, the highest point of the island. I sat in the cockpit choked with emotion. Alongside parties of penguins called "ark, ark" as they porpoised out of the water, landing with a succession of little plops. I was still gazing out upon the scene when the light began to fade with evening. The sky above Anvers was a pastel green and the jagged Graham Coast ranges farther southward turned pale gold. A waning moon hung over the empty land. The ice cliffs of the great bergs turned from blue to mauve to violet and deep purple . . .'

Above all when you are far out at sea, completely cut off from the rest of the world, you come to appreciate profoundly the things in life that really matter. I do not think I could put it more simply and touchingly than our very first contributor, Rosie Swale, as with her husband and young children, she found herself approaching Cape Horn:

'I lay quietly listening to *Anneliese* surfing down these extraordinary seas. You realised that this place which was your home, your boat, the children's nursery, the place where you worked – was now nothing but a box, a shoebox which seemed to spend half its time mountaineering. I caught a glimpse of Colin's orange oilskins through the tiny back windows and I heard his wild singing – and felt a sudden surge of happiness. I wrote in the log: "The thing which keeps us going on this journey is trust. We have to trust *Anneliese* and the biggest thing, of course, is that Colin and I trust each other. After all we hand over the fate of the whole family into each other's keeping for six hours at a time. This trust is something which goes deeper than love. It is one of the things which makes this voyage worthwhile."'

This book – presenting a dozen accounts of how a combination of courage, faith, skill and some kind of indefinable luck has enabled intrepid voyagers to fight their way through, the sea survivors indeed – is one I have wanted to put together for many years, and is very much a labour of love. It is not, I think, the sort of book which could be handled by a landlubber – in order to truly understand what going to sea means you simply have to be a sea-goer. Like most of the contributors to this book I began dreaming my sea dreams a long time ago. Fifteen years back we acquired a sturdy old MFV *Sanu* in which our family have cruised to many places – Sweden, Denmark, Germany, France, Spain, Portugal, Italy, Greece and Turkey. Inevitably we encountered the sea in all its moods, ranging from sunny calms off the South of France to raging gales in the English Channel, from Geta canal cruising in Sweden to force-nine batterings on the West Coast of Scotland, from an unexpectedly tranquil crossing of the Bay of Biscay to an absolutely terrifying encounter with a cyclone in the dreaded Gulf of Lyons. On more than one occasion, with our pumps broken down we have been reduced to chain gangs bailing out overfull bilges. We have even sunk, at Tresco on the Scilly Isles and at Bilbao, Spain – and on both occasions been resurrected. We, too, have survived ... thank goodness.

And that is, essentially, the hub of this volume: it is tales told of the sea by a very variegated group of contributors who are all linked by one common experience – to use Dougal Robertson's expressive title, they have 'survived the savage sea'. Naturally my contents list has had to be an arbitrary one and I am sure there are other names which would equally merit inclusion. One I would like to have included is that of Donald Crowhurst, posthumous author of a rescued logbook which provides a truly traumatic account of what can happen to a man alone at sea – but he, poor fellow, was not a survivor.

The sea, as I said at the beginning of this introduction, brings for us all, sooner or later, our moment of truth. Here then are some personal testimonials – from some very brave men and women – which I hope may entertain and instruct, and perhaps make us more aware that, like the sea, life has profound and seemingly endless depths.

Denys Val Baker

I

Rosie Swale

The saga of the Swale family at sea has been entertainingly told by Rosie Swale in two best-selling books, *Rosie Darling* and *Children of Cape Horn.* Obviously a resourceful young lady, as well as a brave one, Rosie lived an adventurous enough life when single – surviving the inevitable financial and sexual problems of living alone in London and going on to achieve the status of a roving reporter for the national newspaper, the *Sunday People*, including a fascinating job of covering events in Russia. But it was when she met her future husband, Colin, that the real adventures began, culminating in what many people regarded as a foolhardy plan to embark on a 26,000 mile voyage round the world in a catamaran, *Anneliese.*

'I wouldn't advise you to try it,' said a reporter from *Yachts and Yachting* after accompanying the Swales on one of their first nautical outings down the Solent – and he was referring merely to a projected 200-mile trip to Ireland! Nevertheless, Colin and Rosie confounded all their critics by accomplishing their great adventure – and what's more, acquiring a family of two young children literally on the way. As might be expected there are plenty of dramatic episodes in both of Rosie Swale's lively books, but round the world sailing covers a variety of moods. Here, in this extract from *Children of Cape Horn*, Rosie Swale vividly recaptures the growing mood of excitement as in their tiny craft the family approach that dreaded monster of all mariners' dreams, Cape Horn itself....

ALL THE LIES ABOUT CAPE HORN ARE TRUE

Rosie Swale

The dark monster down at the tip of South America was luring us on. There was no going back now, nor any wish to, as *Anneliese* scythed down into the Shrieking Fifties. On the 28th of January it was a glorious day with cold bright sunshine, sparkling sea, white clouds. In this ocean where it was usually overcast grey with a low leaden cloud ceiling, the sudden open feeling was startling.

We were about 6,000 miles from Sydney now; 37 days since we saw any land. The boat was well – so were the children. Each day they still played happily and behaved as though sailing through the stormy Southern Ocean was just part of ordinary everyday life for toddlers. So far, it had not been an ordeal for them. I think they were happy as long as they were with us.

I logged:

With the Horn just 1,200 miles away now, we are bracing ourselves for the worst in the next ten days. But Eve and Jim's greatest concern is still 'Bites', 'Toys', 'Supper', 'NILK PLEASE!'

It was an enormous comfort as well as a responsibility having the children with us, for as Colin put it: 'At least you don't worry about them if they are close to you!' We often worried about our friends far away in England, and hoped they were all right.

It was time to go on watch. Oh dear! The damp down sleeping bag seemed immensely luxurious. Even the knobbly clip of the safety harness sticking into my back wasn't any real encouragement to get up. It was bitterly cold. Objectively I knew it was reasonable to have no heating in the boat. It made it easier to put up with the freezing wind outside. Also, of course, we just didn't have any heater. But there was nothing to tempt one out of bed all the same.

Eve, wearing layers and layers of underclothes, two of Colin's sweaters – and her poncho on top, grinned at me over her partition wall as I searched for my clothes. Colin said it was amusing that when you prepared to go on watch these days you took more trouble getting dressed than for the most important date on land!

I took the safety harness, which I wore all the time now, off temporarily and pulled on two thick Dunlop vests. Then I drew two pink woolly stockings up to the top of my legs – and got a whistle from Colin who was peering in through the small back window to look at the inside compass. The next thing to get on was the lovely warm, woven, cotton track-suit, also a wonderful present from Dunlop, and a thick sea jersey, and a half-inflated life jacket. Then I searched for a dry place on the floor and began the adventure of getting into my Evett Antarctic Sledging suit. It was a beautifully cut garment, light and unbelievably warm, with double sleeves and foam lining all through the inside. There was just one thing you couldn't do while wearing this suit – and I was always having to have freezing strip-teases half way through my watch!

Next I put on my light wet weather gear, another example of the thoughtfulness of Dunlop; and then on top of this I dragged on my heavy orange Marlin foul weather clothing, with trousers up to the armpits and a three-quarter-length coat. Then it was time to put the safety harness back on, with jack knife on a lanyard tied onto the side, so that I could cut myself out of trouble if need be. The next job was to rub Johnson's Baby Oil on my face so that the wind wouldn't chafe it; and onto my hair so that it would not tangle too badly. Then it was time to shake all Jimmy's toys out of my seaboots and pull them on. The last two items were my neoprene hood and gloves. These were really diving gear. They kept the head and hands extremely warm even when soggy. The only bad moments were when you had to take the rather clumsy-shaped gloves off to undo freezing shackles on the foredeck.

At last, after nearly half an hour spent getting into my standard gear, I was nearly ready to go outside – if I could get through the door! I thought enviously of the wife who could welcome her husband home with lovely shiny combed hair and wearing a pretty dress – poor Colin.

He had pumped out the bilges and had changed an engine hose on his watch, and Eve's sleeping bag was setting from the line like a mizzen staysail – getting its last airing before the Horn. Colin had also reduced the crew's mortality rate by fitting eyelets to tie up the engine bay lids. The screw clamps had worn out and the heavy lids had threatened to crash down on our heads each time we climbed into the bays to check the engines' oil level.

I sent my exhausted husband inside to inhabit the still warm sleeping bag – our bed was almost never empty these days.

There was a very strange smell outside as I settled down for the long six hours ahead. Jimmy couldn't be responsible, I thought – the smell was coming from the sea. The wind was about force 5 coming from the north-west, so it couldn't be land smell either. There wasn't any in that direction. Eventually I decided it might be a whale with halitosis!

The icy wind bit at my hand as I took off my glove to pull Jim's nappy in from behind the boat and untie it from the trailing line. The freezing, frothing, bubbles scudding behind *Anneliese* were a long way from the warm soapy suds nappies are usually washed in.

Two hours later it was dark and the quarter-moon became almost dazzling; the stars too were competing for brightness. The freshening wind was struggling unsuccessfully to make the one black cloud in the sky block them all out. The wind increased from force 5/6 to force 7. I reefed the mainsail till at least half of it was curved around the boom. The storm jib was already up. With any luck, I thought, I would not have to go on the foredeck.

Then all at once the wind backed from north-east to south-west and a thick crowd of angry waves fumed around *Anneliese*. We were trying to make our way down south-east to the latitude of Cape Horn at a point about 300 miles west of it. It was no use pretending the wind had not changed. I would have to gybe – the poled-out jib would have to come down and be put up the other side. And the mainsail would now have to be tied out the port side of the boat.

This operation usually took two of us these days, because the boat would not stay downwind in the big seas while you fiddled around on the foredeck with the jib down. The one just dug out of bed would stand shivering and cursing at the inside steering wheel – with one eye anxiously on the deck forward and the other eye glancing at the watch which was ticking away his precious sleeping time. Poor Colin had only had three hours' sleep. I decided to gybe without disturbing him this time.

I let the main well out in the hopes that each time the boat started to head up it would luff and keep her downwind. Then I let the pole topping lift and the jib halyard go, and clinging on to each shroud I made my way up to the foredeck. I clipped my safety harness onto the staysail stay where I could let its loop out or take it in, allowing me to move around nearly as much as needed. Then I lashed down the halyard and clipped the pole temporarily onto the pulpit wire so that it would not slat about.

The deck seemed to drop from under me as I tied the jib down. I just clung on. When the swell had passed it seemed to rear up in front of the boat, leaving a huge terrifyingly deep pit, with abyss sides glinting in the moonlight.

The boat was beam on to the waves now. I could hear objects leaping into action inside the boat as she began mountaineering up them. White fangs yawned at me as I struggled back to the cockpit to reset the bewildered self-steering and gybe the mainsail over. I thought back to the Caribbean – if I fell in now, I would have had it. Colin was asleep and anyway there was no turning back in these seas.

I did not dare unclip the pole in case it was washed over the side. Instead by controlling it via the topping lift and the down haul I pulled it up vertical with the mast and then let it down the other side. Then I ran my numb hands along the edge of the jib to make sure it was the right way round and shakily shone the torch up to see if the halyard was caught around the rigging.

Half an hour later, the sail was up. It was hard to see, because the moon had now set. But the boat seemed to be going along all right again. PHEW! What a struggle – just to get the wind puffing on the other side!

* * *

At last it was dawn. Even the 2,000 fathoms of water below could not act as a fire-extinguisher as the heavy lid of the night sky was pushed up by a burst of golden flame.

Afternoon turned the GMT calendar over to 29th January – the anniversary of the day we had set out from Southampton on our first ocean voyage to Italy before Jimmy was born.

It blew a moderate gale under phenomenally beautiful skies all day. In the evening Colin dressed the tape recorder up in polythene and brought it out into the cockpit. 'The sky where the sun is setting,' he said, 'is so beautiful. I wish I had a fisheye lens for the camera. The clouds are mottled cirrus with two great golden bars where the sun is dropping out of one patch. The blue part is now beginning to go green the way it does when the sun gets near setting. It gives the impression of being clean in the sky. This is probably one of the least polluted parts of the whole world.'

We really felt a kind of power here greater than that of the waves themselves. Maybe it just made more impression on Colin and me because we were not sailors who had been used to the sea all their lives. Also we had to be outdoors most of the time. The worse the weather, the more we had to stay outside!

Dead reckoning on Tuesday 30th January found us about 940 miles from the Horn and about 350 miles from the nearest land – Cape Concepcion in Chile. We were almost on a latitude with the Magellan Straits now. We were also nearing the outer brink of the ice limit and possible shipping lanes. I logged:

We could badly do with some ice information. We are waiting for our radio to burst into life now we are nearing the coast.

The men of the boat are asleep. Eve and I are on watch. We are taking advantage of the unusual peace to have long stories and eat dried apricots.

This didn't last for long, though. Two hours later the wind began howling in from the south-west. The waves were huge and irritated by constant wind changes. It was a grizzly and damp afternoon. I worked out two stolen sun sights and ran them up to each other to get a rough fix which put us 91 degrees 03 West, 52 degrees 13 South – on a longitude with the Galapagos Islands 3,200 miles north.

Everything outside was now covered with a blanket of grey fog. I could hear the thunder of the waves, but I couldn't see them. I mopped the dampness and spray off my Marlin with one of Jimmy's nappies so that it would not drip all over the place. Thank goodness it was time for Colin to take over.

When Colin woke me up again six hours later, he had a strange look on his face. 'It certainly doesn't do to have too much imagination round here,' he said shakily.

He had spent most of his watch enveloped in thick fog. All he had been able to see had been huge waves coming and going in about 100 yards. They had not looked like waves at all. Just weird deep fog valleys. The wind had fallen off light and he had been on the cabin roof putting away the mainsail which was banging about – when all at once he had seen an extraordinary illuminated patch where the western horizon should have been ... It was very creepy. And to the east, where we were heading, great banks of fog were turning orange. Then suddenly the western sky had cleared and become greeny blue and the glorious sight of the sun just a couple of degrees above the horizon was revealed! The calm didn't last long.

Things are getting a bit hectic when you have to hand-steer all the time. It means that the waves have reached a point when it is dangerous to let the boat broach or surf out of control.

It had been blowing south-south-west force 9/10/11 for 36 hours. I was too exhausted to be really frightened any more. I just clung to the wheel and steered on and on. Each wave was a crisis. I did not dare look behind. Each time I turned round and saw what towered there, my mind turned inside out and I lost my sense of the balance of the boat, and the ability to steer her out of difficulties. I understood now why the helmsmen of the old clipper ships used to have iron protecting cages round them. There was always something really dreadful three or four waves away!

It was the sort of storm which made even the tiny spitfire, which was all we had up, seem a big sail. *Anneliese* was behaving really wonderfully. Her escape route was always upwards. She insisted on sitting on top of the waves, rarely allowing them to come even partially on board. When we weren't surfing, we were trying to keep at about six knots, slightly slower than the waves, which were then boiling up slowly in front of us. They seemed to fold up in patches of foam and then draw back on themselves in a sort of circular movement. You got the feeling of the boat's nose going down and her stern lifting almost vertically as she followed the shape of each steep wave. In among the big waves were mad little ones which would rush up and fling themselves at *Anneliese*'s sides.

Suddenly I felt a really huge wave break just behind us. The top of it seized *Anneliese*'s stern – and off she went. We seemed to be flying. I had never seen anything go so fast. Water whirled past. There was a deafening roar. Her nose rose and she started to leap over the next wave as well. We must have been going at 35 m.p.h. The cockpit floor was vibrating. I looked down. The port engine was on, roaring full throttle. The force of the wave had actually bump-started the engine, which had been left in gear to spare the props. Giddily fighting with the steering wheel, I throttled down and looked round at the foaming aftermath of seething water. Perhaps our boat had known best what was needed to save her. I was shaking all over.

Inside the boat everything had taken off and landed in a different place. The emergency barrel with the fragile sextant in it had crashed down into the port hull. Charts had skithered off the seats, tins rolled in the cupboards, a teddy bear had leapt onto the floor. Eve and Jimmy were shrieking with laughter. During all this Colin had somehow managed to keep hold of the kettle he had been boiling for coffee.

We thought thankfully of *Anneliese*'s planing hull, which had allowed her to behave like a boat even at phenomenal speeds. We realised that if she had had a hull speed limitation as single-hull boats do, she might have dug her nose right in and pitchpoled the way the Smeetons' gallant yacht *Tzu Hang* had.

Two hours later Colin was outside steering. Whenever I heard him singing and whistling, I knew things must be getting bad.

The sight out of the top forward windows was really amazing. *Anneliese* seemed to be 60 feet above the horizon – and then 60 feet below it – and then in seconds up again. There were many sensations of being at a first-class fun fair.

I sponged my oilskins down with a nappy, wriggled out of the outer layers and lay down. It really took far too long to take it all off and put it all on again now. Zealously I had kept all the oilskins' chinks sealed. Colin and I both knew that our underlayers getting wet would be a disaster. It would be impossible to dry them. We also had to dress to be just warm enough, but not hot enough to perspire and again make the underclothes damp.

I lay quietly listening to *Anneliese* surfing down these extraordinary seas. You realised that this place which was your home, your boat, the children's nursery, the place where you worked – was now nothing but a box, a shoebox which seemed to spend half its time mountaineering. I caught a glimpse of Colin's orange oilskins through the tiny back windows and heard his wild singing – and felt a sudden surge of happiness. I wrote in the log:

The thing which keeps us going on this journey is trust. We have to trust *Anneliese* and the biggest thing, of course, is that Colin and I trust each other. After all we hand over the fate of the whole family into each other's keeping for six hours at a time. This trust is something which goes deeper than love. It is one of the things which makes this voyage worthwhile.

We encouraged each other as much as possible. 'You know how to jump horses over fences – you'll manage all right,' Colin would tell me, before I went out to steer. And when it was his turn to go on watch I'd say 'Remember you know how to race motor cars.' I was always being reminded of the old Irish saying 'Put your heart over first!'

Those lovely little birds with black curved beaks seemed much more friendly now there was a storm on. They looked remarkably like the flying fish of the Atlantic trade winds. But after all, what are birds but fish who have taken to the air? They came and visited us, orange webbed feet stretched to windward as if they were going to land. It was very clever of them, I thought, to approach against the wind – so that they could get away easily if they didn't like what they saw.

Grey sky, grey sea with white snarling teeth greeted me when I next came out to steer. The only colour anywhere was where the sea was 'shipping it green'. The last time *Anneliese* was floating in green water she had been anchored in the lovely little lagoon in Rarotonga. Now here she was in green water again. But this time the green was the frenzied surface of a thousand fathoms of writhing ocean.

I kept seeing what looked like snow falling onto the waves to leeward. It turned out to be the white silken pieces of our Irish flag which Colin had made out of spinnaker-mending material as we approached Sydney Harbour last September. Now our flag was just tattered Irish green and gold – no white for surrender!

'Well, we've made it into February – just!' I wrote unsteadily in the log.

The gale had eased a bit, but you still had to watch which way you opened the cabin door in case some of the sea came into the boat with you. We were beginning to see what Alan Villiers had meant by 'the headlong dash to the Horn'!

It was still 280 miles to the latitude of the Horn. We knew it might be quite a fight to get down to it. The wind was still south-west – and our current theory was that you couldn't do anything but run with the wind on the quarter in a gale. We didn't dare head up to the seas, even if this was necessary in order to go in the right direction.

But by afternoon the wind had veered westerly. We were even more cheered up when a large gang of those black and white penguin-coloured dolphins came to visit us. They seemed to be the water's answer to the albatrosses – big-eyed, friendly, humorous and absolute masters of their environment.

None of these creatures seemed keen to eat our scraps. No wonder, I thought, they looked so tremendously fit on their natural diet. I wondered how they managed their cuisine in the stormy ocean. We really felt it was a privilege to be out here among them. Colin and I often thought how lucky we were even to have a chance to sail past Cape Horn. The seas round here were very humbling.

I logged:

This is not a battle with the Southern Ocean with its giant powerful waves. It is too strong to make it any kind of a competition between us. It has just been a gracious gesture on the ocean's part to allow us to ride on its foaming back during the last month. I hope that this magnanimous spirit won't end before we are round Cape Horn safely. I hardly dare to think of what lies ahead. If we manage it, it will be a credit to the sea's unusual patience, rather than to our skill.

The important thing, we felt, was to be happy. To revel in the sunrises, the rare wild beauty of this part of the world, the birds, our children – our few precious hours of kip. If 2nd February was to be our last day, we might as well enjoy it. If not – well then there was nothing to be cheerless about.

The seas became a bit kinder during the afternoon and pink puffy clouds softened the horizon. They looked a bit like those packets of coloured pieces of cotton wool that Boots are always offering as special bargains!

Towards evening we finally managed to tempt one of the albatrosses with a piece of shortbread. I threw in half a biscuit and he missed it – or disdained to notice such a trivial offering. Then I chucked in a whole piece – and the enormous bird swooped down. By the time he'd got there, the shortbread had disappeared under a wave. So he did a beautiful surface dive, his purple feet sticking up above the water like a neat pair of diver's flippers.

Albert had been following us for several days now. He really was magnificent, with giant cloud-coloured wings, a characterful curved orange beak and a friendly gleam in his black eyes.

Next day the wind backed south-westerly again. It was blowing force 5/6. We were reaching south trying to get to the latitude of Cape Horn before a southerly buster came and kidnapped us back up north. In the afternoon I baked a pre-Cape Horn batch of brown bread. It rose to the occasion for the first time on this cold part of the voyage.

That evening we turned on the radio which had been silent since the Chatham Islands a month before, and there was an English voice calling: 'Hello Victor Juliet 4405 yacht *Anneliese* ... This is Victor Papa Charlie ...' It was coming from the other side of South America – from the Falkland Islands. Colin had arranged for a schedule with them morning and evening, from 1st February onwards, but until now nothing had come through.

We didn't feel so alone any more. We pressed down the transmitter and began to ask for ice information and to thank them for listening out for us – it was difficult not to go on a bit. We had been alone for so long. Then we turned the radio to 'receive' and listened eagerly.

The operator repeated: 'This is Victor Papa Charlie calling yacht *Anneliese*, yacht *Anneliese* . . . nothing heard so far . . .' and his voice faded a bit. We realised sadly that though we were listening to him, he could not hear us at all. Vainly we tried to will the pleasant-sounding man at the other end to pass us the ice information we needed so much, and a weather forecast, on the off-chance that he could hear us.

LOG:

22.00. A patch of sunlight in the distance is being blown towards us – I must sneak out and catch it with the sextant to get our first position line for two days.

The wind had eased temporarily, but the swell still stayed enormous. We turned on the engines to keep *Anneliese* at the vital 5/6 knots. We had found the fact that *Anneliese* was actually a motor-sailer very useful. Many of the old clipper ships which managed fine in the worst gales had foundered and been lost afterwards when the wind had eased and they had lain helplessly in the troughs of the huge waves.

At last it was 4th February – *Colin's birthday*. What a change from this time a year before, when we had just sighted the loom of Barbados! The wind had piped up to north-west force 8 – at least we wrote force 8 down in the log book. It was more comforting than thinking it was force 9. During seconds snatched from steering the boat during my watch, I helped Eve and Jim make up birthday cards for Colin. Then we dug out the lovely new fleecy Dunlop vest we had been saving and wrapped it up.

Colin was really delighted. He couldn't believe that when he was a boy he had actually hated being given clothes!

Birthdays are meant to be exciting, I thought, as I struggled to get the cabin door shut with the long liferaft painter in the way – but not perhaps like this. The seas were really huge again today. The struggle did not seem near stopping. Cape Horn never seemed to get any nearer. The waves were filled with a maniacal power. They seemed to want to race round and round the world endlessly, becoming furious when they met the baffling continent of South America and had to squeeze through Drake's Passage which is only 500 miles wide.

I did not think Colin would ever forget this birthday. 'Twisters', 'roaring swooshes', 'trouser-browners'! were some of the entries in the log book describing these seas. What was happening now made what we had had in mid-Southern Ocean seem like a mill pond. It was becoming impossible to divide the gales. The wind just shrieked all the time now; and the seas really didn't need to get much worse.

LOG:
Our good friend Albert and his wife have been around all day, sometimes almost flying into the mizzen-mast with a loud 'CHIRRRRRRRRRRRRRRUP!' to remind me it is time for Colin's celebration lunch. They like chocolate pudding better than bread – because my bread sinks immediately and they have to dive for it! Unfortunately for the albatrosses, Colin likes chocolate pudding too – and we all had to finish off a birthday feast of ham and baked beans.

A rough fix of two square sun position lines put us 79 degrees 19 West, 55 degrees 10 South. We were now south past the latitude of Darwin's Beagle Channel, and abeam of Isla Hoste. We didn't dare turn east too soon in case we were driven onto land by a southerly gale. But we did not dare go too far south either. For we didn't have any information as to the movement of ice this year. Somewhere down there was another lethal razor-sharp shore. At least Cape Horn and its grim surrounding islands did not move about!

That evening there was a dreadful scrunching sound as Colin stepped down into the port hull. Oh no! Not Cuthbert Cockroach! With tears in our eyes we wrapped the remains of our little six-legged friend up in paper and popped them into an empty watertight Vitamin C tube. Then Colin engraved: 'CUTHBERT COCKROACH – Master Mariner' on the top, and we launched him over the side to have a seaman's burial.

But just as we were changing over watches later that night, a large golden brown creature ran out from behind the emergency radio and wriggled his antennae. It was the real Cuthbert!

He was all right after all! We decided that the casualty must have been one of his unpleasant relations.

February 5th put us 350 miles to Cape Horn; 500 till we cleared Staten Island. The wind was north-west now – with a shrill bargaining whine in its voice. Will it let us through? I wondered.

During the afternoon we turned due east for the first time. We couldn't help thinking of False Cape Horn and Deception Island and the poor misled sailors who had named them. We hoped fervently that our navigation was right and that it was Drake's Passage to the Atlantic which lay ahead – not land. Cape Horn might be known as the worst place for a boat in the world. But now we were longing to get to it. There was so much to be worried about – the waves, the wind, ice, lee shores, whales turning the boat over, navigation ... But somehow Colin and I never seemed to be too frightened at the same time – and so together we somehow managed to keep things going.

The wild scrawls and blank spaces in the navigation log which we usually tried to keep every hour were better indications of the violence of that storm on the night of 6th February than any description could be. Colin had the worst of it. 'Biggest ever wind and waves – OO-ER!' he scribbled. He had to hand-steer all night. It was really blowing. We were about 200 miles from Cape Horn. It was a snorting north-westerly storm, force 12 at times. Never ever had *Anneliese* been in wind as strong as this. It absolutely screamed and shrieked. There was no moon. Everything was black. You could just see the foaming crests. It was pretty much the limit of what we could put up with. It was the sort of conditions in which Colin did a great deal of singing and whistling!

Suddenly we realised that all the things people had said about the Southern Ocean – well, they were happening now. The terrific, unbelievable seas were not just from where the wind was blowing, but from every angle. Colin told me afterwards: 'This great black shape roared up to the side of the boat – and then there was an avalanche from the top of it. I had to shout at myself to tell myself what to do. We were in the actual curl of a wave. There was a foaming foaming mass of water. I just hung on ...'

Colin said he had felt like Slocum who had leapt up into *Spray*'s rigging when he met 'the culmination of many waves, roaring as it came!' Incredibly *Anneliese* stayed level. Most of the water went under her. Colin had had the engine on all night, not in gear, but simply because he thought that the heavy flywheel spinning round might act as a gyroscope and stabilise the boat. Perhaps it had. We never knew how near the end we came.

We bitterly regretted having left our bar steering seat in Sydney. People had said it would be swept overboard. But now our legs ached as we stood for hour after hour steering the boat. The inside steering wheel was a help at times, but often in these conditions it did not seem safe not to be near the sails and fully aware of everything, outside.

Often the things you do in life turn out to be easier than people say. But sailing through the Southern Ocean and around Cape Horn was being as hard as anybody had ever told us it would be. Colin said 'All the lies about Cape Horn are true!' as he came off watch.

He lay down with his neoprene wetsuit hood beside him on the pillow. I went outside and clipped myself tightly to the cabin top, so (I hoped) that nothing could sweep me overboard. We really seemed to be fighting for our lives. 'GOOD LUCK "ANNELIESE"' I wrote in huge scrawled letters in the log.

I kept the wind well on the quarter, and prepared to steer till dawn. A mistake now and all our journey across the whole of the Southern Ocean could have been for nothing.

Gradually, almost imperceptibly, the wind eased. At last it was morning. *Anneliese* was still upright. The children were demanding porridge for breakfast. More or less normal family life was going on. I really admired those people who had faced storms like this in a monohull. I don't know if the children could have managed in a boat which leaned over when the wind blew.

'Oh what a marvellous, marvellous feeling ...' Colin sounded intoxicated, a bit like he had just after James Mario was born. But there is something about great tiredness when things go right after a struggle, which is better than being drunk.

It was 19.00 GMT mid-afternoon on 7th February. We had just had the greatest thrill any navigators could have. The mileage recorder was just turning on to 7,000 miles across the Southern Ocean, the loneliest, emptiest, coldest, windiest sea in the world – and there, dead ahead, was South America! Colin and I clung to each other and gazed at the line of the Diego Ramirez Islands which had just appeared in the distance in front of us. They are the southernmost group of all the islands of South America – 60 miles in front of the Horn, but further south. Chichester and Knox-Johnston had gone between them and Islas Ildefonso. But it looked as if *Anneliese* might make it round the outside of the whole lot.

The three main islands of the group, Roca Norte, Isla Bartoleme and Isla Gonzalo stood in a line north to south. They seemed like stern sentinels – perhaps deciding who was going to be allowed to go through Drake's Passage to the Atlantic. Drake himself had in fact discovered and anchored off these islands after a three-week easterly gale had blown him there.

The wind was now slight easterly. The sun was setting as a golden bar with rays as we motorsailed closehauled round what was in a way the end of the world. As we approached close to Isla Gonzalo and its entourage of rocks, the sight was worth every long mile through the Southern Ocean getting there. We had never really expected these islands to be beautiful or for there to be so many live creatures around.

About twenty of the biggest albatrosses we had ever seen swooped out from the rocks and flew around *Anneliese*'s masts, while beneath them in the icy water black and white Antarctic dolphins spouted and played around her hulls. A little later, a whiskery seal – the southernmost citizen of South America – swam out to greet us. Eve and Jimmy were wild with excitement. We found it pretty hard to manage the excitement of it all ourselves. It was difficult to sound sane or coherent as we tried to record our impressions on the tape recorder and in the log book.

As we passed close we could see that all the rocks were thronged with seabirds sitting in lines, gazing at us. The rocks themselves were black with a hint of bright green when we got close. They were fantastic shapes. They looked like the work of some eccentric sculptor, exhibited in an ocean art gallery. One rock was shaped like a huge bell sticking up out of the sea. Another looked like a calf lying down; another like a crouching lion. The rock nearest us reminded us mouthwateringly of a kind Australian friend's Christmas pudding which we were still keeping for a really special occasion.

A wildcat sea was clawing at the base of some of the rocks, sending up huge sheets of white foam which reared up for a few seconds then ran down again. The white faded gradually as the water ran off.

Grunts of sealions and dolphins and albatrosses came out of the darkness as I took over watch from Colin three hours later. We were about 15 miles east of the Diego Ramirez Islands now. The wind was still south-easterly and fairly squally. We were lurching along at about five knots. Above us was the world, below us was the ice. We had reached the southernmost point of the whole voyage. An hour later, I eased the sheets and *Anneliese* headed on a slightly northerly course – for the first time for 25,000 miles.

Cape Horn was only 45 miles away now, and *Anneliese* and an unknown current were taking us closer all the time. I still felt that getting there was rather like trying to lift a cup of tea to one's lips in a small ship in a hurricane. So much could go wrong before the morning. I jumped nervously each time a dolphin blew. I kept shining the Aldis lamp around for icebergs. I reefed the mainsail at the slightest sign of a squall. The moon was gone. It was pitch-black outside. I think I must have been in rather a strange state of mind by the time Colin took over again.

Colin woke me just before dawn. He looked as though he had swallowed a cocktail of excitement and fear and relief on an empty stomach of exhaustion! I wrenched myself out of the sleeping bag. Both children were already in the cockpit.

'Mummy, *Mummy*, LOOK!' Eve shouted.

Outside, standing out clearly in the early morning sky about 20 miles away – was Cape Horn Island. It was huge and bold and blackly unmistakable. On each side of it I could see the Lower Hermite group and Wollaston Islands. Behind there was a high mountain rising up from the distance with a shining glacier like a crown on top. We would be past it in a couple of hours. I thought – *Well done Anneliese, well done Anneliese!*

'She's a good boat – in port!' someone had once said.

Colin and I hugged each other through thick layers of clothing, then got our three-month-old bottle of champagne out of the bilges and toasted the decks of *Anneliese* and ourselves – even James Mario had a swig. Then I went and prepared our celebration breakfast of the last tinned ham and beans – and put the Christmas pudding on to steam for lunch!

Half an hour later, the strangest thing of the whole voyage happened. Here, off Cape Horn itself. The wind suddenly almost stopped. *Anneliese* was bobbing peacefully in the clear, black, green water. We hadn't enough fuel to motor through Drake's Passage and to the Falkland Islands, and we hadn't enough sail – unless we put the spinnaker up we were becalmed!

Echoes of the gales of the last weeks screamed in our ears, warning us to get out of this part of the world before it was too late. But there was nothing we could do in this uneasy calm. The monster we had been dreading for so long was showing secret kindliness. Cape Horn was being courteous to us. We were stopped where the weather does not usually allow boats to delay.

We gazed and gazed and tried to saturate our minds with this place which we felt we would never see again like this. It seemed we were gazing at a forbidden part of the world; a place where human beings should not be.

It was less sinister and frightening and yet more magnificent than we had ever imagined. There was beautiful visibility. We got out the cameras and took as many pictures as possible. Colin bent over the back of the boat to the self-steering rudder – and brought long trails of yellowy brown seaweed on board, which the children loved playing with. It had bladders as large as pears and flat strops along the edges. Among these lived all sorts of little beasts and shellfish.

We switched on our radio for the 10.30 schedule with the Falkland Islands; and as usual tried to answer their call. Our spare aerial was not as good as the masthead one had been. We were getting used to nobody hearing us.

Suddenly the operator said: '*Roger, Roger!*' We were through! We were abeam of Cape Horn – and for the first time for months we were in touch with the outside world. It was wonderful to hear an English voice at a time like this.

By midday, storm clouds had begun to gather round Cape

Horn again, and five hours later the Horn's family of islands and headlands – False Cape Horn, Grupo Wollaston, Isla Decepcion, monuments to those who had been less fortunate than us and had perished there – faded into the distance as a brisk northerly wind took us away on a close reach. The 1,400-foot-high giant of Cape Horn stayed in sight, looking more and more like its picture on the chart, till we were over 40 miles away.

Bill O'Brien once told us that he had built the 'Oceanic' like a seagull – because 'You never see a seagull, designed by nature, get its back wet in a chop!' During the long weeks behind us Colin and I had steered *Anneliese* from wave to enormous wave, we had come to admire Bill O'Brien's genius more and more. *Anneliese* was just a standard 'Oceanic' built for cruising – and yet Bill had somehow given her enough strength and resourcefulness to manage the Southern Ocean.

We felt proud of our boat not only because she was the first catamaran to go round Cape Horn but also because she had managed it as a happy home, with Eve and Jimmy living normal nursery lives of toys, potties and sweeties inside. It had been the equivalent of sailing your cottage around Cape Horn!

We were nearly through Drake's Passage now. We decided to learn from Chichester and steer a course well clear of Staten Island with its chronic overfalls.

But we were in a sort of daze really. We had never actually thought past Cape Horn. We had not dared to. We had assumed that once we were round the corner we would immediately be in sheltered waters – and an easy sail away from home. As a welcoming committee of dolphins came in from the Atlantic, we realised we had not even got the proper charts out for this new ocean.

II

Miles Smeeton

Miles Smeeton is one of that tough breed of dedicated sailors (like Eric Hiscock and the late Peter Pye) who has spent most of his adult life roaming the high seas – later writing about his voyages in a series of very professional travel books, such as *Sunrise to Windward*, *The Misty Islands* and *Once is Enough*. Many of these voyages have been made in an old and much beloved ketch, *Tzu Hang*, and sometimes the journeys' ends have been very distant indeed – the Seychelles, Ceylon, Malaya, Indonesia, Japan – later to Alaska, America, Iceland, Norway and Sweden. On most of these trips Miles Smeeton has been accompanied by his intrepid wife, Beryl, herself both a fellow explorer and author (with books on lone trips through Persia, China and Russia). It was with his wife, and another well-known world yachtsman, John Guzzwell, that Miles Smeeton endured the harrowing experience of having his boat completely turned over by a freak wave in the Pacific. Almost unbelievably the Smeetons experienced exactly the same disaster a year or two later – hence the seemingly cryptic title of the book, *Once is Enough*, from which this dramatic account is taken....

PITCHPOLED

Miles Smeeton

IT must have been nearly five in the morning, because it was light again, when the noise of the headsails became so insistent that I decided to take in sail. I pulled on my boots and trousers. Now that I had decided to take some action I felt that it was already late, and was in a fever to get on with it. When I was dressed I slid back the hatch, and the wind raised its voice in a screech as I did so. In the last hour there had been an increase in the wind, and the spindrift was lifting, and driving across the face of the sea.

I shut the hatch and went forward to call Beryl. She was awake, and when I went aft to call John, he was awake also. They both came into the doghouse to put on their oilies. As we got dressed there was a feeling that this was something unusual; it was rather like a patrol getting ready to leave, with the enemy in close contact. In a few minutes we were going to be struggling with this gale and this furious-looking sea, but for the time being we were safe and in shelter.

'Got your life-lines?' Beryl asked.

'No, where the hell's my life-line? It was hanging up with the oilies.' Like my reading glasses, it was always missing.

'Here it is,' John said. He was buckling on a thick leather belt over his jacket, to which his knife, shackle spanner, and life-line were attached. His life-line was a thin nylon cord with a snap-hook at the end, and Beryl's, incongruously, was a thick Terylene rope, with a breaking strain of well over a ton.

'Got the shackle spanner?' I asked. 'Never mind, here's a wrench. Is the forehatch open?' Someone said that they'd opened it.

'Beryl, take the tiller. John and I'll douse the sails. Come on boys, into battle.' I slid the hatch back again and we climbed up one after the other. We were just on the crest of a wave and could look around over a wide area of stormy greyish-white sea. Because we were on the top of a wave for a moment, the seas did not look too bad, but the wind rose in a high-pitched howl, and plucked at the double shoulders of our oilies, making the flaps blow up and down.

The wave passed under *Tzu Hang*. Her bowsprit rose, and she gave a waddle and lift as if to say, 'Be off with you!' Then the sea broke, and we could hear it grumbling away ahead of us, leaving a great wide band of foam behind it.

Beryl slipped into the cockpit and snapped her life-line on to the shrouds. John and I went forward, and as we let go of the handrail on the doghouse, we snapped the hooks of our life-lines on to the rail, and let them run along the wire until we had hold of the shrouds. The wind gave us a push from behind as we moved. I went to the starboard halliard and John to the port, and I looked aft to see if Beryl was ready. Then we unfastened the poles from the mast and let the halliards go, so that the sails came down together, and in a very short time we had them secured. We unhooked them from the stays, bundled them both down the forehatch, and secured the two booms to the rails. As we went back to the cockpit, we were bent against the pitch of the ship and the wind. Beryl unfastened the sheets from the tiller and we coiled them up and threw them below.

'How's the steering?'

'She seems to steer all right, I can steer all right.'

'We'll let the stern line go anyway, it may be some help.'

John and I uncoiled the three-inch hawser, which was lashed in the stern, and paid it out aft. Then we took in the log-line, in case it should be fouled by the hawser. By the time everything was finished, my watch was nearly due, so I took over the tiller from Beryl, and the others went below. The hatch slammed shut, and I was left to myself. I turned my attention to the sea.

The sea was a wonderful sight. It was as different from an ordinary rough sea as a winter's landscape is from a summer one, and the thing that impressed me most was that its general aspect was white. This was due to two reasons: firstly because the wide breaking crests left swathes of white all over the sea, and secondly because all over the surface of the great waves themselves, the wind was whipping up lesser waves, and blowing their tops away, so that the whole sea was lined and streaked with this blown spume, and it looked as if all the surface was moving. Here and there, as a wave broke, I could see the flung spray caught and whirled upwards by the wind, which raced up the back of the wave, just like a whirl of wind-driven sand in the desert. I had seen it before, but this moving surface, driving low across a sea all lined and furrowed with white, this was something new to me, and something frightening, and I felt exhilarated with the atmosphere of strife. I have felt this feeling before on a mountain, or in battle, and I should have been warned. It is apt to mean trouble.

For the first time since we entered the Tasman there were no albatrosses to be seen. I wondered where they had gone to, and supposed that however hard the wind blew it could make no difference to them. Perhaps they side-slipped out of a storm area, or perhaps they held their position as best they could until the storm passed, gliding into the wind and yet riding with the storm until it left them.

I kept looking aft to make sure that *Tzu Hang* was dead stern on to the waves. First her stern lifted, and it looked as if we were sliding down a long slope into the deep valley between this wave and the one that had passed, perhaps twenty seconds before; then for a moment we were perched on the top of a sea, the wind force rose, and I could see the white desolation around me. Then her bowsprit drove into the sky, and with a lurch and a shrug, she sent another sea on its way. It was difficult to estimate her speed, because we had brought the log in, and the state of the water was very disturbed, but these waves were travelling a great deal faster than she was, and her speed seemed to be just sufficient to give her adequate steerage way, so that I could correct her in time to meet the following wave.

Suddenly there was a roar behind me and a mass of white water foamed over the stern. I was knocked forward out of the cockpit on to the bridge deck, and for a moment I seemed to be sitting in the sea with the mizzen-mast sticking out of it upright beside me. I was surprised by the weight of the water, which had burst the canvas windscreen behind me wide open, but I was safely secured by my body-line to the after shroud. I scrambled back into the cockpit and grabbed the tiller again, and pushed it hard over, for *Tzu Hang* had swung so that her quarter was to the sea. She answered slowly but in time, and as the next sea came up, we were stern on to it again. The canvas of the broken windbreak lashed and fluttered in the wind until its torn ends were blown away.

Now the cloud began to break up and the sun to show. I couldn't look at the glass, but I thought that I felt the beginning of a change. It was only the change of some sunlight, but the sunlight seemed to show that we were reaching the bottom of this depression. Perhaps we would never get a chance again to film such a sea, in these fleeting patches of brilliance. I beat on the deck above John's bunk and called him up. I think that he had just got to sleep, now that the sails were off her, and there was someone at the helm. I know that I couldn't sleep before. He looked sleepy and disgruntled when he put his head out of the hatch.

'What about some filming, John?'

'No, man, the sea never comes out.'

'We may never get a sea like this again.'

'I don't want to get the camera wet, and there's not enough light.'

'No, look, there's a bit of sun about.'

As he was grumbling, like an old bear roused out of its winter quarters, he looked aft and I saw his expression change to one of interest.

'Look at this one coming up,' he said, peering over the top of the washboards, just the top of his head and his eyes showing. 'Up she goes,' he ducked down as if he expected some spray to come over, and then popped his head up again. 'Wait a minute,' he said, 'I'll fix something up,' and he slammed the hatch shut and disappeared below again.

He came up in a few minutes, fully equipped. He had the camera in a plastic bag with the lens protruding through a small hole. He took some shots. The lens had to be dried repeatedly, but the camera was safe in its bag, and we had no more wave tops on board. Presently he went down again.

John relieved me for breakfast, and when I came up it seemed to be blowing harder than ever.

'How's she steering?' I asked him.

'Not bad,' he said. 'I think she's a bit sluggish, but she ought to do.'

I took over again, and he went below; no one wanted to

hang about in this wind. I watched the sixty fathoms of three-inch hawser streaming behind. It didn't seem to be making a damn of difference, although I suppose that it was helping to keep her stern on to the seas. Sometimes I could see the end being carried forward in a big bight on the top of a wave. We had another sixty fathoms, and I considered fastening it to the other and streaming the two in a loop, but I had done this before, and the loop made no difference, although the extra length did help to slow her down. We had oil on board, but I didn't consider the emergency warranted the use of oil. For four hours now we had been running before this gale, running in the right direction, and we had only had one breaking top on board, and although I had been washed away from the tiller, *Tzu Hang* had shown little tendency to broach to. To stop her and to lie a-hull in this big sea seemed more dangerous than to let her run, as we were doing now. It was a dangerous sea I knew, but I had no doubt that she would carry us safely through and as one great wave after another rushed past us, I grew more and more confident.

Beryl relieved me at nine o'clock. She looked so gay when she came on deck, for this is the sort of thing that she loves. She was wearing her yellow oilskin trousers and a yellow jumper with a hood, and over all a green oilskin coat. So that she could put on enough pairs of socks, she was wearing a spare pair of John's sea-boots. She was wearing woollen gloves, and she had put a plastic bag over her left hand, which she wouldn't be using for the tiller. She snapped the shackle of her body-line on to the shroud, and sat down beside me, and after a minute or two she took over. I went below to look at the glass and saw that it had moved up a fraction. My camera was in the locker in the doghouse, and I brought it out and took some snaps of the sea. Beryl was concentrating very hard on the steering. She was looking at the compass, and then aft to the following sea, to make sure that she was stern on to it, and then back to the compass again, but until she had the feel of the ship she would trust more to the compass for her course than to the wind and the waves. I took one or two snaps of Beryl, telling her not to look so serious, and to give me a smile. She laughed at me.

'How do you think she's steering?'

'Very well, I think.'
'We could put the other line out. Do you think she needs it? The glass is up a bit.'
'No, I think she's all right.'
'Sure you're all right?'
'Yes, fine, thanks.'
I didn't want to leave her and to shut the hatch on her, and cut her off from us below, but we couldn't leave the hatch open, and there was no point in two of us staying on deck. I took off my oilskins, put the camera back in its plastic bag in the locker, and climbed up into my bunk. The cat joined me and sat on my stomach. She swayed to the roll and purred. I pulled my book out of the shelf and began to read. After a time, I heard John open the hatch again and start talking to Beryl. A little later he went up to do some more filming. As the hatch opened there was a roar from outside, but *Tzu Hang* ran on straight and true, and I felt a surge of affection and pride for the way she was doing. 'She's a good little ship, a good little ship,' I said to her aloud, and patted her planking.
I heard the hatch slam shut again, and John came down. He went aft, still dressed in his oilskins, and sat on the locker by his bunk, changing the film of his camera. Beneath him, and lashed securely to ring-bolts on the locker, was his tool-box, a large wooden chest, about 30 inches by 18 inches by 8 inches, crammed full with heavy tools.
My book was called *Harry Black*, and Harry Black was following up a wounded tiger, but I never found out what happened to Harry Black and the tiger.

When John went below, Beryl continued to steer as before, continually checking her course by the compass, but steering more by the wind and the waves. She was getting used to them now, but the wind still blew as hard as ever. In places the sun broke through the cloud, and from time to time she was in sunshine. A wave passed under *Tzu Hang*, and she slewed slightly. Beryl corrected her easily, and when she was down in the hollow she looked aft to check her alignment. Close behind her a great wall of water was towering above her, so wide that she couldn't see its flanks, so high and so steep that she knew *Tzu Hang* could not ride over it. It didn't seem to be breaking as the other waves had broken, but water was cascading down its front, like a waterfall. She thought, 'I can't do anything, I'm absolutely straight.' This was her last visual picture, so nearly truly her last, and it has remained with her. The next moment she seemed to be falling out of the cockpit, but she remembers nothing but this sensation. Then she found herself floating in the sea, unaware whether she had been under water or not.

She could see no sign of *Tzu Hang*, and she grabbed at her waist for her life-line, but felt only a broken end. She kicked to tread water, thinking, 'Oh, God, they've left me!' and her boots, those good roomy boots of John's, came off as she kicked. Then a wave lifted her, and she turned in the water, and there was *Tzu Hang*, faithful *Tzu Hang*, lying stopped and thirty yards away. She saw that the masts were gone and that *Tzu Hang* was strangely low in the water, but she was still afloat and Beryl started to swim towards the wreckage of the mizzen-mast.

As I read, there was a sudden, sickening sense of disaster. I felt a great lurch and heel, and a thunder of sound filled my ears. I was conscious, in a terrified moment, of being driven into the front and side of my bunk with tremendous force. At the same time there was a tearing, cracking sound, as if *Tzu Hang* was being ripped apart, and water burst solidly, ranging into the cabin. There was darkness, black darkness, and pressure, and a feeling of being buried in a debris of boards, and I fought wildly to get out, thinking *Tzu Hang* had already gone. Then suddenly I was standing again, waist deep in water, and floorboards and cushions, mattresses and books, were sloshing in wild confusion round me.

I knew that some tremendous force had taken us and thrown us like a toy, and had engulfed us in its black maw. I knew that no one on deck could have survived the fury of its strength, and I knew that Beryl was fastened to the shrouds by her life-line, and could not have been thrown clear. I struggled aft, fearing what I expected to see, fearing that I would not see her alive again. As I went I heard an agonised yell from the cat, and thought, 'Poor thing, I cannot help you now.' When I am angry, or stupid and spoilt, or struggling and in danger, or in distress, there is a part of me which seems to disengage from my body, and to survey the scene with a cynical distaste. Now that I was afraid, this other half seemed to see myself struggling through all the floating debris, and to hear a distraught voice crying, 'Oh God, where's Bea, where's Bea?'

As I entered the galley, John's head and shoulders broke water by the galley stove. They may have broken water already, but that was my impression anyway. John himself doesn't know how he got there, but he remembers being thrown forward from where he was sitting and to port, against the engine exhaust and the petrol tank. He remembers struggling against the tremendous force of water in the darkness, and wondering how far *Tzu Hang* had gone down and whether she could ever get up again. As I passed him he got to his feet. He looked sullen and obstinate, as he might look if someone had offended him, but he said nothing. There was no doghouse left. The corner posts had been torn from the bolts in the carlins, and the whole doghouse sheared off flush with the deck. Only a great gaping square hole in the deck remained.

As I reached the deck, I saw Beryl. She was thirty yards away on the port quarter on the back of a wave, and for the moment above us, and she was swimming with her head well out of the water. She looked unafraid, and I believe that she was smiling.

'I'm all right, I'm all right,' she shouted.

I understood her although I could not hear the words, which were taken by the wind.

The mizzen-mast was in several pieces, and was floating between her and the ship, still attached to its rigging, and I saw that she would soon have hold of it. When she got there, she pulled herself in on the shrouds, and I got hold of her hand. I saw that her head was bleeding, and I was able to see that the cut was not too serious but when I tried to pull her on board, although we had little freeboard left, I couldn't do it because of the weight of her sodden clothes and because she seemed to be unable to help with her other arm. I saw John standing amidships. Incredibly he was standing, because, as I could see now, both masts had gone, and the motion was now so quick that I could not keep my feet on the deck. He was standing with his legs wide apart, his knees bent and his hands on his thighs. I called to him to give me a hand. He came up and knelt down beside me, and said, 'This is it, you know, Miles.'

But before he could get hold of Beryl, he saw another wave coming up, and said, 'Look out, this really is it!'

Beryl called, 'Let go, let go!'

But I wasn't going to let go of that hand, now that I had got it, and miraculously *Tzu Hang*, although she seemed to tremble with the effort, rode another big wave. She was dispirited and listless, but she still floated. Next moment John caught Beryl by the arm, and we hauled her on board. She lay on the deck for a moment, and then said, 'Get off my arm, John, I can't get up.'

'But I'm not on your arm,' he replied.

'You're kneeling on my arm, John.'

'Here,' he said, and gave her a lift up. Then we all turned on our hands and knees, and held on to the edge of the big hole in the deck.

Up to now my one idea had been to get Beryl back on board, with what intent I do not really know, because there was so much water below that I was sure *Tzu Hang* could not float much longer. I had no idea that we could save her, nor, John told me afterwards, had he. In fact, he said, the reason why he had not come at once to get Beryl on board again, was that he thought *Tzu Hang* would go before we did. After this first action, I went through a blank patch, thinking that it was only a few moments, a few minutes of waiting, thinking despondently that I had let Clio down. Beryl's bright, unquenchable spirit thought of no such thing. 'I know where the buckets are,' she said. 'I'll get them!'

This set us working to save *Tzu Hang*.

Beryl slipped below, followed by John, but for the time being I stayed on deck and turned to look at the ruins that had been *Tzu Hang*. The tiller, the cockpit coaming, and every scrap of the doghouse had gone, leaving a six-foot by six-foot gap in the deck. Both masts had been taken off level with the deck, the dinghies had gone, and the cabin skylights were sheared off a few inches above the deck. The bowsprit had been broken in two. The rail stanchions were bent all over the place, and the wire was broken. A tangle of wire shrouds lay across the deck, and in the water to leeward floated the broken masts and booms – the masts broken in several places. The compass had gone, and so had the anchor which had been lashed to the foredeck.

There could be no more desolate picture. The low-lying, water-logged, helpless hull, the broken spares and wreckage, that greyish-white sea; no bird, no ship, nothing to help, except that which we had within ourselves. Now the sun was gone again, the spindrift still blew chill across the deck, and the water lipped on to it, and poured into the open hull.

I think both John and I had been numbed with shock, but he recovered first and was working in a fury now, and a hanging cupboard door, some floorboards, and the Genoa erupted on to the deck. I hung on to them, so that they would not be blown or washed off, while he went down again for his tools. He found his tool-box jammed in the sink, and when he groped under water for the tin of galvanised nails in the paint locker, he found them on his second dip. I had intended to help John, as the first essential seemed to be to get the hole covered up, but he was working so fast, so sure now of what he was going to do, his mouth set in a grim determination, oblivious of anything but the work in hand, that I saw he would do as well without me, and now Beryl, who was trying to bale, found that she could not raise the bucket to empty it. I climbed down to where Beryl was standing on the engine, the water washing about her knees. We had to feel for some foothold on the floor-bearers because the engine cover had gone. A 70-lb keg of waterlogged flour floated up to us.

'Overboard with it,' I said.

'Mind your back,' said Beryl, as if we were working on the farm.

I picked it up, and heaved it on deck, Beryl helping with her good arm, but it seemed light enough, and John toppled it over into the sea, out of his way. Anything to lighten the ship, for she was desperately heavy and low in the water.

'We'd better bale through the skylight,' Beryl said, 'I'll fill the bucket, and you haul it up. We'll need a line. Here, take my life-line.' She undid her line from her waist and handed it to me, and I noticed that the snap-hook was broken. I tied it on to the handle of the plastic bucket.

We waded into the cabin feeling with our feet, because there were no floorboards to walk on. I climbed on to the bunk and put my head and shoulders through the skylight. Beryl was on the seat below with the water still round her knees. She filled the bucket and I pulled it up and emptied it, and dropped it down through the skylight again. It would have floated if she had not been there to fill it. It was the best that we could do, and although we worked fast, to begin with, we could just keep pace with the water coming in. No heavy seas broke over the ship and when a top splashed over, I tried to fill the aperture with my body as best I could.

John was doing splendidly. He had made a skeleton roof over the hatch with the door and floorboards, and nailed it down, and he had made it higher in the middle, so that it would spill the water when the sail was nailed over. He was nailing the folded sail over it now, using pieces of wood as battens to hold it down. It was a rush job, but it had to be strong enough to hold out until the sea went down. As soon as he had finished he went to the other skylight and nailed the storm-jib over it. Beryl and I bailed and bailed. As the bucket filled she called 'Right!' and I hauled it up again. Her voice rang out cheerfully from below, 'Right . . . Right . . . Right!' and John's hammer beat a steady accompaniment. *Tzu Hang* began to rise slowly, and at first imperceptibly, in the water.

When John had finished with the skylight, he called to me to ask if he should let the rigging screws go, so that the broken spars would act as a sea-anchor. I told him to do so, and he then went round the deck and loosened all the rigging screws, leaving only one of the twin forestays attached to the deck. He had not much to work with, as the topmast forestay and the jibstay had gone with the mast, the forestay had smashed the deck fitting, and the other twin forestay had pulled its ringbolt through the deck, stripping the thread on the ringbolt. All the rigging was connected in some way or other, so now *Tzu Hang* drifted clear of her spars and then swung round, riding head to wind, on her single forestay. This forestay was attached to a mast fitting, on the broken mast, and the fitting was not equal to the strain now put on it, and it carried away. *Tzu Hang* swung away and drifted downwind, sideways to the sea, and that was the last that we saw of our tall masts, and the rigging, and the sails on the booms.

We bailed and bailed. We had two pumps on board, but the

water that we were bailing was filled with paper pulp from books and charts and labels. They would have clogged up with two strokes, and to begin with the pump handles themselves had been under water. John was now in the forecabin, standing on the bunks and bailing through the skylight. Both he and Beryl were wearing the oilskins that they had been wearing when we upset, but I was still only in a jersey, and was beginning to feel very cold. I was continually wet with spray and salt water and lashed by the bitter wind and my eyes were so encrusted and raw with salt, that I was finding it difficult to see. A broken spinnaker-pole rolled off the deck, showing that *Tzu Hang* was coming out of the water again, and was getting more lively. I saw a big bird alight by it and start pecking at it, and I supposed that this was also a sign that the wind was beginning to abate. I peered through rimy eyes to try and identify it, and saw that it was a giant fulmar. It was the first and only one that we saw.

After a time I became so cold that I could no longer pull up the bucket, in spite of Beryl's encouragement from below.

'This is survival training, you know,' she said.

It was the first joke. Survival training or no, I had to go below for a rest and we called a halt, and John came back from the main cabin and we sat on the bunk for a short time. Beryl found a tin of Horlicks tablets in a locker that had not been burst open, and she pulled off one of her oilskins and gave it to me.

'Where is Pwe?' I asked. 'Anyone seen her?'

'No, but I can hear her from time to time. She's alive. We can't do anything about her now.'

We were making progress, for the top of the engine was showing above the water. There was over a foot less in the ship already, and we were getting down to the narrower parts of her hull. We went back to work, and I found that now I had some protection from the wind the strength came back to my arms and I had no further difficulty. All through the day and on into the evening we bailed, with occasional breaks for rest and more Horlicks tablets. Before dark, almost twelve hours after the smash, we were down below the floor-bearers again. After some difficulty we managed to get the primus stove, recovered from the bilge, to burn with a feeble impeded flame, and we heated some soup, but Beryl wouldn't have any. Now that the struggle was over for the time being, she was in great pain from her shoulder, and she found that she couldn't put her foot to the ground into the bargain. She had injured it stumbling about in the cabin, with no floorboards. Some blood-clotted hair was stuck to her forehead. Like a wounded animal, she wanted to creep into some dark place and to sleep until she felt better.

We found a bedraggled rag of a cat, shivering and cold, in the shelf in the bow, and with her, the three of us climbed into John's bunk to try and get some warmth from each other.

'You know,' I said, 'if it hadn't been for John, I think that we wouldn't have been here now.'

'No,' he said. 'If there hadn't been three of us, we wouldn't be here now.'

'I don't know,' said Beryl. 'I think you were the man, the way you got those holes covered.'

'I think my tool-box having jammed in the sink, and finding those nails is what saved us, at least so far.'

Beryl said, 'If we get out of this, everyone will say that we broached, but we didn't. They'll say that there was a woman at the helm.'

'If they know you they'll say that's how they know we didn't broach, and anyway, we didn't: we just went wham. Let's leave it.'

'How far are we off shore, Miles?' John asked.

'About 900 miles from the entrance to Magellan I should say.'

'If we get out of this, it will be some journey. If there is a lull tomorrow, I'll fix these covers properly.'

'Get her seaworthy again, and get her cleaned up inside. I think that's the first thing to do.'

Beryl was restless with pain and couldn't sleep. In the end we went back to our own soggy bunks. As we lay, sodden and shivering, and awoke from fitful slumber to hear the thud of a wave against the side of the ship and the patter and splash of the spray on the deck, we could hear the main-sheet traveller sliding up and down on its horse. The sheet had gone with the boom, but the traveller was still there, and this annoying but familiar noise seemed to accentuate the feeling that the wreck was just a dream in spite of the water which cascaded from time to time through the makeshift covers. The old familiar noises were still there, and it was hard to believe that *Tzu Hang* was not a live ship, still running bravely down for the Horn.

For several days to come, although all our energies were spent in overcoming the difficulties of the changed situation, it seemed impossible to accept its reality.

III

John Ridgway

John Ridgway is the Royal Marines Captain who first caught the headlines when, with Chay Blyth, he successfully rowed the dinghy *English Rose III* from Cape Cod, America, to Inishmore, Ireland, a journey of some 3,000 miles which took 92 days. The little boat was like a Nova Scotia dory, the sort of open boat traditionally used by fishermen off the coast of North East America. The dory men who made her ready promised the two Englishmen, 'a fighting chance', and they certainly needed it, living for more than three months in a cockpit measuring eight feet by four feet. *English Rose III* was battered by storms, by Hurricane Alma, by huge and often almost overwhelming waves – salt water got into the rations and food became short. Nevertheless the brave rowers kept going. It was, naturally, an experience that brought new dimensions to both their lives. . . . In the case of John Ridgway he has gone on to take part in several other long distance voyages by yacht, as well as starting his own 'outward bound' type of training school up in Scotland, where businessmen, schoolboys, students, working men, people from all walks of life, are trained to be able to cope with the physical demands of adventurous living – including, of course, sailing! Now an accomplished lecturer and writer John Ridgway still looks back with a special feeling to his first epic-making voyage – the flavour of which is well captured in this breathtaking glimpse of life in an open boat during Hurricane Alma. . . .

HURRICANE ALMA

John Ridgway

I may not be a Master Mariner, but I had covered many thousands of miles of sea before the day that Chay and I set out in *English Rose III*. I had studied navigation, sailed with the Merchant Navy and spent many happy hours in small boats, so I knew something about life at sea and the strange wonderment that comes over you when you feel at one with the ocean. I knew the glories of the brilliant sunrises and sunsets when the whole of the sea seems to be a moving flood of reds and golds and purples.

I had found peace at sea before. I had also found that you have to be an exceptionally strong man to be a seaman. I do not mean a great, tough thug of a person. But you have to be a complete person – mature, sensible and responsible if you are going to consider any type of voyage over the great oceans of the world.

You also have to realise – for the very breadth and hugeness of the sea forces this upon you – that you must be humble. There can be no flouting the sea. Foolhardy gestures, flamboyance, bravado lead to your undoing. Relax your guard for one second and the sea will have you.

Certainly the North Atlantic is a cruel sea, and with every day that passed we both came to realise the truth of this. But it has its wonders and delights. Some of these I had seen before and they had been half-forgotten and left lying in some small, tucked-away portion of my memory.

Chay had seen nothing before. At the beginning there was almost incredulous disbelief on his face as the ocean opened before him. The flicker of the sun through flying spume, the lift of the bow of the boat rising to the never-ending succession of waves, the gurgle of water rippling along the sides of the boat and the grace and freedom of the seagulls as they swooped and circled a few feet from our heads – all these things were some small miracle to Chay.

I shall never forget the look on his face when he saw his first whale. I had seen whales before, but this first sighting of the enormous mammal from a small boat which was only inches off the sea certainly had me worried for a moment or two.

'Chay, do you see that – a whale?' and I pointed over the sea towards the back of the monster, which looked like a small, barren island that the sea had just regurgitated.

It was not the biggest whale in the seas, but I suddenly realised what this must look like to Chay, who, after all, had rarely seen anything bigger than a large salmon. It was the look on his face that told me what he was thinking as it seemed to amble through the water towards us with an idle flick of its mammoth tail.

'God,' Chay said – and it was a prayer, not an exclamation. 'What a size – just look at the jet it's blown out. That's it breathing, I suppose.'

It spouted again and the wind caught the water and sprayed it close by. There was an odd smell, a deep fishy smell similar to that you might find on a summer's day walking down Billingsgate Market. It really was huge. We seemed to peer up at it as though at the side of a passing double-decker bus.

Suddenly the great head of the giant turned. It was pointing straight at us and came towards us slowly, inexorably. It was menacing, and I do not care who knows it, I was frightened. Only feet away from the side of 'Rosie' it dived – not the lightsome, frolicking dive of a porpoise or a dolphin, but the steady, sinking, rumbling dive of a submarine. It passed right under the boat, and I felt 'Rosie' stir and shiver from the disturbed water set up by the whale.

'We'll be lost, look out!' cried Chay.

He dived too – for his safety harness – and buckled it on quickly.

'That thing will overturn us and everything will be lost. Hang on, John!' Chay shouted.

I can understand his anxiety – he had never seen a whale that close before. But neither had I, and I was feeling exactly the same. But if we were going to be overturned, then we were going to be overturned and there was nothing we could do about it. So I sat tight and waited.

After a minute or two nothing happened. I looked at Chay and he looked back. I am sure the exchange of looks would be very similar to that swopped by a couple of elderly spinsters who had seen a mouse run under their chair a minute earlier and were waiting for the first touch of a twitching nose on their ankles. Another minute passed. Then we just grinned. The whale must have gone.

'I don't want many more shocks like that,' Chay said. I agreed. It had been frightening. But it was memorable. There are not all that number of people in the world who have seen a whale at such close quarters while they were voyaging in a tiny boat far from land. I will not forget it, neither the fear of it nor the wonder. And I know Chay will not, either. It was an incident, too, which took our minds off the greater terrors – the sea itself and the enormity of our task.

The sea was not something you could forget for long. Although Chay and I had a yarn about whales and their habits and their extraordinary powers which enabled them to swim thousands of miles and navigate as expertly to a landfall as the Captain of the *Queen Mary*, the sea soon intruded once again into our thoughts.

I remembered the horror of Hurricane Alma. I knew about hurricanes – in theory. I knew the power of the winds at their centres could reach more than 120 m.p.h., that ships had disappeared in them never to be heard of again. I knew, too, that the winds built up mountains of water with breaking peaks that weighed hundreds of tons.

I knew, too, that there were sudden shifts of wind which brought seas from a completely different direction in a very short time indeed. I shuddered when I read of the cross seas that could run at the height of a hurricane. Seamen who had experienced them said that it was like two mountains approaching each other at the speed of a racehorse and crashing together. I thought that if we were ever caught in a hurricane it would be the end for 'Rosie' and ourselves.

I had also remembered reading, as a boy, some of the great stories of disaster at sea caused by hurricane or tornado or just a plain, straightforward gale.

As a soldier I had obviously been interested in the other two Services, the Royal Navy and the Royal Air Force, and had studied the problems that they faced. I had read of ships in the last war which were caught in North Atlantic hurricanes. These were horror stories of guns and boats being carried away, of breaking seas ripping armour-plated tops off turrets, of bridges being crushed and their occupants crushed to death or swept into the wild waters like leaves in an autumn breeze.

So it was with some concern that I heard a radio broadcast at 12.20 p.m. on 13 June. The announcer interrupted a programme – I cannot recall what – and read a brief message. 'Hurricane Alma is due off Cape Cod this evening and is expected to turn north-eastwards.' Turn, in other words, right at us.

I was astonished by this report as well as alarmed. It was, of course, a reassuring message for those on shore, and I was relieved that our many friends back in Orleans would not have to suffer the havoc of Alma. But I was astonished – for Alma was too soon. The hurricane season was August and September – at least that was what I had been taught. And then I remembered that in some years, perhaps ten or fifteen years apart, the hurricane season began early.

It looked as though hurricanes were a little early this year.

I told Chay what I had heard and said that we could expect Alma to arrive in a few hours' time. But he had heard the message as well, and his face showed me that he was as worried as I was.

'What do we do now?' Chay said.

I knew that my limited experience would be tested to the full and that any sea lore I had picked up on my way through life must be remembered, for our lives would depend on my memory. I explained to Chay what we must expect and did not pull any punches when I talked about the dangers of hurricanes. Chay was not too surprised, I suppose because the very word 'hurricane' conjures up to an alert and imaginative man the perils of the sea.

'Well, Chay, we must make everything ready. We must think ahead so that when the seas and the winds are high we don't have to risk our lives trying to secure things in the boat,' I told him. 'We must put the sea anchor out as soon as the first winds start up so that we are not blown back to the Cape if the wind comes from the East.'

It was by now a pleasant day, a little misty, with lots of birds about. The boat looked fine, still freshly painted with everything in good shape. So I decided to take some ciné and still photographs with our cameras.

I saw Chay looking at me a little anxiously, but I thought this was because he was still worrying about the broadcast. He put me right in a moment. 'What on earth are you up to, John? Don't you realise we might be dead in a few hours, that we've got work to do if we're to try and stay alive. And yet all you do is take pictures as though you were a Francis Drake playing bowls. Let's get moving.'

I could see his point, all right, but I was not playing this thing cool. I had not meant to seem like Drake. What I needed was time. Time to think and scrape that memory of mine for sea lore, and taking pictures was a good way of gaining time.

I have got this approach to life which some people mistake for courage. I do not make this conscious effort to impress – it just happens. It is like this. I think of everything that can go wrong – or, at least, I try to – and then work out how to answer the challenge. Once I have made out the list of 'things to do', that is that. I say to myself, 'John, you've thought of everything and done everything you can to ensure your safety. There's nothing more you can do except sit.' So I sit. People think I am brave. In fact, it is a form of laziness.

So I took Chay's point and we did get cracking. We lashed everything so that if we should be capsized we would not lose any kit or be hit by a heavy piece of equipment.

We prepared our sea anchor ready to stream it and we had some food. If we were to be hit by Alma at least we would have a good meal inside us.

But even though we were dreading the night before us, we realised that we must press on as best we could towards our goal. So when Chay and I had made all our preparations we decided to row just a bit more that day. Out came the oars again and we rowed and yarned trying to hide our apprehension by talking about the past.

At 8 p.m. we felt the first breath of wind. Soon there was a stiff breeze, although there was still some mist about. Chay suggested we called it a day and got some sleep before Alma caught up with us. He quite rightly said that we might not be able to sleep for a long time and that our physical reserves would be strengthened by sleep. We got the tarpaulin out, snuggled as best we could into our uncomfortable beds with their mattresses of life rafts and water bags and prepared for the worst.

I could not drop off that night. I lay on the bottom of the boat listening to the water swirling round the boat and nervously heard the wind freshen and the seas begin to increase. The seas were not strong nor the wind high – we were to go through far worse – but it was my wretched imagination at work. I could not get out of my mind those stories of storms at sea and I could see in my half-sleep those men being plucked off their wartime ships and cast into the ocean. But in the end I slept.

We slept for nearly twelve hours, a dreamless night so far as I can remember now. We were both awoken at the same moment by Hurricane Alma and hundreds of gallons of swirling, grey Atlantic water which crashed on to our backs and half filled 'Rosie'. One moment asleep, the next fighting for our lives. I can never remember waking up so swiftly or so completely before. The scene on that roaring frightening morning was awful.

The wind was screaming, whipping the tops off thirty-foot-high waves and flinging them more violently than any rainstorm straight into our eyes. We could only see by half turning our backs and screwing up our eyes to keep out the slashing, stinging salt water.

'Rosie' was alive, the sort of aliveness that you might find in a demented animal crazed by the nearness of death. She was bucketing, pitching and rolling in the seas despite the enormous amount of water swilling inside her. For a moment I seemed completely detached as though I was sitting in the front row of the stalls at a London theatre on a first night. I saw our beds were under water. I noticed that Chay's face was green with the stain from the tarpaulin cover. It was a mad world, a world made up of punishing noise, violent movement. I suppose I took all this in within a few moments, but I shall always remember the sheer terror of that Atlantic awakening to Alma.

Chay and I screamed at each other over the roar. 'Bail, for God's sake bail.'

We grabbed a bucket each and bailed. We did not seem to be gaining on the water, for as soon as we threw ten bucketfuls out another ten would come inboard, either from the breaking seas as we were rocketed like maniacs on a watery switchback or from the driving white spume.

As we battled I remembered saying to myself: 'Thank God for that training, those daily runs. Thank God I'm fit. I could never face this if I was a soft, white-collar worker.' So we bailed. I don't know for how long – it seemed like years – and gradually we got that water in the boat under control.

We both then huddled down as best we could to rest. Our lungs were gasping for air from the enormous exertion we had put into our fight for life. After a few minutes we were able to look at each other and raise a kind of smile of encouragement to each other. I know Chay's grin, not quite as carefree as it normally is, bucked me up a lot.

So I started to think again. I realised that 'Rosie' was not a dying boat. Certainly she was still being thrown around, but she was riding well. I had a sudden surge of affection for those phlegmatic Northerners from Bradford who had built her. She was all right, a great boat.

I did a quick check of our gear. Everything was still lashed. We did not appear to have lost a thing. It just shows that you must look ahead when you are on the ocean. If we had left the job of lashing until the weather got bad we would have lost a large proportion of our vital gear.

What of ourselves? I asked Chay if he was all right. 'You must be joking,' he shouted back. 'I'm drenched through, I'm cold, I'm hungry and I'm frightened to death. It's all right for you, you're used to mucking about in small boats. I'm not. I suppose I'm okay. I'm alive and no bones broken.'

We had to get organised again. We could not relax, for the wind still continued to scream and the water still came inboard and I saw that while we had taken our breather the bottom boards were already awash again.

So we decided that one would use the pumps, which were capable of getting rid of eight gallons of water a minute, while the other rested as best he could under the tarpaulin. There was no hope of getting dried out or of changing into dry clothes. But at least the tarpaulin would keep the chill off and give the man resting a chance to regain his strength. Looking back, it was a miserable, depressing way to have a rest. But at the time it seemed like heaven to snuggle up under the tarpaulin out of the wind and wet.

I took the first stint on the pump while Chay went under cover. He even managed to sleep, for I saw his eyes close and his regular, undisturbed breathing. He looked rather like a young boy asleep on that chaotic morning. I did not have much time for brotherly thoughts, however, as there was a job to be done. I grabbed the pump handle and pumped. Each time the boat lurched I seemed to be thrown against a sharp projection on our equipment. But the pumping had to go on. It was agonising. The strain was on my arm and the monotony of pump, pump and pump, pump, was enough to drive one stupid.

But I kept at it, for I knew that this was not the moment to give up. One piece of relaxation and we might be lost, for I kept thinking over and over again that the cruel sea would only strike if you gave it a chance. So pump, pump and pump, pump.

At the end of half an hour I woke Chay and he took over the pump and I tucked myself up in the tarpaulin. I could not understand how I could feel so cold on a June morning, but I was shivering, worn out and glad to get under cover.

However, I found that although there was some comfort being out of the spray and wind, another discomfort crept in. I suddenly felt seasick. I had been sick early in the voyage, a thing that I had half expected to happen. I should have got used to 'Rosie's' movement by now. I had not – and I felt very sick. Part of it was anxiety, I suppose, part the astonishing gyrations of our tiny boat, which seemed to do everything except loop the loop or capsize.

So it was agony for me to struggle out from under the canvas to relieve Chay. He looked old now, strained and anxious. I suppose I must have looked the same. We did not look like soldiers from the Parachute Regiment. We looked like old tramps who had spent a week under old newspapers in the pouring rain in a draughty corner of a Midland slum. We certainly looked horrible.

And so it went on until noon. The wind did not abate and

it was still causing heavy seas and the spume was still flying and we were still screwing our eyes up as a shield against the salt spray.

I was frightened all the time and so was Chay. 'I'm plain worried,' he told me. 'Why do I do these things? I've had nine years in the Army and I should've learned by now that you never volunteer for nothing "not nohow".'

Both of us prayed. As I worked at the pump I would pray for help and guidance. I felt that I was responsible for 'Rosie' and Chay. I had asked him to come with me and I knew that he trusted in my seamanship and navigation. So I prayed that God might aid me in my task to save us from Hurricane Alma.

Chay prayed as well. I would see his lips moving as he laid down in the boat. I knew he had seen me pray. There was no feeling of self-consciousness – we knew that we were right to pray.

I was pumping one moment and I caught a movement out of the corner of my eye, a tiny flash of white. I screwed my eyes up and peered closely to where I had seen this on the swirling water close to the boat, and I saw an astonishing sight. For there, tucked up close in the lee of *English Rose III* were a dozen or so sea-birds. I thought of the hundreds of birds there must be over the ocean and wondered what happened to them when a screaming hurricane hit an area. Did they drown, were they smashed in the seas? I was happy to know that a dozen of them would be alive because of us. It was good to know that 'Rosie' was saving us and the birds.

I watched them; their feathers ruffled when an eddy of wind caught them. They were really close to the boat, only feet away. As 'Rosie' rolled I thought that they must be crushed by the gunwales, but each time they seemed to sense the danger and just paddle an inch or two to get clear. It was fascinating to watch them, and doing so prevented me thinking quite so much about our own peril.

I changed places with Chay again. He was in better shape than I was, and I think that this was because I picked a bad position to pump from. I kept getting drenched and water was running constantly through my clothes and down my body. As the water temperature was only 48 degrees Fahrenheit it did not take much of this to make you feel you were sitting in an icebox. I think that I was on the verge of suffering from exposure, and looking back, that coldness and exhaustion was probably the cause of my seasickness.

That morning seemed unending. The seas showed no sign of abating and the wind still roared. The spume and spray that lashed us seemed to be as vicious and as determined as birds of prey – they tore and worried and harried us.

I was dozing at about lunchtime when Chay shouted at me and I stirred, but did not make any real effort to answer him. I was more or less comfortable and it took too much energy even to say, 'Yes.'

Then I was wide awake again. I had heard Chay shout my name and he was a good six feet away. Up to then we had had to put our heads almost together and shout to be heard above the noise of Alma. But here I was hearing him quite clearly. The noise had decreased.

'John, wake up. I think we're through it. I think we'll live. We've made it,' came Chay's shouts. His eyes were laughing.

So we were through it. We had beaten a hurricane in a twenty-foot open boat. The seas were still high and the wind was still blowing hard, but it was no worse than an earlier gale. We were through the worst.

It was an uncomfortable afternoon, as we were still wet and aching in every limb from fighting the crazy movements of 'Rosie'. We were bruised too, from the constant bumps against the sharp edges in the boat. Morale began to suffer as well after an hour or two, and we both longed to be out of that wearying, miserable, never-ending motion and on land again.

Chay had the idea that finally got us back to a proper mental state.

'John, how about some grub? We should be able to get the stove going. A hot meal, curry and rice and a cup of cocoa, how about it?' he asked.

Of course it was the answer. Chay set to. How he managed in that violent motion I do not know. He dragged our cooking utensil out; at that time it was a shiny new, aluminium pressure cooker. He broke into the first of our full ration pack, found the curry – a dehydrated bar containing meat and sultanas and looking like a large crumbly Oxo cube – and the packet of rice that went with it.

Then out came the water which he poured over the concoction in the bottom of the pan. He got the stove going and suddenly there was that smell. I can recall it now, the rich, spicy smell of curry. I lay there sniffing. It was then I realised how hungry I was; my mouth watered and I became more and more impatient.

Chay handed the pan to me at last with our one and only spoon, a long-handled wooden thing. I gulped the first two or three mouthfuls and food had never tasted better. I could feel it going right down. I was alive again and feeling warm. I stopped when I had eaten half, which was about half a pound of solid grub. I handed the pan over to Chay and I watched him wolf his portion. Every mouthful he took was an agony because I could have eaten four helpings and still have felt hungry.

But Chay had not finished with the meal yet. 'I've got a sweet, John, just to round the day off,' and he gave me a bar of rum fudge. My goodness, how delicious that was.

And so Hurricane Alma went her way and we ours. We were left alive and with the thought that nothing worse than that 14 June could come along.

We slept and awoke to fog and a ship. It was the trawler *Winchester*, who stopped, and her skipper and crew chatted with us. It was good to hear new voices, but the news they gave us was bad. We found that after twelve days at sea we had only covered 120 miles – ten miles a day. That was really bad.

We had been blown back for the third time to the Georges' Bank. It was the hurricane and the easterly winds that had stopped our progress, and we were both thoroughly depressed. One of the crew shouted down that the trawler was going to Boston, Massachusetts. 'Why don't you give up now, Mac, pack it in? It's much too far to row. Use your heads.'

For a fraction of a second I was tempted. Dry clothes, a good meal, sleep and the stillness of land – what a prospect. But it was only for a fraction, and both Chay and I shouted back, 'No thanks. It's good of you to offer us a lift, but we'll press on.'

When she slipped away into the mist of the fishing grounds Chay and I had a good long, down-to-earth talk. We decided that we had been messing about too much, not spending enough time at the oars. We had somewhere lost the drive that we needed to conquer the Atlantic.

So we worked out a routine. Both of us would row from eight each morning until half an hour before last light. One would make the grub and eat and switch round when the other fellow's turn came up. That would mean that the boat would always be driven through the water. At night we would row separately, two hours' sleep, two hours' row and so on.

I felt encouraged by this decision. We had our drive back. We were in top gear again. But the weeks to come were going to strain us and our rigid ideas. At this time we did not know that, which was probably a good thing.

I must say that when I thought about this voyage back in my home with my wife and my friends in the Regiment, I thought that there would be a dreary, dreadful monotony about life and that time would hang heavy. But I began to find that there was never enough time to keep the boat and the equipment in good order. And there was always something happening on those broad waters.

June 16 was a sunny day, a clear blue sky and the water was flat calm – what a difference. We started to row a bit later than we had planned, at about 10 a.m., mainly because we had rowed until nearly midnight the night before.

At eleven-thirty we saw a large ship about four or five miles away, but we did not make any signals to her. She just kept on her way, serene, imperturbable. A little while later I had a look for some rations out of the polystyrene box that Chay had opened the night before for our curry. I found that part of the week's rations were damaged and uneatable – soaked in salt water despite all the protective coverings.

I felt a bit anxious at this and checked some more of the unopened boxes. Some of these had been ruined. That was obviously Alma's doing – we had not got away scotfree as we had both thought. We talked this over and thought that we might have to reduce our rations later on. Even then we had not realised the damage that Alma had left in her wake.

We rowed some more after I had made lunch from a dehydrated fish bar brought almost to life again by boiling in water. In fact, it was pretty horrid and mushy. But it was food. Later on we were to long for these mushes when food got short.

In the afternoon the wind got up again, but we kept on rowing until seven-thirty when we had dinner – curry again! And so to sleep. That day, a quiet one for us, had kept me full of interest from the time I awoke until the time came for me to get under the tarpaulin and go to sleep. There was never enough time.

During the next few days we had fogs and mists, we saw porpoises and whales – one which seemed like a travelling Nissen hut, it was so huge. It was worrying being in the fog, as we heard sirens and once or twice the rush of a ship travelling fast through the water not far from us. I had doubts about our position again – surely we were not back once more among the fishing fleet on the Georges' Bank – and I felt rather depressed about our progress. But 19 June was to cheer me up considerably, for we saw a ship and I found my estimated position was very nearly spot on with the position she gave us.

We saw four ships close together at about 10 a.m. and one saw us and came towards us. Chay thought it was a fishing factory ship first of all, as there was a smaller vessel close by, and he thought she was transferring her catch.

The ship turned out to be the *Albatross IV*, an oceanographic vessel from Woods Hole. They asked if we needed anything, but I refused everything they offered – we had wanted to be independent of anyone on the ocean. But I changed my mind when I remembered that our torches were out of action, so we took two torches and spare batteries which they kindly offered us. We had a general chat about weather, ocean currents and the position which had so delighted me. She then rang on, there was a tinkle of telegraphs deep below and a swirl from her stern and she was gone.

We knew at least from the *Albatross* that the course we had set was right and that we were heading correctly towards the Gulf Stream with its warmer waters, its brilliant blue and the gentle drift which would help us on our way. It was a very satisfying morning.

Better than this, though, was their intention to report our position to Lloyd's of London. It would mean that our wives would know in a short time that we had survived Alma and that one of their worries was behind them.

We ran into another gale the next day and I was impressed

by the way Chay managed to get to sleep during it. We had put the sea anchor out and got together under cover of the tarpaulin. I could not close my eyes and hung on in terror as the water and spray hit the tarpaulin and sloshed its way into the boat. I can only think that he was more tired than I was and just could not keep awake – but that would be strange for my tough comrade, who, I feel, has greater physical strength than I have.

Later the wind dropped, and all was well and we progressed gradually to the longest day, 21 June, through a series of uneventful hours disturbed only by seeing sharks galore.

We managed to get a good sunbathe in the afternoon, rowing in really excellent weather. As I rowed I looked at my body and at Chay's as we took our steady pull at the oars in the nude. I was looking for damage, bruises, cuts, abrasions. We looked fine. To date we were unscarred by the Atlantic. It was a situation we knew could change – suddenly!

IV

Ann Davison

Ann Davison had led a pretty adventurous life before she ever went to sea. She was trained as an air pilot and for many years worked in a travelling air circus, giving performances all over Britain. It was during this work that she met her future husband, Frank, who nursed a life-long ambition to buy a boat of his own and sail off on some great adventure, such as round the world. Soon Ann had got the bug, too, and after much scraping and saving the Davisons finally acquired an old fishing trawler, *Reliance*. Unfortunately, preparing the boat for the projected voyage entailed so much extra expense that everything seemed to come to a dismal full stop at the Lancashire port of Fleetwood, where *Reliance* had a writ pinned to its mast by one of its many creditors. Determined not to be thwarted of fulfilling his great ambition, Frank Davison persuaded his wife to join him in the hazardous and, of course, highly illegal exploit of slipping from the berth and sailing out of Fleetwood literally at dead of night. The idea was to escape to some foreign land, but the sea, alas, had other ideas, and a series of gales and engine breakdowns led inexorably to a tragic end, both for *Reliance* and its skipper. Ann Davison survived, and indeed went on to accomplish one of the first women's single-handed crossings of the Atlantic in her sloop, *Felicity*, as well as other formidable voyages. These are recounted in several books, such as *My Ship is so Small*, but in none of them is told such a terrible tale as in this extract from *Last Voyage*. . . .

LAST VOYAGE

Ann Davison

Frank had restored order in a remarkable manner whilst I was unconscious. He had pumped the ship out, by hand, working the long stiff arm of the deck pump, an exacting job at the best of times, until *Reliance* was dry and riding buoyantly. He had put up the stay-sail, a headsail of number-one canvas and no pocket handkerchief to handle. He had – how like him – cleaned down the inside of the wheelhouse ('Distempered with soup. What has been going on?'), had made coffee and porridge for breakfast. Found out where we were, which must have been a bit tricky for him under the circumstances, and set the ship to sail herself with lashed wheel out to sea.

Apparently *Reliance* had drifted, early on, very nearly to the entrance to Plymouth, where he had tried to anchor, using the kedge, with main halyard for a cable, and somehow lost them both. He was exceedingly put out by this, which he said was rank carelessness on his part. The fact of there still being the spare bower available and a spare halyard did nothing to appease him. It was after this he hoisted sail. He had even made a simple and ingenious little gadget to drive the water out of the wheelhouse and keep it drained, which worked most successfully.

It was altogether an astounding achievement for one who had but a short while before reached the ultimate in exhaustion, but Frank had more guts than anyone I ever knew. It made me bitterly ashamed of my recent lapse and I was never so humbled in my life.

Over breakfast whilst *Reliance* lopped slowly out to mid-Channel, we did some mental overhauling. Throughout the meal we kept up a pretence of cheer, but there was this thing between us, and when he said abruptly, 'What did happen last night?', I was glad of the chance to bring the horror into the open. We had shared all else, and could share this too. Better by far to bring it out and have done with it than to leave it rotting in the recesses of our minds. Or so it seemed to me, and I told him all that had happened. He listened silently, holding his head in his hands, and looked up, when I finished. 'How awful,' he said, 'how bloody awful. My poor Ann. To think that I . . .

'But you know,' he went on thoughtfully, 'it is extraordinarily interesting. I must tell you my side of the story.'

Which was totally unexpected because somehow I had imagined he would have no recollection of what had occurred.

He remembered the gale as I did up to the time I brought him the coffee. By then he was mentally and physically beaten. Dizzy with looking out of the window, back to the compass, out of the window again. Worn out by the bellowing assaults of the sea . . . One of the most subtle tortures and unrecognised contributory factors to fatigue on a small ship in heavy weather (if it goes on long enough) is the utter inability to relax. For all the time muscles are in play, flexing, working, contracting, whether you are awake or asleep, upright, moving or sitting down. On they go, automatically, relentlessly, never letting up for an instant – until you could scream . . . He was worn out by sheer physical exertion at the wheel – *Reliance* was just about as heavy on the steering as it was possible to be, the only bad thing about her. After I had left him he had passed right out, and came round lying on the wheelhouse floor with water swilling over him. It was pitch dark and bitterly cold. He had not the faintest notion of where he was on what was going on. He thrust his head out of the window and was stung by flung spray, and was utterly and completely lost.

After that it was a phantasmagoria of the macabre.

He unfolded a nightmare tale to me there in the galley, standing as it were on the borderline of sanity and looking both ways.

He knew who I was when I came into the wheelhouse with the soup, but otherwise his mind was a blank. All he knew was that something was wrong. His mind was shut against reality, so that nothing I said about the gale had meaning and he thought I was keeping something dreadful from him. Then when he went below he passed out again in the saloon, and came round with the conviction he had been attacked and laid low by a blow from behind. The chaos in the saloon being evidence of a fight having taken place there. He knew, as one knows in a dream without question or reason, there was a plot afoot, in which I was involved together with other unknown invisible persons (presumably responsible for the attack) to deprive him of the ship. Make away with him, in fact, and take *Reliance* off on some unspecified, nefarious purpose.

When we went up the deck together he was convinced we were in harbour, tied alongside a quay-wall, dear God! But after he passed out for the third time, he awoke to normality but hazily.

It was the most terrible experience I ever heard of. And it showed clear in his ravaged face.

'Dingbats,' he said, when he finished his account. '... and to think it happened to me.'

'But of course,' I said, desperately anxious to settle this and drive the fear of it from his mind, 'it would happen to you. Look what you have been through since we sailed. Before we sailed for that matter. Look at the mental and physical energy you expended yesterday. And on what? When did you last sleep? I don't suppose you averaged more than an hour a day since we sailed. And when did you last eat? There is a limit to endurance. You reached it and went beyond. A less conscientious person would have packed up long before – like I did this morning – but you forced yourself on until your conscious brain could stand no more and the sub-conscious took over.

'And the subconscious can have a particularly nasty way of explaining things.' I grinned tentatively.

The psychology may have been shaky, but it had the desired effect.

Frank brightened. 'Do you think that?'

'I know it,' I stated positively. 'I was in no better state, but it took me a different way.' And I told him about the black-outs. He looked very grave. 'It can't go on,' he said. 'This ship ... she's had everything we possess. She's not going to have our sanity too.'

'She won't. Sleep and rest, and food. That's all we want. And we'll pull out, never fear.'

It was all very well to put on a show of heartiness and talk like a character out of a paper-backed adventure story. I never felt less hearty in my life. I was scared, not of dying or death or losing the ship or failing in our ultimate purpose, but of the thing that had happened to Frank. Until that, the voyage, for all its hardships, had been a kind of splendid fun, at once terrifying and magnificent (and there is a real retrospective joy in hardships overcome), but now it was as if there was an evil force at work, a malignant cancer in our adventure, against which we were helpless. And the horror of it brooded over us, for all we bolstered each other up with a brave display of heroics.

Plymouth was on our doorstep so to speak, but we never mentioned it.

Last night I would have thrown in my hand to save Frank and today I withheld for the same reason. And the choice was mine, for he was at the stage of leaning on me for decisions and drawing on me for strength. To have put in to Plymouth would not have given us the rest we craved. It would have brought on legal miseries which might well, I feared, put Frank out of his mind for ever. I would see those lawyers, and ourselves too, for that matter, in hell first.

We were going to be fit before attempting to scale that mountain.

So *Reliance* plugged out to clear the Eddystone, whence we intended to beat out of the Channel. But the wind died and died away, just when we could have done with a bit, and I spent the day at the wheel juggling with every puff, steering between the light-house and Start Point. And fretted fearfully over Frank, who had agreed to turn in, and then spent the entire day filtering paraffin, sorting things out and testing the fuel tanks to find out how much there was left.

I dared not fuss and chivvy him off to bed, because it was essential for his recovery to show absolute confidence in him, so I held my peace in the wheelhouse and worried myself sick. He brought a cup of cocoa at dusk and we had a gusty meaningless row because we were so strung-up. We were clear of the light-house then, bobbing up and down in the Channel, like a rocking-horse not getting anywhere. So we left the ship to look after herself and went below for a meal, switching on the navigation lights as we went.

Afterwards we went on deck in the dark, to find *Reliance* had drifted into a steamer lane and ships were thick about us like trees in a forest. Bearing down was a colossal steamer winking wrath from an Aldis lamp. There was hardly a breath of a breeze to stir the staysail and we were powerless to alter our course in any way. The steamer steered round us, flashing fury with the lamp turned aft, and continued to do so as she stormed on her way down Channel. I leant over the bulwarks and bellowed, 'And you!', which was entirely wasted, but an eminently satisfying thing to do.

Frank turned in then, saying, 'Don't worry about these guys – we're under sail, they have to get out of our way.' And I spent a hectic night drifting, not quite out of control, but very nearly, across the bows of outraged steamers. There must have been some pretty fruity commentaries taking place on various bridges that night. *Reliance* was a pigmy among giants and the giants were not looking for navigation lights at her level. After a few heart-twisting turns I switched on the riding light, stern light and decklights as well, which may have been unorthodox, and illegal for all I know, but at least rendered the ship visible.

By dawn we were across the steamer lanes and rid of the ships. I was exceedingly tired. The wind started to fuss and moan after its quiet night, then grumbled and blustered, whipping up a steep little sea, in an early morning temper. *Reliance* became rather a handful. The staysail lunged and jerked and thundered whatever I did. Frank had had about eight hours' sleep, so I thought it fair enough to go and ask his advice.

He was sound asleep and bounded up in a great fright when I touched him. 'What's this?' he rasped. 'You've got the cable running out freely, haven't you? It's buoyed, isn't it? Well, then what's the trouble?'

With sinking heart I tried to explain what I had come about, and wished to God I had not disturbed him.

'I don't see what your worry is.' He was very brisk. 'There's nothing jamming the cable, is there?'

'No,' I said wearily, 'never mind. Go back to sleep.'

'Nonsense. You come to me with your troubles, then you won't tell me what they are.'

'I'll tell you in the morning.'

I went back to the wheelhouse wondering if it would be wise to put back to Plymouth after all. But the thought of the lawyers intervened. Best to wait and see how he was later. He wasn't properly awake then; he would be all right after plenty of rest and sleep. I decided to wait and see ...

The wind grew no stronger but steadied and *Reliance* settled down. I lashed the wheel and went on deck to tidy up. Ropes and halyards and things were loose and swinging. There is a technical jargon for doing things to ropes just as there are technical names for the ropes themselves, but I never got round to learning the language. I knew roughly what the various ropes did – and what they shouldn't do, so I tightened them up and made proper little hanks of their running ends and hung them on their cleats and belaying pins and felt very responsible. Then Charles gave a bit of bother and broke away. He was a tremendous block with a hook to hoist the jib. I christened him Charles after a friend, whose wife in a moment of stress had once referred to him as being 'so big and angry', and I never knew anything so big and angry as that block when it was at large. I caught him eventually after an exciting dodge and chase (one cosh from Charles, bigger than a man's head, and you'd had it), and hooked into an eyebolt in deck and knitted a cat's-cradle round him to keep him there, which it did, and wondered very anxiously about Frank.

He turned up about six in the morning, looking remarkably cheerful.

'What were you nattering about this morning?' he said. 'I wasn't awake properly. Damn funny. Thought you were foreman of a cable-laying gang.'

'Frank,' I begged, 'for Pete's sake, don't do it again.'

'No,' he said sombrely, 'I won't.' And he didn't.

It blew steadily all day (from a westerly direction, of course, it never blew anything else for us, unless it was south-west) what would have been a good sailing wind if we had had any sails, but the mizzen wanted mending, and the main halyard was gone and the spare needed rigging, a task we boggled at, neither of us having the strength to play the daring young man on the flying trapeze or hoist the other in the bosun's chair; so we slogged on the long beat down Channel as best we could under the old red staysail.

A test heave on the flywheel lever confirmed the suspicion that the for'ard cylinder was seized again, gummed up through slow running; the reason for the engine stopping when the throttle was closed. Fuel was so low now that it was to be conserved against the time we chose to make port – or an emergency. But we shirked the job of an overhaul until we regained the strength to handle the heavy engine parts, and spent the day catching up on our food intake, preparing and gobbling prodigious meals. At the end of each one Frank fell sound asleep.

By nightfall we were doodling off the French coast, marked by a long row of shore lights. Just where it was exactly escapes me now; we seemed to know at the time, but were more directly concerned with the rapidity with which *Reliance* was approaching. So we came about, and the staysail rent asunder. Whereupon *Reliance* with an air of saying that will be all for tonight, drifted smugly out to sea. Up Channel, I could have taken an axe to her.

We stooged about till dawn and got up the jib, Charles being rather more than we cared to handle in the dark just then. As it was he was exceedingly obstreperous, swinging us off our feet and slinging us into the mast or anything solid at hand. It was a relief to get up out of the way.

There were one or two fishing boats at work in the vicinity. A large blue one came up to us, attracted no doubt by the tatty appearance of our ship. An immense crew hung avariciously over the side and offered to help. Frank refused and offered to buy some fish. I had hopped below at their approach and hopefully counted the four pound notes. But they said they had no fish and went away. They returned later offering to tow us into some place or another, and were quite disgruntled that it was not their day for easy money and they had to go fishing after all.

We concentrated on the mizzen-sail; Frank fixed the mast rings, and I stitched the bolt rope on the sail. *Reliance* rolled nowhere in particular in a merry-hearted fashion, scooping up small bucketfuls of water which sloshed playfully down the deck. We hoisted the mizzen on the topping lift, using the handy billy to help with the last few feet, and had it set just as the blue fisherman was making towards us for a third try. Evidently the fishing wasn't too good that day. But when he saw the mizzen go up he realised we were no good either and departed.

We lashed the float in place again against the wheelhouse, and generally the ship looked less of a shambles. But Frank seemed very depressed, and to set him up I said with ample food and water aboard we had every chance of completing the voyage; talked glibly about putting into Lisbon or the Canary Islands if we found it was getting beyond us. I have no idea whether I believed in this myself, being quite beyond faith in anything, but it was a show of confidence, and cheered Frank no end, and that was all that mattered.

A row of red lights turned up at night, still on the French coast, to give us light fever, and we stood watch and watch about. Frank slept all right on his watch below, but I could not, and spent the time in the galley listening to the radio.

Actually after that last deplorable blackout I did not close my eyes in sleep aboard again.

Our time was drawing to an end. There were but three more days of our voyage left, though we were not to know that of course.

We strove desperately to get out of the Channel, beating from side to side against a relentless westerly wind and with available sail not getting much forrarder. Had we been at the top of our form we should have done better. We were inundated with offers of assistance from passing vessels of all sorts, from small fishing boats to large steamers. It was most embarrassing. Frank used to deal with them, whilst I (having become a very desperate character) watched from a vantage-point below, ready to launch a surprise attack in the event of any funny business. This amused Frank vastly. He said there was no likelihood of any trouble from that kind at sea. But I have no faith in humanity. He always tried to buy fish off the fishermen, but either the fishers are mean or the fishing in the Channel is bad for we never got any. The last fisherman to accost us asked if we intended making port; Frank said no and he grinned, saying, 'I wouldn't if I were you.'

We got trapped by wind and tide in Lyme Bay and flogged up and down between Start Point and Portland Bill, unable to clear either point, and seeming likely to spend a Flying Dutchman existence in the Bay for the rest of our lives. We then put up the balloon jib which was really too light a sail for the weight of wind blowing, but it pulled like a horse, and *Reliance* sailed closer to windward. It seemed at last we might clear Start Point. Towards nightfall (this I think would be 3 June) the wind increased, and the question arose as to whether we should take the big jib in. It was obvious that the blow would continue, which suited us fine if it got no worse, but it was just as much as the sail could stand. If we replaced it with the smaller headsail then we could not clear Start Point, and faced the prospect of at least another day ploughing up and down in Lyme Bay. On the other hand if we were to take it in, now was the time to do so.

Frank said furiously, 'Whatever I do will be wrong,' decided to play for a straight win and left it.

So it blew up into a snorting gale; the silk sail burst with a clap of thunder and flogged itself to ribbons.

We spent another night in the familiar bellowing maelstrom of a maddened sea. Hawklike, I watched Frank with anxious intensity, but there was no need. He was undistressed. By dawn we were tossing in an ominously green sea in the south-western corner of Lyme Bay, with the Devonshire coast far too near, and getting nearer every minute.

Charles had taken the opportunity to create an inextricable tangle above the hounds and refused to come down. We wrapped the remnants of the sail round the winch and wound him down. So that the twist would not be transferred to the sail Frank made a rope grommet, and strenuously we hauled up the little jib, by hand and by winch.

By this time we were so close in I was yawning my head off in exasperation at the difficulty of it all. *Reliance* refused to turn through the wind and had to be gybed round, losing valuable sea-room. The water looked positively translucent. Then we were slogging up towards the Bill once more.

'What a game,' said Frank.

Inevitably the wind eased off: we bucketed slowly away from the shore, out of green into grey water, up towards Portland Bill. If only we could clear one of the horns of this damned Bay and get into mid-Channel again. If only this infernal wind would blow from another direction...

It was in melancholy mood I waited in the saloon for a weather report from the radio. The sky had been still full of wind at dawn, and I hoped to hear that the sky was a liar. The radio bleated a song popular in my early flying days, 'There's a Small Hotel', evoking a host of memories – was life really so gay, so carefree? – all sounding both appropriate and incongruous. It had changed to 'Put Your Shoes On, Lucy', when Frank came in and we giggled at it foolishly.

We listened to a gale warning and Frank said, 'We'd better fix the engine in that case.' He seemed quite brisk and cheerful. I picked a book at random from the top of the pile at my feet. *Ulysses.* Flicked the pages – '. . . made weak by time and fate, but strong in will to strive, to seek, to find, and not to yield.'

Not to yield. I followed Frank into the engine-room.

It was an easier task to free the piston this time, knowing exactly what the trouble was and how to tackle it. We felt when we left it ready for starting that it was a good job done, and that we were catching up on the work bit by bit. But we hadn't got round to the mainsail yet. It was still pretty wild though not yet the gale of the warning and we were too jelly-boned to cope with a halyard up the pendulum-swinging mast. Tomorrow, we promised ourselves, if it is fit.

By night we were coming up to the Bill, having pinched and scraped all the sea-room possible. The sou'westerly wind had hardened considerably. *Reliance* under jib and mizzen was tugging away to clear the Bill, upon which the light flashed brightly. Frank took a last look round; satisfied that all was well, he turned in. It was tacitly understood that rest for him was all-important.

For a while I stayed in the wheelhouse watching the Portland light and our steady progress. We were going to have ample margin. The movement of the ship underfoot had become second nature and I did not notice it. Nor hear the shrilling of the wind. But I felt the cold and lashed the wheel and nipped below for a cup of coffee.

As one is oblivious of the noise of a well-known engine and is instantly aware of a change in the beat, so I recognised when *Reliance* changed direction. Immediately I was on deck to see what she was up to.

For no known reason she had swung off course and was belting downwind for the Bill.

Knowing her reluctance to go through the wind and the

amount of sea-room she required gybing, and desperately anxious not to lose all we had gained, I called Frank.

As she was coming slowly round, Charles, way up at the top of the mast, played his ace – the rope grommet parted and the jib blew over the side.

Reliance drifted stern first.

'Engine,' cried Frank. On the way down I slipped into the galley and turned off the stove. It was bound to be an all-night session. It always was. And I knew the situation was going to be tough by the waves of drowsiness that swept over me. A sure sign.

As the torches roared I looked out of the hatch. Bright were the lights behind Chesil Bank. Bright were the lights on the Portland radio masts. Brilliantly swept the beam of the light-house.

The tide was making six knots, or more. Taking us with it...

'We haven't much time,' I said to Frank, who nodded as if I had said it was raining.

The engine started on one cylinder. I went to the wheel-house and Frank wedged the fuel injector on the for'ard cylinder. There was no time to play around. We had covered an amazing distance whilst the heads were heating and were very near to the high cliffs of Portland Bill. But half-power was not enough. With the throttle wide *Reliance* was going astern. Stern first she passed under the light, its white beam slicing the night sky overhead.

Frank took over and put her into reverse in the hope she would steer better.

I looked out of the door aft. Black waves were breaking high and white on outlying pinnacles of rock. Right in our path.

'Don't think we'll make it.'

I felt faintly surprised and automatically unhooked the lifejackets. Each time she lifted we listened – waiting...

Ahead or reverse it made no difference. *Reliance*, fast in the grip of wind and tide, passed under the end of the Bill, missing the rocks by a matter of inches. The swift immutable current swept round the point and up the eastern side of the Bill. *Reliance* went with it, stern first round the point, then broadside, bow on to the cliffs, closing nearer and nearer in every long-drawn minute.

We dropped the mizzen, and Frank went to try and clear the atomiser on number one.

'Bring her round,' he said, 'If you can.'

With unusual docility she turned, was coming round, was nearly round, then a sharp bark, and the engine stopped. She swung back to face the cliffs. And plunged towards them, inexorably.

I thought: I know this. I've been through it all before.

As Frank bounded up through the hatch, cursing, I switched on the deck-lights and together we ran up the deck. The anchor was already shackled to wire and chain, but as we tore at the lashings, he looked up at the towering cliffs above us and straightened.

'No use. No time,' he said. 'We'll have to look to ourselves...'

Quickly he got the paraffin and as I handed him a bundle of garments for a flare, he hesitated – 'Won't you want these again?' – and laughed shortly and soaked them in paraffin. The flare cast an orange glow over the deck and by its weird light we unlashed the float and moved it over to the lee side, ready for launching.

We were putting on lifejackets, Frank grumbling he couldn't work in one, when she struck. Lightly at first then harder and harder. We were in front of the wheelhouse. He shouted, 'Hold tight!' and we grabbed the mainsheet. Jolting and bumping on the bottom, louder and louder she crashed. Each crash the knell for our hopes and beliefs. Sounding the end of all for which we had laboured and endured.

And I could believe none of it.

I heard Frank saying, 'What a shame, what a shame,' as the ship rent beneath our feet.

Then the tall cliff face was upon us with a tremendous splintering crash. The bowsprit snapped like kindling. The flare was out. The night was dark. We clung to the mainsheets in a pool of light thrown by the lamps in front of the wheelhouse. She began to roll. From side to side, rails under, with incredible speed, as if she would roll right over. A colossal jolt; the shock travelling from stem to stern. The mainmast sagged, came over, seemed to hang suspended. The boom dropped and we leapt from under. Before our horrified eyes the bows of the vessel buried into the very face of the cliff.

And above the roaring sea came the terrible noise of a dying ship.

Frank yelled: 'Float!' and we heaved it over the side. It swung in the water, level with the deck, in the depths below, streaming away under the counter.

'Jacket OK?' he shouted. 'Over you go!'

I swung over the side, facing it, and, as the ship rolled, felt out with my feet for the float, missed it, and was left hanging by my arms. He leant over and gripped my wrists. But the ship, rolling prodigiously, flung me off. I shouted: 'Let go!' and dropped into the sea.

In the float I got a leg in the ropeworks. Each time the ship came over, the mizzen-boom on the counter rail drove within a hair's breadth of my chest. I was trapped, helpless and infuriated. Frank, not seeing this, shouted, 'Right?' and without waiting for a reply climbed on to the bulwarks and leapt overboard.

I happened to look up, got an imprint of him silhouetted on the rail high above – the ship having rolled the other way – then he jumped clear into the sea, swam to the float, clambered aboard and handed me a paddle as, panting and angry, I wrenched free. Muttering about the dangerousness of the ropeworks in the float (incomprehensible to Frank) I dug in a paddle and sculled away to the end of the line out of reach of the boom. Frank said, 'Got your knife?' and cut the painter.

It struck me as an unnecessarily dramatic gesture, just as making a flare from a bundle of real clothes had appeared to him. It was impossible to believe in our predicament.

As far as we could judge – it was too dark to see more than the faint outline of the cliff-tops and the white smudge of waves dashing against the face – *Reliance* was aground at the foot of a bluff round which the coast fell back a bit. There was no landing for us there, the cliffs were sheer, and the high-flung spray of the bellowing breakers warned us to keep off. We struck out along the coast in the direction of Weymouth, taking care to keep clear of the boiling turmoil at the foot of the cliffs.

Our queer little craft was a lozenge-shaped ring of cork, or some other unsubmersible substance, canvas-bound and painted red and yellow. The ring was woven about with an intricate system of life-lines, and in the centre of the ring, suspended by a rope network was a wooden box. It was in this network I had got entangled. The box was double-sided, with two compartments either side with sliding lids, for the containing of provisions (a point we had not taken advantage of, unfortunately). It was immaterial which way up it floated, for both sides were the right side.

We sat on the ring and paddled, with our feet on the box and water up to our knees. Sometimes the water swept across our laps. The float swooped gamely to the top of a wave and dived down into the trough. Frank said she was a good little craft – but wet. We were very cold.

We were both wearing woollen sweaters and jackets but our clothes were soaked through, of course. Frank had cast off his shoes and his feet gleamed very white in the black water. I was still wearing the light rubber-soled sneakers that had hardly left my feet since we sailed from Fleetwood. In my pockets was the 'shipwreck' equipment carried since the night off Land's End, torch, four one-pound notes, watch, knife and lucky photograph. The watch was still going in spite of its immersion. We left the ship shortly after 2 a.m. and it did not stop until twenty-three minutes past eight. Then it stopped irrevocably.

As we paddled along the coast, careering up and over and down the swift waves, we saw terrific activity burst out on the cliff-tops. A rocket shot up with a bang, leaving a white trail against the night sky. Torch, bicycle and car lights appeared and ran about in a purposeful manner. An organisation was going into operation. We visualised telephonings, shouts, orders; a lifeboat launched, coast-guards in action ... because of a ship in distress ... *our* ship, we realised, unable to rid ourselves of astonishment and incredulity. Simultaneously we looked back. A yellow pinpoint of light still burned at the foot of the bluff.

'What a shame,' burst out Frank, thinking of his beloved ship, 'what an utter, bloody shame.'

Right back to the beginning again ... with four pounds and a pocket-knife ... No *Reliance*, no future, no hope. I made some boy-scout remark about everything going to be all right. But apart from the overriding surprise I was beyond feeling anything but a thankfulness that Frank and I were together and a yearning to lie down and sleep for about a week.

He said, 'Aren't we getting too far out?'

It was hard to say.

'No. Yes. We are a bit.'

There was a point a mile or so ahead along the coast, and we thought if we could get round that we might find a lee and a landing, and paddled towards it for all we were worth. Yet we seemed to draw no nearer.

A steamer making for Weymouth passed on our starboard hand, not too far away. We shouted, competing ineffectively with the roaring sea, and shone the torch, but the battery was almost spent, and it gave only a feeble glow. At the same time we spotted the lights of a lifeboat coming round the point we were trying to make for.

By now we realised that the fierce current that had wrecked *Reliance* was turning and carrying us out to sea. Inexorably, we were going back, some distance out, and parallel to the way we had come. But the ship's lights were consoling and the knowledge there was a lifeboat looking for us, comforting. We had complete faith in being picked up.

We could see the masthead light of the lifeboat rising and falling. From the tops of waves we could see the navigation lights. Then it moved close inshore, and passed us.

We yelled at the top of our voices and waved the torch. The torch went out irrevocably, and our shouts were drowned in the tumult of wind and water.

Our puny efforts with the paddles were no match for the sea. Drawn relentlessly away we watched the lifeboat work up the coast to *Reliance*, then down and back again, shining a searchlight on the cliffs.

Frank said peevishly, 'What the hell do they think we are? Goats?' And I said, 'It will be dawn soon, and then they'll see us.'

We passed *Reliance*... the end of Portland Bill.

When daylight came they did not see us. Nor by then could we see them. Only from wave-crests could we see land at all. The seas were tremendous, and very steep. From the top we looked down into impenetrable depths, from the troughs we gazed, awestruck at huge walls of water. The cold was intense.

Wilder and wilder came the seas. Wilder and whiter.

Instead of the float riding over the crests, the crests rode over the float. We paddled one-handed, holding on to the life-lines.

'I do not see' – I found it extraordinarily difficult to move my frozen lips – 'how anyone could pick us up in this . . . even if we were seen . . .'

Frank did not reply, but looked round and round at the awful sea as if he did not believe what he saw.

The current took us into the very centre of Portland Race. The sea was white with insensate rage. Towering pinnacles of water rushed hither and yon, dashing into one another to burst with a shrapnel of foam – or to merge and grow enormous.

From the level of the sea itself it was as the wrath of God, terrifying to behold.

Seated on the bottomless coracle, filled with wonder and awe, we worked away with the paddles to meet the seas. Bravely the little craft tugged up the precipitous slopes and plunged into the depths. I was thinking I would rather be in her than in a dinghy, when suddenly I was in the sea, underneath the float, looking up through the centre where the water was bright green.

There was time to wonder – is this drowning? – and – how green the water is from this side – then I surfaced, found I was gripping a life-line.

The float was swinging uneasily at the bottom of a trough. There was no sign of Frank. Terror-stricken, I shrieked for him at the very top of my voice.

He came up about ten yards away. Swam strongly to the float, still holding his paddle, whereon I realised I had lost mine.

We heaved aboard, and lay athwart the ring, gasping, clinging to the life-lines.

'What did that?' I panted.

'Don't know. This is *not* funny.'

Then we saw my paddle, swung upright and set off in pursuit, chasing it up hill and down stormy dale, but it remained forever out of reach.

Suddenly we were in the water again. Under the float. Green water above. This time we were slower getting aboard. Took longer to recover. We looked at one another in great fear.

'What do we *do*? How do we fight this?'

The upset was so sudden, happened so quickly, we had no notion as to the cause of it. And that was the frightening part.

Dizzily the float tore up and down, swinging and swaying. Tensely we watched the advance of each white-headed mountain. Frank had lost his paddle in the last upset and we could not even make a pretence of fighting.

Then we were flung into the sea again. And this time saw how it happened. Saw with slow-motion clarity how the float was sucked up under a great overhanging crest, and thrown over backwards in the boiling tumult as the wave broke.

This time it was very hard to get back on to the float.

Frank threw an arm about my shoulders: 'All right?'

'Yes.'

'Good-oh.'

We got right inside the float, crouching on the wooden box with water up to our armpits.

There must be some way of stopping it turning over, I thought.

He shouted: '*Look out*!'

Instinctively I leant forward, head down on the ring to meet what was coming. And we did not turn over. But took the full force of the wave as it exploded upon us.

I found myself shouting: 'That's it. That's it. Lean forward. Head down. That foxes 'em.'

Shivering violently with cold I remembered something once read about the mechanics of shivering and put up a great show of exaggerated shudders, partly to offset the numbing cold, and partly as a manifestation of triumph. Frank smiled wanly.

But the conquest was short-lived. The seas grew worse. Boiled in a white lather all about us. Breaking in endless succession... We hardly recovered from the onslaught of one before gasping under the next. The weight of water and shock of cold were stunning. Each time a wave broke over us it was with the effect of an icy plunge, although we were actually crouching in water all the time.

Hours dragged out in immeasurable misery as the sea struck with a sledge-hammer to kill a pair of gnats.

No longer buoyed by the slightest hope of rescue we sank into an apathy of endurance, huddled together, heads on the ring, hands grasping life-lines with the prehensile, immovable grip of the newborn. Or the dying. Passively fighting for the lives which were a little less living after every blow.

In a comparative lull, from a wave-top, I glimpsed land, Portland Bill, thin and attenuated in the distance. Pointed to it. Frank slowly stood up and called in a whisper for help.

It was such a pitiful travesty of his usual stentorian bellow I was inexpressibly shocked, and with a surge of protective energy reached up to pull him down, dreading a recurrence of the horror of the other night. Then I saw it was not that ... and looked wildly round for help. But there was none.

He did not speak. He put out a hand, pressed mine, reassuringly, smiled at me.

And gradually, the smile fixed and meaningless and terrible, faded into unconsciousness, into a slow delirium when, blank-eyed, he tried to climb out of the float. I held on to him and feebly tried to rub his hands, my own unfeeling.

A monster wave rose above the rest. Fury piled on fury. Curling foaming crest. Sweeping down on us. Inescapable. I threw an arm round Frank, leant forward.

The little float drove into the wall of water and was lost within it.

When it broke free Frank was dead.

I stared at the edge of the ring. At the ropes intertwined about it. At the froth and bubbles on the water.

Nothing mattered now. No point in trying any more. The fight was over. I laid my head on my arms and closed my eyes, engulfed in a blessed darkness.

But Fate, or whatever governs the chances that influence our actions, is entirely without mercy.

A wave thundered down on the float which should have been the end of me, but instead, woke me from oblivion to anger. A bitter impotent rage, so that I struck out, beating the air with my fists, fighting a tangible battle with an intangible foe.

It was the last wave to break over the float then, and I was left alive and miserable and waiting to die. Bethought me of the knife in my pocket and how the end could be hastened, but the knife was gone. I was too stupefied to think of the obvious.

(*That* only occurred three days later, then it was too late.)

So I waited.

A puffin landed near-by and sculled round the float evincing great interest in it. I had an unreasoning impulse to touch it, but it was just out of reach. It seemed entirely without fear and its presence was infinitely comforting. It made no effort to fly away, but drifted alongside, preening its feathers.

As I watched the bird thoughts came into my head, peopling an empty stage, and I listened to what they had to say and looked at their actions as though they were no part of myself. As indeed they were not, for they came without conscious evocation.

I saw the headlines ripping out – and vultures picking over the bones of our beliefs. Heard the speculations of armchair sages, wise to another's trouble, not to truth. Heard the baying of the wolves...

And listened to rumours, whispers and suspicions...

They say... You ran away. You purposely wrecked the ship. You dared not face your responsibilities. You could not face what was coming. You killed yourselves. Shirked... Ran ... Suicide...

They say...

By God... No! Furiously I turned on the thoughts and scattered them for those of my own choosing.

There was one of us left. One to carry on what both had begun. The application may have been unorthodox, but the principles were sound, of that I was convinced. To have faith in one's beliefs, to follow an aim to the end is a fundamental necessity. Otherwise the whole pattern of life is pure chance, a miasma and a mockery, and nothing is worth the doing or trying. As life be a blade of grass and one must live out one's unknown purpose unreasoned.

To leave that which we had begun uncompleted, to give in without a fight to the very end, would be to nullify all that had gone before, admit defeat, and to a worthlessness of all we had tried to do, and be.

'All right,' I cried to the fleeting clouds, 'you shall have your blood money.' And to the empty sea I shouted: 'I'm going back. Going back. Do you hear?' And got up to stand on the float and shout it again, racked with rage and madness and utmost despair.

As if some purpose had been accomplished the puffin flew away.

As the long, long morning wore on and the sun climbed high, the sea moderated somewhat, the clouds swept away, and it turned to a day such as we had loved, blowing and blue, but the life-giving warmth of the sun had come too late.

I sat on the ring to dry out and the float hurried on to an unknown destination, taking me within twenty yards of a large brown buoy. Afterwards I discovered it to be twelve miles from land, marking a sunken aircraft. But I had seen it before, in a gale, and knew our surmise then had been correct. I wanted to tell Frank. Then the buoy moved away, disappeared over the leaping waves, and it was some time before I had the wit to realise that the float had changed direction. Turning to see whither it was bound I found land ahead and on the port hand.

Gradually features became discernible, recognisable as the west side of Portland Bill and the long strand of Chesil Bank.

The float was making straight for a beach below Portland town at the mainland end of the island. It looked to be a good landing, but there was a tremendous surf. Waves swept past the float, hurrying landwards without a moment to lose, growing bigger and bigger and roaring mightily.

About two miles off the float changed direction again as the current took it diagonally towards the Bill and out to sea. I broke off a wooden handhold attached to the life-line, for use as a paddle and tried to work inshore. It was pretty inadequate but enabled me to steer to a certain extent. The stream ran in fairly close but at the same time carried the float seawards, sweeping down the coast, passing good landing places until there was nothing but sheer cliff, rock bestrewn at foot, where the sea dashed with huge columns of spray and smoking spume. It did not seem possible to land there, or even having landed to scale the cliffs.

Nearing the end of the Bill the float was very near in.

The place was a mass of rocks and giant boulders. The noise of the sea was thunder. But it was either that or making the whole miserable circuit over again.

Feeling, for God's sake let's get it over, I dug away with the handhold for all I was worth. Then was caught up in a blind white rush, hurled towards the rocks. The float turned over and I was flung into the sea. Surfaced for a moment, still gripping a life-line. High overhead hung a wave, breaking. Instinctively I let go and was lost in a green confusion, rocks beneath, sea above.

The water receded, I was lying on my back on a rock with the float on top of me.

The float was empty.

I tried to push it off. Failed. Tried again and succeeded. Another wave towered. Tumult. Then air and peace and the float atop again. Again I pushed it off. Crawled to another rock, clung to it as the next wave broke.

Between waves I had glimpsed a cavern whose floor was above the level of the breaking seas, and between waves I worked towards it, pursued by the float, and thinking with idiotic simplicity: So this is how you land on rocks, cling like a limpet and keep your head down.

Then I was standing in the cave. Alone. No sign of the float. Nothing. I stood and looked at the sea and my thoughts were my own.

The cave was tall and vaulted, running parallel to the cliff with an out-wall protecting it from the sea, and it was open both ends.

I looked up at the cliffs, sixty or seventy feet, maybe not so much, I was in no state to judge, except that they were sheer and over-hanging, quite beyond my capabilities to scale. I had come in to a small rock-hidden cove bounded by the cave and a precipitous wall of cliff. I knew it was almost at the end of the Bill but could not see what lay round the corner. There was no way of finding out except by going into the sea. I looked out at the other end of the cave. The entrance there was almost blocked by great rocks, and beyond was more sheer cliff, seeming to tumble down into the sea. There appeared to be no way out either way.

I shouted until my voice gave out and all I heard in reply was the scream of seagulls and the thunder of surf.

My pockets were inside out and there was nothing left but the lucky photograph and the useless watch with which to fight the fight I had come back for. So much for all that high-flown thinking. I laughed helplessly and blacked out and fell about until I had the sense to lie down and rest. It was cold and the cavern floor was wet. I thought of going below to get a coat, and stirred and found where I was.

A small brown bird was hopping inquisitively round my feet.

I was pretty far gone by then and knew if I stayed where I was there was no point in having come ashore, so I crawled over the boulder-blocked entrance to find a way along the coast and look for that place where the cliffs had seemed possible of climbing. I don't suppose the going was really as tough as it seemed. There were rocks and boulders to be surmounted all the way, some as big as cottages and presenting interesting problems for there was no way round with the sea on one hand and aloof heights on the other.

I came to the place I was looking for and started to climb. The surface was not rock but loose dry earth with here and there a patch of turf. It was very steep. Where there was nothing to give a grip, I dug out hand and footholds with my hands. Ten yards from the top I lost my grip and slid back for several yards, arms outspread, pressing hard against the side, until my feet were brought up against a small outcrop. It was a straight drop fifty feet into the sea, when I looked over my shoulder, and this was somehow profoundly irritating. I dug very careful handholds then and climbed to the top.

What I expected to find there I don't know. The reason for all this effort was lost in the effort itself. I was dimly aware of being geared-up for a fight. Though with whom or why was not clear. Maybe I expected to see the battleground laid out ready and waiting. I beheld a gentle slope of turf leading up to a radio mast. Nothing more.

Beyond?

Slowly I walked towards the top of the slope.

V

Francis Chichester

Francis Chichester may, alas, be gone, but surely will never be forgotten – the Grand Old Man of single-handed ocean voyaging who not only accomplished so many formidable 'firsts' but wrote so well about his experiences in a whole series of books, such as *Alone Across the Atlantic*, *The Lonely Sea and the Sky*, *Along the Clipper Way*, *Gipsy Moth Circles the World.* In any assessment of this rather unique adventurer, his early days should be remembered, for he was originally an air pilot of great ability, making several dramatic long distance flights about which, again, he wrote entertainingly in *Solo to Sydney*, *Ride on the Wind* and *Alone over the Tasman Sea.* In all his many accomplishments Francis Chichester showed a meticulous attention to detail, indeed exactitude, so that he was not merely a gifted yachstman but, for instance, a quite intrepid and brilliant navigator. Ever ready to try out new equipment he probably helped more than anyone to push yachting into its new era of almost computerised technology. Needless to say this is not a trend which has met with universal approval among those who like to go to sea in small ships essentially for the sheer pleasure of the experience – however, in this extract from one of Chichester's last books, *The Romantic Challenge*, technology hardly enters into what is a very vivid account of coping with a straightforward 'knockdown'....

KNOCKDOWN

Francis Chichester

I left Horta on 30 April. João took the helm until *Gipsy Moth* was in the Canal do Faial, the channel between Faial and Pico. Then he signalled to his pilot launch which came and took him off. I was sad to leave Horta, although I was longing to be home again.

All day it was slow going but in fine weather, with gentle breezes. For a while in the evening *Gipsy Moth* was becalmed and only sailed six miles over a four-hour period. In one way I was contented enough to go slowly because I was in a lazy, listless mood, but I could not clear the archipelago of islands before dawn next morning so I had very little sleep. I had the same trouble when leaving Horta in 1960 with Sheila – of not being able to settle down to a sleep until Graciosa was astern.

At 0630 the next morning I could see Praia, the town of Graciosa, on the north-east side of it, and at 0900 I noted that with the big runner boomed out to starboard '*Gipsy Moth* had a businesslike press-on gait, with a slight roll to port, a gurgle of water along the hull as she rolled back which gave a feeling of power and speed.'

Sunday 2 May, noon. 'Run fix-to-fix 115 miles, sailed 121·25. Distance to Plymouth 1,091. Distance sailed since leaving Plymouth 17,400 miles.'

Nightfall came with heavy rain and poor visibility. I dropped the mizen-stays'l, which was making a lot of noise, clanking and flapping, and seemed to be obstructing the air-stream on to the heads'ls for most of the time and only pulling periodically itself. *Gipsy Moth* was playing her devilish trick time after time of imitating a steamer's engine beat, which never fails to make me apprehensive and nervy. Half an hour after midnight I was woken by the change of movement of the boat and waves, to find *Gipsy Moth* heading south instead of north-east. The wind had veered, bang! from

S to NW; so *Gipsy Moth* was now headed into the seas raised by the southerly wind which had been blowing all day. The movement was horrible, jumping, twisting, snatching and rolling. I could not stand, even in the cockpit, without holding on to something. I was faced with getting the runner down, then the pole, then gybing and coming up to the wind. However, I plugged away and it was not as bad as I had feared. I had to be very careful how I moved about and it was a long job because of having to hang on to something all the time. Going up the mast, working at the heel of the pole and then lowering the pole turned out the easiest part because I had things to hang on to there. I used the topping-lift to lower the pole off the mast after I had freed it. The whole operation took two and a half hours.

I changed the windvane down to a smaller one but it was decidedly not my night; by the time I had finished *Gipsy Moth* was becalmed and aback and I had the tiresome job of working her round to her proper heading as she bounced about on the old sea. When the wind came I expected it to go back to the south so that I should have the joy of rigging the boom and all that once more. However, I decided to turn in. *Gipsy Moth* could do what she bloody well liked. I was chilled, shivery and seasick, and above all I was fed-up with the extraordinary antics of the wind.

At 1100 on the 3rd I donned my harness to go and raise the tops'l, only to find that *Gipsy Moth* was on the wind and no tops'l could be used. I could not see anything wrong with the weather to account for the wind's odd behaviour. It seemed that a tiny secondary with wide open isobars giving near calm winds had passed through on a north-easterly track. The barometer was high and had scarcely moved. I had only recorded it twice in the past twenty-four hours, 1,023 mb at 1,300 and 1,022 mb at 1,825 on 2 May; the next reading given was not till 2,000 of the 3rd.

Monday 3 May, noon. 'Run only 91 miles for 124·5 sailed. Position 40° 51′ N 23° 21′ W. Distance to the Hoe 994 miles.'

At 1733: 'A dull, dreary, grey sea, grey sky and grey light, with drizzly fog cutting visibility to about half a mile. I spent two hours on deck clearing up after last night. This included freeing the mizen topping-lift which was wound round the backstay insulator at the top. The wind is veering once more and I could do with a poled-out sail again but not today, thank you. I am grateful I am not racing and can take it easy if I want to. I am now looking forward to lunch; I am keenly hungry for once and have some sweet potatoes on the boil. I wish I had something appetising like Peter's red mullet to go with them. My remaining tinned fish is dreary, though I may have one tin of bonito left which is the best. However, the sweet potatoes fried after parboiling are delicious on their own. I slipped up in not looking for tinned fish at Horta; the Portuguese turn out good stuff.'

In the middle of lunch (at 6.30 p.m.) the wind began to veer considerably, so I dressed up again and gybed. The gybe was needed and it was better to do it before dark, which was just falling. The result was good, giving the heading required and a knot extra speed, though to be fair I think the extra knot was due to increased wind speed. The true wind now was from nearly west, speed 17 knots. I ought to have worked out the true wind sooner and gybed earlier instead of eating. Barometer 1,016·5, a drop of 5·5 mb in the past twenty-three hours. This was a steady drop, indicating a weather change on the way.

The log entry for 0330 on the 4th reads: 'With the wind piping up and in the upper 30s at times, *Gipsy Moth* was beginning to run wild. Chiefly due to the old pal, the tops'l. So I hoicked myself out of my very comfortable sleeping-bag and dropped the tops'l. I also dropped the mizen-stays'l to give the wind a better run into the big jib forward of the mizen-stays'l. This also allowed the mizen to be squared off more with more effectiveness.... However, the barometer is dropping steadily and the wind rising, so there may be too much of it presently. The barometer is 1,012, down 4·5 mb in seven and a half hours.' This was an average drop of 0·6 mb per hour. I expected the wind to freshen but it was nothing to worry about.

An hour later: 'The true wind is 216°, SW by S, 25 knots. *Gipsy Moth* is running before it so the relative wind is only 18 knots. Sailing speed 7¾ knots. I had to change the big vane to the smaller one. The big fella was bending over below the horizontal and I think this was reversing the effect because *Gipsy Moth* put in one or two noisy gybes. The noise came from the mizen. I had it vanged down so fortunately it could not come right across, otherwise there might have been breakage. Now I want to gybe but am pondering on dropping the mizen first. The barometer has dropped a millibar in half an hour. Although the wind is not very much yet, the sea is getting up and the riding pretty rough. I think it would be much easier for the self-steering gear without the mizen. A nuisance because it is a cow to muzzle, that mizen.'

0550: 'Dropped and furled the mizen – quite easily in spite of my criticism of it. *Gipsy Moth* is under good control now, though rolling uncomfortably. Two or three seas boiled over on to the stern, but I hope they go with a front passing through. I hope the Met set-up is much like last night and that the weather will ease presently in the same way. But I don't really believe it will because the barometer is now dropping pretty fast; 1·5 millibars in fifty-six minutes speaks to me of a gale or worse. Anyway it is daylight and the sun shone for a minute or two which was cheering, but it looks pretty grey and murky now. I had one small casualty in the night's operations: I lost my favourite little torch; it slipped out of my mouth while I was changing the windvanes. It was most valuable for such jobs, enabling me to see the blacked-out side of the vane while using both hands to fasten it. Now I think some soup before something else cries out to be dealt with. This is the third night out of four since leaving Horta that I have been done out of most of my sleep. – There's a big sea just come aboard; I suppose I must fit a washboard or two in the companion. I don't want a sea down below.'

0831: 'I was having a zizz after a bowl of pea soup and was woken by a squall. The windspeed instrument showed over 40 knots, which with *Gipsy Moth*'s 10+ knots – I had the log on the double scale which only reads to 10 knots – meant *Gipsy Moth* was bouncing along with a wind of at least 50 knots. The rigging had a relentless tone, not a screech or a scream but a tone sounding powerful and irresistible. The important point for me was that *Gipsy Moth* was going too fast in a rough sea, slueing, twisting and rolling. I had to act or breakages would occur. I felt awful, roused out after what seemed only minutes of sleep. I felt weary to the marrow. However, that big jib had to come down. It turned out an easy job. The jib made a shattering, ear-hurting din as I lowered it, but din wasn't going to hurt, as long as the jib didn't flog itself into pieces. The foot and bunt of the sail went into the sea and I hoped *Gipsy Moth* wouldn't overlay it with the keel as she bored and heeled when a wave pushed the stem; but when I returned to the stem after securing and hardening the halyard fall at the mast, the sail was docilely lying on deck against the sail net along the stem life-lines. A wave must have obligingly dumped it there for me. I didn't even get splashed until I returned to the cockpit after bagging the sail and stowing it in the forepeak, when a wave washed my legs. I think, and hope, it was only a squall causing the hurroush, but the barometer had just dropped 3·5 millibars in the past two and a half hours, 1·4 mb per hour. I have only three more actions left me now, that I can think of at the moment:

1. Reef the remaining sail, the main stays'l. I had a row of reefing eyes added to it for that purpose.
2. Set the storm-jib which is about half the size of the reefed stays'l but needs two blocks for sheeting inboard; or
3. A smaller vane. My No. 2 vane is doing excellently at present and I hope it will be all right.

As far as the foresail is concerned, I have to have something forward whatever is blowing, otherwise *Gipsy Moth* won't steer downwind, but broaches and lies broadside on to the waves which is a bad position. The true wind is now 241°, 48 knots. Well, breakfast seems a good idea. Thank heaven I'm not feeling seasick. I think I will skip my exercises this morning though. I feel weary and I did have a lot of exercise in the past nine hours even if the wrong sort.'

1155: 'Baro. 1,002·3; down 1·6 mb in one hour and 26 minutes. True wind 254°, 45 knots. *Gipsy Moth* is sailing at eight knots under the one sail, the main stays'l. A lot of spray is flying along horizontally with sundry swishes of water into the cockpit. I fear this is getting worse and I am debating whether to rig the storm-jib.'

1445: 'I dropped the main stays'l after rigging the storm-jib, which required quite a lot of jobs doing for it; such as, finding a shackle for its tack and shifting the mizen-stays'l vang to make way for a snatchblock to lead the storm-jib sheet along the deck to the cockpit. It was blowing hard and raining hard and there were batches of big seas which made it all rather a long job. In the end it did not seem to have slowed down the speed at all. I noticed nine knots on the dial just now but I suppose it might have been worse if I had left the bigger stays'l because the wind is now gusting up to 57 knots. My next worry is the windvane; will it hold out or ought I to change it for a yet smaller one. I have an R/T session due tonight and I notice that the mizen topping-lift is around the top insulator on the backstay aerial again. As the mizen is down and furled on the boom, the topping-lift is holding the boom, and I shall be unable to free the backstay unless I drop the boom right onto the deck. A snorter sea has just filled the cockpit and the water is pouring into the cabin under the washboard, but there is nothing I can do about it for the moment. The drains in the cockpit are small and the cockpit big. I think the drain is blocked or partially so. I suppose I had better don my armour again and go and bail it out. What a chore and a bore. Later; O.K., it has drained off. The duckboards are jammed above the floor with general confusion of sheets etc., but that can soon be cleared up. I'm for a wee snooze.'

1742: 'The wind vane bust in two and hell was let loose as *Gipsy Moth* headed across wind. I put on my stormwear at once and hunted for another vane. I got the old vane disentangled and off but needed to turn downwind to fit another one. I could not get *Gipsy Moth* to point downwind using fixed tiller lines. In the end I fixed it. All I worry about at present is that I was thrown across the cockpit and landed on my kidney against a wooden edge. It hurts like hell although I rubbed it well with arnica. Having only one kidney I am concerned. If that one is bust I shall be poorly placed in an hour or two's time.'

I figured that if the kidney had been bust, the body might not be affected for several hours though I would have had it when the blow occurred. For four hours I waited fearfully and then joy surged back that I had escaped. Other troubles dwindled by comparison. It continued horribly painful whenever I made the slightest movement.

'The cabin is getting into a rubbish heap as waves throw the boat one side or the other and anything loose flies through the air. Water is coming over the floor and I must bail some out. I let the mizen down on to the stern deck to try and free the topping-lift, but it was quite impossible because of the wind. One good thing, the barometer which dropped 2 millibars between 11.55 a.m. and 2.0 p.m., has practically stopped dropping since then; but even if it starts rising now I reckon it will be a long job, this storm, and the worst is usually just after the barometer starts to rise. What I do not understand is having all this dirt with such a high barometer, which I consider 1,000 mb to be. The true wind was 278°, 57 knots. *Gipsy Moth* was doing nine knots downwind. The rough DR since noon yesterday was 200 miles, less, say, 10 per cent = 180 miles in a direction 45°, which placed *Gipsy Moth* at 43° N 23½° W. The sea was an impressive sight. The flying spray from the whipped off wave crests made a carpet 6–10 ft deep covering the ocean as far as one could see, like a layer of ragged sea-mist.'

2026: 'The baro. has gone up 0·5 mb in the past two and three-quarter hours. It is hellish on deck. I did several jobs. Rigged a snatch-block to port for the storm-jib sheet. This enabled me to bring the clew of the storm-jib nearer amidships which would decrease the speed a little. (I was hit then, my hand, while writing, by a tin flying over from the other side of the boat.) Also I slacked away the boom of the main stays'l because its topping-lift was chafing against one of the storm-jib sheets. I rigged a light in the port shrouds, but I doubt if it will be any good on a night like this. I doubt if visibility is more than half a mile. Below, I bailed out four bucketfuls of oily water under the cabin sole. I don't think there is any more I can do and I shall turn in. It is a good thing to get some rest if possible so as to have some ginger in case of emergency. I have not seen the wind indicator go over 60 knots but there are some very hefty gusts.'

The next narrative log entry in the main log was not until 9 May, five days later, at an hour before midnight. The 2026 entry in my log of 4 May was also the last entry in the navigation section until 0640 the next morning, the 5th, when I noted the rough position for putting out an SOS; but that was only half a line of figures. It was not till 1500 on 5 May that I again wrote log narrative, and then it was in a notebook which I could use while lying in my bunk.

Exactly what happened and when is hazy in my mind. For

one thing my sense of time went completely haywire. It seemed an age between some of the events which later proved to be only hours. Before midnight I was lying on my back on my bunk, tensely braced against the starboard side next to the engine casing. Presently I slept. I was woken when *Gipsy Moth* was struck by a wild wave which nearly threw me out of the bunk. I lay still for a few seconds and then decided that the leeboard would not keep me from being thrown out. I must get out and fasten a rope somehow from above to underneath the bunk. I had just got out to do this when the first big knockdown occurred. I felt the boat start to hurtle, grabbed the handhold and held on like a fanatic. Stuff from the galley shelves flew across the cabin to the chart table. I thought, 'Christ! What luck; thirty seconds earlier I would have been still in the bunk and thrown across the cabin over the engine casing.'

I left things where they landed; it wasn't any good putting them back. I fixed a rope from the handhold above to the lug near the head of the bunk. Also I unfastened the galley belt and anchored it to the handhold farther aft. I got back into the bunk and lay trying to sleep but I was too tense. I don't know how long it was before I decided the speed was dangerously fast; the speedometer read 12 knots at times with only the little storm-jib set. *Gipsy Moth* was taking a terrific pounding. I thought I must be using the wrong tactics in running downwind. Every yacht behaves differently in a storm. Maybe I ought to head her into the wind to take the way off her. I got out to go and lash the helm down a-lee. As I stood beside my bunk putting on hard weather clothes, *Gipsy Moth* was thrown again. As I began to leave the floor, I grabbed the rope or strap and hung on with all my strength. 'God!' I thought, 'this is no good.' I felt desperate. 'What can I *do*?' This knockdown was more violent than the first; I expected it to be. I went into the cockpit, disengaged the windwave and lashed the helm hard down to a winch at the lee side of the cockpit. *Gipsy Moth* refused to head up to wind and would only lie beam on to wind and seas, and she was *still* doing four or five knots. I told myself it was better not to go forward and drop the storm-jib, that I might need it to control the boat. The truth was I shirked going forward to work the foredeck. Violent seas were breaking across. I was not sure what was best to do and, just out of my bunk, took the easiest course. I decided to leave her as she was until daylight.

I went below and lay on my bunk in oilskin trousers and seaboots. Suddenly I had a premonition. The seas were far worse. Anything would happen and it was only a matter of how long before it did. That rope and strap would never hold me in with a worse knockdown. I was lying there like a trapped animal. God! How weary I was. What could I do? I got out to put on my life-harness and hook it to the steel beam above the bunk. It might keep me from being thrown more than two or three feet. I was scarcely on my feet before the third and biggest knockdown occurred. I was aware of terrific forces and had a lonely feeling as if I was being hurled into space, lost to the world, a feeling I have known in earthquakes.

I was pinned against the cabin roof looking down, as if from a dream-like height, at the frames in the bilge, stripped of all the floorboards. My back was against the roof and my thigh against the mizen-mast where it passes through. I was lying on the cabin roof and the boat was above me. I had a spasm of fear that it was going to fall on top of me. Then I was only curious to know what was going to happen. I had flashing images of the mast torn off and tearing open the deck to let the boat go down like lead. I was tumbling from the ceiling. I was seeing badly. I remember putting up my hand and noting that my spectacles had been knocked half off; I remember pushing them back and being surprised that they had survived. I think all this occurred while I was tumbling. Then I was lying partly on the piece of floor beside my bunk. I began to lose consciousness and made an effort to flop into the bunk before I passed out. Things went distant and unreal but I recovered.

My impression was that *Gipsy Moth* had been hurled with terrific force off the crest of a wave into the trough ahead. The first thing I did was to look at the mizen-mast beside me; it was still there. It looked all right, but I could see that the engine casing had moved and I feared that either the engine had moved on its bed or that the mizen-mast had bent. Everything moveable on the port side of the boat had been catapulted across to starboard and I could see a shambles.

Below the chart table, debris was feet deep; broken plates, bottles, food, fruit – as if a cartload of rubbish had been tipped there. The light, however, was still on; a marvel on a black night of storm. How long would it last if the batteries had been upside down? There was a light in the main cabin. I did not remember having one there. It was the light at the head of Giles's bunk, switched on by the impact.

It had happened at two minutes to midnight. The clock had stopped when hit by a bottle. Hundreds of fragments of the bottle were stuck into the woodwork as if embedded there for ornament. The clock was at the top of the cabin doghouse between two windows. If the bottle had struck and smashed the window water would have been cascading in.

I must look to see what the damage was. I could hear above the din of the storm heavier regular thumps and bangs. Something had broken adrift on deck. I scrambled over the debris in the main cabin, going forward to look at the main mast where it passed through deck. The deck appeared intact and the mast all right up to it. I worked my way aft, hopefully switching on the mast spreader lights and wading through the heaped-up debris beside the companion. The hatch would not open and I had a nasty clutch of panic that I was shut in below. My side and thigh were so painful that I was feeble. I got myself into a better position on the companion steps where I could use both hands to tug at the hatch end. It opened a crack. I worked it open; but still feared that I could not get out. The hood with its steel frame was crushed down on top of the hatch and at first it seemed as if there was not enough clearance to slide the washboards up out of their grooves and away. It was only fear; I worked the top board up and free and it was easier to get the second one out of its grooves, making a gap big enough to squeeze through. In the cockpit I trod on a rubbish dump of duckboards, entwined with ropes. At the time it did not strike me as amazing that they were still there. Both masts were still standing. Both spreader lights were on. What astonished me more than anything was to see both paraffin lamps hanging still alight in the mizen shrouds. The life-lines were sagging, but all else appeared more or less secure. I felt a surge of great relief. I had had enough worry with broken booms to dread a broken-off metal mast bashing the hull in a storm. I looked for the storm-jib; all that remained were a lot of streamers up the forestay, flogging with loud cracks and bangs. Pieces of the mizen-stays'l had been broken out from the ties holding it furled to the boom and were banging about. The sail was already torn and I shut my mind to it. Then I was amazed to see the self-steering windvane waggling normally. It was agonising to move about because of my thigh and the pain in the small of my back.

I must have blundered heading across wind. I freed the helm, engaged the self-steering and trimmed to run dead downwind. I left the storm-jib alone. Its loss seemed to make no difference to the speed and once again *Gipsy Moth* was charging downwind at 10 knots. Once I saw the speedometer reading 12·5 knots. *Gipsy Moth* was now under bare poles but I daresay the fragments of the storm-jib and the flapping pieces of the stays'l would increase the speed. I could think of nothing to do about it. I think the wind was not very great; I never saw the indicator over 60 knots; even with *Gipsy Moth*'s own speed added, the wind did not, I think, exceed 70 knots except in gusts. The seas were the danger; they were terrific. During the day I had seen them like Cape Horn stuff, but steeper and shorter, with more frequent breakers. They had looked vicious. If only I could take way off the boat; *Gipsy Moth*'s own speed through the water caused the danger. What possible ways were there of doing this? It was a waste of time to put out a sea anchor, the warp would not last ten minutes before it parted due to the snatching load. The same thing applied to streaming warps by themselves. I had been through all that. I could not think of anything.

I went below and lay down in my life harness, which I fastened round the steel knee bracing the deck beam to the mizen-mast chainplate beside my bunk. I hadn't been lying there long before I became aware that the water in the bilges was increasing fast. The floorboards had been floated free and were knocking against each other. I got up and looked for a leak. There was already about a foot of water in the main cabin. It was dark stuff, like black coffee, impossible to see through. I could not find any inrush of water. The leak must be under water. The violent impact when the yacht landed must have started the bolts holding the 7½-ton iron keel to the wooden keelson or else pulled the keelson away from the frame. There wasn't a hope of finding a leak in that foot-deep black water.

I felt depressed and frightened. How many hours before *Gipsy Moth* sank? I was deeply sad. There was so much in Life. It was dreadful for death to tear me away from all the people I loved. But it looked as if this was it. There could not be a rougher sea or a rougher night for trying to launch the rubber dinghy from the foredeck. It would be blown away at once. Even if not, how could I get into it, or get water and provisions aboard? Why, I shouldn't even be able to keep them on the deck of the yacht. For God's sake, where is the brandy? A half glass would be like a comforting friend. I craved that warm glow, that dulling of fear, that damn all, who cares. But I turned it down; only clear thinking and good judgement would give me a chance here – and I had forgotten that the galley bottle was in fragments.

'God helps those who help themselves.' I fossicked out two plastic bags and a spinnaker bag and began filling them with any suitable food handy. I worked my way through the main cabin, treading on the edge of the settee bunk which was now being washed by the water, swishing from side to side. Thanks to Sheila's storage plan, some most suitable foods were to hand – dried fruits and nuts, peanut butter, biscuits, some rolls of bread and a lot of oranges from Horta, which would give me some liquid if unable to get water. I put aside the five-litre jar of honey which Peter had got me. If I could get just that on board it would be food enough for months of existence. Water would be the big problem. All the 20-litre jerricans and five-litre flasks of water were in the fore-peak and I doubted whether I could open the hatch in the foredeck to get any of them out from under the pile of bagged sail. There was nothing to be done about that before leaving the ship. After the big knockdown I thought it would be safer to lie on the floor between my bunk and the engine casing, instead of in the bunk. I pulled the heavy wooden ditty-box into the cabin beside the chart table, where it was useful as a stepping-stone to pass over the water to the main cabin settee. It was three to four feet long, and over a foot high. Then I thought 'to hell with it! I'd rather risk the bunk in a dry sleeping-bag'. I looked round for somewhere to put the food bags but there was nowhere dry now, except my bunk. I regretted having moved the ditty-box; I could have piled them on top of it. I piled them on the floor beside my bunk. They got wet inside which I think may have been due to condensation.

'Am I being stupid not putting out an SOS?' I hate asking for help. And it was a rdiculous thing to do; how could any ship rescue me in this stuff? In any case I had been running before the storm for several hundred miles without a fix and couldn't give an accurate enough position for any ship to find me. On the other hand if I did get into the dinghy, the 400 miles to the nearest land, Portugal, would be a long drift without a sail and I might have no water. I was being stupid; there might be a ship nearby and it might mean the difference between life and death. I went over to the set. To my surprise it was working. I could hear quite well through the receiver but when I used the transmitter to put out the SOS, the meter indicated no signal passing through the aerial. The mizen topping-lift was twisted round the top insulator on the backstay aerial again.

I could think of nothing else I could do. I reckoned this was one of the tightest jams I had been in; I was dead beat with sheer fatigue, fear, tension and depression. Only a sleep could give me a chance of a clear brain to think up something to save me. I looked at the water level. I reckoned I had several hours before it reached the level of my bunk. I decided to sleep. To hell with it all! I flopped into my bunk, fell into a deep sleep and did not stir for two or three hours. When I awoke it was daybreak. I felt refreshed and clear-brained. 'What can I do to help myself?' I started to review and think. The water level in the cabin seemed about a foot below the level outside, perhaps somewhat less. Was there a chance of its rising no farther as soon as the two levels were the same? I wished I knew the answer. Even if the water continued to rise above the waterline, that is to say if the yacht continued to sink, would there be enough buoyancy forward and aft of the two watertight bulkheads to keep the hull afloat even if the cabin was full up and the decks awash? They had a considerable capacity between them. If so, I should still have a chance of bringing the boat to port, camping meanwhile in the cockpit with my bags of food and sleeping-bag. In any case when the water levels inside and out of the cabin were level, surely the inflow would be slower. Would I not have a chance of keeping the level there with bucket-bailing? One thing I was determined on; nothing would make me abandon *Gipsy Moth* until she sank under me.

I had one Thermosful of hot water and I mixed up a honey and hot water to get over my queasiness. I think it was also excellent food though I did not feel hungry. After that I had a spoonful of honey at intervals.

The water was now up to the level of the settee and the noise of its surging to and fro, with the floating floorboards banging from side to side of the cabin, was like the seas breaking on Brighton beach after a storm. It nearly damped out the noise of the storm and deck gear. 'Of course I must send out an SOS. There might be a ship quite handy, and she might possibly rescue me.' I worked out what I thought *Gipsy Moth* had done and in which direction she had sailed since the rough DR position of the previous evening. I jotted down 43½° N 19½° W, and logged the time as 0640 GMT. I set about transmitting an SOS. The receiver was working well but no transmitter light came on. I gave it a biff with the palm of my hand and to my surprise it lighted up. I duly put out an SOS. I hoped it went on the air, though the instrument indicated almost no signal passing through the aerial. There was no response. I felt deserted. I was on my own.

After the knockdown when I had first heard the water in the bilges I had tried the electric pumps. The switches were at the foot of my bunk. They hummed for a while and then I tried the switches separately; only one hum. Then I thought 'How stupid to waste current on bilge pumps!' When I was in the cockpit to re-set the helm, I had tried the manual bilge pump. It required a lot of pumping to lift the water from the bilge just to the pump. I had to sit on the edge of the cockpit seat, bent double, head down level with my knees to avoid the sweep of the tiller. The water only spurted out intermittently until I had drawn off a bucketful, and then the pump jammed. I thought of opening up the pump to clear it but what was the good of a pump which had jammed after a bucketful? The idea of trying to empty a half full yacht with it was ridiculous and I left it, with a surge of anger at the futility of the thing.

I was gradually firming up my mind to keep the yacht

afloat somehow or other until I got it to land. At first after the knockdown I had hated the idea of losing my life, now I began to hate the idea of losing *Gipsy Moth.* I got a bucket and staggered along from the chart table to the cockpit with ten buckets of water, which I emptied on to the side deck. In those seas it would have been difficult enough to carry a bucket of water through the boat if fit and fresh; with my damaged thigh and side it was agony. I went back to my bunk, flopped down, and fell asleep for a few minutes. When my kidney area had such a bang I thought the kidney must have been bust or so badly damaged that it wouldn't last more than a few hours; but I was still alive. Then I had thought that *Gipsy Moth* would be foundering in a few hours and that that would be the end of the road for me; but *Gipsy Moth* was still afloat and I was still alive. So I got up and dumped another batch of bucketfuls into the cockpit, to let it run away through the drainholes. With each bucket I carried I modified the drill in some small way. Bending my body a little forward and to the side eased the pain in my back; there was an important handhold above the chart table seat and the engine casing gave support to my right thigh when I moved my left leg forward, and so on. I kept a tally, making a cross for each bucket, and always aimed at a definite number, holding out for reward: a flop down and a short rest on completing the batch. Then I would relax completely and often slept for a few seconds.

I think it was after the thirtieth bucket that I noticed a hole in the deck inboard of the toerail. It was on the lee side and was either under water when *Gipsy Moth* was heeled or else the seas swishing off the deck would run along the toerail from both fore and aft down to it, swirling into the boat with a kind of whirlpool action just like water emptying out of a bath. It was near the forward end of the cockpit where I had emptied the first buckets of water over the side of the cockpit on to the side deck. Hell! What a joke. The water from those first bucketfuls must have mostly returned at once through the hole. It was so ridiculous that I couldn't help laughing. But although there was enough swirling in from the water on the deck to sink *Gipsy Moth*, I still felt sure there was a big underwater leak.

I remembered almost the last thing that Sid Mashford had

said to me when I left Plymouth: 'Don't forget that if you have a leak, a piece of towelling is an excellent stopgap if you can pack something over it.' I tore a corner off a green towel. I could not think of any suitable piece of plywood which was handy, so I cut a piece from the side of a Tupperware box. I hunted out the glass jar of tacks, stuffed a dozen into my mouth, and with a tomahawk which I kept to hand, crawled along the side deck. A stanchion had torn out, leaving the hole in the deck. I stuffed a torn-off piece of my underpants into the hole, spread my square of towelling over the top and held it there by firmly tacking down the piece of Tupperware. It wasn't easy because the hole went right up to the toerail. Every few seconds the sea would wash over the side deck while I knelt there.

In the afternoon I lay in my bunk, and resumed my narrative log in the notebook. Wednesday 5 May, 1500: 'Wind 25 knots, gusting to 45 and more occasionally. Speed 5·5 knots under bare poles. I had got together all the things that I needed for leaving ship in the dinghy except four, which I did not want now because of the storage difficulty. It was hard to find anywhere to put anything except on my bunk. The four were water, lifejacket, sailing gear and spare pump for the dinghy.'

1905: 'Wind 35 knots. Speed six knots. Still no sail up and won't be for the foreseeable future till the gale is over and the sea down. I have a strong impression that the water level inboard is a little lower. So far I have removed 124 buckets two-thirds full. I would have done more this spell had it not been for pressing jobs on deck.'

My biggest, longest sheet, which had been attached to the storm-jib, had been chafed through and washed overboard. It had then got itself wound round the steering oar several times. To free it I had to lie full length on the counter and use a boathook plus a long arm. Then I noticed that one of the self-steering tiller lines was nearly worn through and would part at any time, though I felt sure it would happen at night when it would be most difficult to deal with. Replacing it was quite a job as it passes through four blocks or pulleys and the main tiller must be kept operating while fitting the new line. 'I cannot get at the galley for something hot to eat because of the water. It makes an incredible row with all the floorboards afloat, knocking against each other and bottles and half the yacht's stores and gear. However, yesterday I was sure it was only a question of how long before she sank.' This shows how my sense of time had gone haywire; the knock-down had occurred that same day.

At two o'clock on the morning of the 6th the relative wind was 23 up to 40 knots, and *Gipsy Moth* was running at a speed of three to five knots with the wind on the quarter. Two or three big waves swept over the deck and poured quite a lot of water below the companion, but two and a half hours later the wind had eased to 28 knots, and while massaging my thigh and my back with arnica ointment with my left hand while I ate digestive biscuits and peanut butter with my right, I was planning to set the main stays'l first thing after daylight.

An early job was to get to the chronometer, which I had forgotten about completely. I suppose it had stopped for want of winding, as it only runs for 56 hours.

0835: 'The chronometer is O.K. It records that it is only forty-four hours since I wound it. All this in less than forty-four hours! It seems incredible. A bonanza! I found a roll of dry paper.'

1009: 'Well, I have done several jobs. Item 1 – Raised the main stays'l. Item 2 – Secured the pieces of mizen-stays'l with some more ties. It looks as if it is simply that the seam sewing has given way. It wasn't hoisted at the time but the wind got into the furl. Item 3 – I noted that the starboard navigation light and its housing have carried away. Item 4 – Charged the batteries to full meanwhile. Item 5 – Freed the mizen topping-lift from the backstay insulator. I should be able to use the R/T now. Item 6 – bailed out 21½ bucketfuls of water, making a total of 145½ buckets. Water obviously lower. I had to use the small bucket at times to fill the big one. Of course I am working at the near end of the lake, which is shallower than the midships part. All this would be easy if it were not for the pain when moving. I am having a rest and will then try for a sun shot and then have another go at the water. If I could get rid of that and start drying things it would be a cheering step forward. I was quite dry working on the foredeck but got a souser in the cockpit just as I was finishing. I don't mind that except for its keeping my padded jacket wet. Now for some cold fodder. Another

40-bucket go at the water and I reckon I could use the galley and get something hot.

'I got a sun shot at 1139 and a second one at 1243 which gave me a fix at 43° 45′ N 16° 25′ W. Course for Plymouth 52°, distance 651 miles. Rather a rough position due to big seas. More precision later, I hope.

'Another 40½ buckets; total 186. Full ones too. Now dipping in the main cabin. I am getting a drill for it now. One learns to avoid the movements which hurt. I reckon that another 80 buckets will quieten the noise and get rid of swishing water. I have fond memories of Brighton beach but don't want to have it in the same small room for too long. I want to raise the mizen but I am determined to mop up this water first because my supply of energy is limited at the moment....

'I bailed until I had the deepest bilge empty. It has started filling again but that does not necessarily mean there is a leak. There may be a leak below the waterline, but the pockets of water lying outboard of the stringers and timbers will be finding their way to the deepest part of the hull for some time. I kept a tally and emptied 155 buckets. I measured the bucket, a two-gallon one, and reckon on average I filled it to 1¾ gallons. Total for the operation, 186+155=341. It may not sound much but carrying a full bucket 10 or 20 ft in a yacht is a long way in a rough seaway....

'What changes of fortune in a man's life. Two or three days ago I was as smug as can be with everything clean and tidy in the yacht ready for Sheila to come aboard at Plymouth. I was just reckoning the time to arrive. A few hours later I was collecting hurriedly the necessaries to keep me alive for a few weeks in a dinghy, thinking it only a matter of how long before *Gipsy Moth* sank. A few hours later I am still in the whole yacht, apparently undamaged below, making again for Plymouth.

'Some odd things turned up when I was bailing out the ship. At the 106th bucket this afternoon, while bailing in the main cabin, I noticed something under the water. I put my hand in the water, which is as thick as soup – or coffee perhaps would be a better description because I know there is at least 1 lb of coffee in the water – and found my longest woodsaw lying at the bottom of the bilge. It had travelled all the way from a locker under Sheila's bunk in the forecabin, found its way round the mast, along the alleyway past the heads and half-way through the main cabin. How did it get so far aft? It is 2½ ft long. How did it get moved anyway with its row of teeth? At bucket 107 I drew out a full vacuum flask; this was Sheila's and it had been fitted with quite a tight fit into a slot above the little table beside her bunk; how did that get loose? Alas, it was smashed inside and only full of bilge water. At bucket 109 I drew out a full bottle of Courvoisier brandy. There were no labels left on the bottle but the stamped bottle glass identified it. It is my favourite brandy, given me by Raymond Seymour of Whitbread's. It was undamaged, another bonanza.

'These finds started me thinking and at bucket 113 I thought "Why not try to light the Aladdin heater?" It had been under water for some time but you never know unless you try. I opened the door and there was a large clump of nasty pulped trash inside, pulped paper and debris washed into the bilge. To my surprise a 24-watt opaque bulb was sitting on top of this heap. There is certainly an opening to the side of the stove so that one can put in one's hand to adjust the wicks, but it seemed very odd to find that bulb there above all that. Also it boded ill for the fate of the drawer containing all my bulbs, fuses and electrics generally, because that is where it had come from. Well, I put a match to the wick and it lighted at once. Astonished, I tried the second burner and that lit too. Now they are still going full blast, another big surprise. More good luck, because they are badly needed with everything in the boat more or less soused. I stopped work when I touched rock bottom, so to speak. Every bilge must be loaded with gear. Item – Where are nine bottles of paraffin and probably the same number of grog of various kinds? There is no sign of any of them. Now for a try at a hot meal, the first for years it seems. I must log the heading, etc. but now I have dug out the proper log from the plastic bag where I had it ready for abandoning ship, and will resume entering up in that.'

On Friday 7 May, I was recording at 0600 that 'all's well. It seems to me that it is only comparison (though that's not quite the right word which I want) which counts in life. Here I am feeling happy, contented, undoubtedly pleased with the prospect of a whole lot of interesting problems to solve and actions to take'. I wondered how many people have been damaged by being hurled against the roof of a boat cabin? Thinking about it I figured that my leg hit the mizen-mast where it goes through the cabin roof. Everything else shot right across the cabin so I would have done the same had something not stopped me, and that could only have been the mast. I know I was pinned to the roof because I was looking down into the bilges straight before my eyes. But they appeared to be above me. At the time I recall saying, 'Oh God, she's upside down; will she right herself?' But that must have been some effect of centrifugal force as she was picked up physically and thrown by the sea or the wind or both. She could not have been upside down because the masts were quite undamaged and not even displaced as far as I could see. Recalling the leeway *Gipsy Moth* made in rough cross seas in the Caribbean and the reasons I deduced for it, I am certain that this was the answer.

'Massage first, then as many exercises as I can do in the bunk. There is nowhere to stand for the others yet. One can't very well do leg swinging à la ballet school or 300 jogs while balanced on the curved frame timber of the bouncing hull. After that if I'm as mobile as I seemed to be when I got up just now, I'll be a devil and double the sail area by raising the mizen. Then a temporary aerial is needed so that I can get the Colorado time signal. The chronometer is probably still accurate because it has stood some pretty hefty shocks already successfully, but of course I can't tell. The previous aerial made use of one of the life-lines but evidently was put out of action when the stanchion pulled out of the deck. Voorwaarts! Oh! and then I must have a hunt to see if I can find an egg intact. How delicious fried eggs would be for breakfast! I know one egg that won't answer the roll call because it stuck my chart folds together and when I tried to open the chart the paper surface pulled off, spoiling the chart.

'Anyone reading this might say, "Why on earth is he meandering along over the paper when there is so much wanting to be done?" My answer would be that I am not in a hurry; at present I am not going to do a single thing unless I have to. I want to recover from my body blows first and that requires time. I don't want even to feel hurried. The only way to make a success out of a situation like this is to act as if it were one's normal way of living. I am going to turn it into a normal way of life, sailing this craft with my body damaged. I learned this from that great explorer Stefansson. His maxim was that successful polar travel depended on first making Arctic travel one's way of life. And there is dear old Lao-Tsze's remark, "The journey of a thousand miles begins with a single step".

'It is all a little overpowering when I start working on the debris. I feel like an earthquaked peasant picking over the ruins of his cottage. This job needs a month to clean up. I simply cannot get into Sheila's cabin. It is one great dump of interlocked boxes, gear, all my clothes, two suitcases, one of which I can see open upside down while there is no sign of the other, stool, curtains, vacuum cleaner, newspapers, all hotch potched in a cabin-filling heap 3½ ft high. If I pull anything out where can I put it? First I must hunt for my navigation instruments. I took two sun sights and want to work out an accurate position. Perhaps this tin of anchovies, these saucers, bowls, cups and vacuum flask tops won't mind if I move them off my chart table. There is a place to put them in the galley. What oddities turn up. When I opened my cutlery drawer in the galley which is usually filled with many knives, about 20 forks, spoons, teaspoons and the rest, so that there is not a blank square inch in it, there was not a damn thing except one solitary fork. The drawer was closed. I needed one of the spoons and hunted round for a while and finally ran them to earth in the adjoining cupboard in the dustpan and under some big scrubbing brushes; but many are missing. Where do these things get to?'

Friday 7 May, 1407: 'Run 113 miles. Sun fix 44° 53′ N 14° 19′ W. Distance to Plymouth 532 miles. Rig: mizen and main stays'l.'

2255: 'Just now I slipped with a saucepan half full of water and went a purler. Critics might assert it was due to this champagne cocktail I'm drinking. If so I shall be having a worse fall after this second one. I fear, however, that this is going to be a rough night.'

Saturday 8 May, 0629: 'Out of my bunk after donning oilskin pants and sea boots. I have a technique now for putting on boots while in the bunk; I make use of the engine casing to push my foot against it. I had to get out to gybe because the heading had fallen off to 120° instead of 65°. A horrible movement due to heading across the seas raised by the previous wind. I felt slightly seasick by the time I got back to my burrow but a spoonful of honey fixed that. I've just had to go out again because the mizen-boom was whanging across with gear-breaking force due to the lumpy sea and *Gipsy Moth* being so close to sailing downwind. I thought the vang tail had worked loose but it had not. The trouble is that the eye to which I usually downhaul the boom when running carried away with the stanchion which pulled out of the deck. Why worry, the sun is shining and *Gipsy Moth* is 140 miles nearer home than this time yesterday. 424 to Plymouth.

'Today, after some breakfast, I emptied the bilges which are too full again; I still think that may be due to blocked up water working through the limber holes and past the frames and stringers. Up forward I think all the bilges are still full because of the limber holes being blocked. Last night I penetrated to the heads. It really is somewhat depressing; my razor, hairbrushes and all such accessories gone. They may be in the bilge, but there is still too much black water there to see through. Even if I recover them, I don't fancy using them. I may not find the razor in which case I shall have to turn up in Plymouth looking like Rip Van Winkle escaped from jail. I spent quite a time mopping up and clearing limber holes to let the water find its way to the lowest part of the hull, where I could scoop it up. As a result, with 14½ bucketsful taken out, the hull is pretty clear of water. It would require a cloth to mop up most of the rest. This of course is wonderful, but when I look round I want to shed a tear to see the boat I had clean and tidy for Sheila and Giles to sail in with me. Now it is as if living on a rubbish dump. Total bucket talley 362½.'

That Saturday evening, I had a blessed nine-minute R/T call to Sheila. She told me not to come into Plymouth on the Monday or Tuesday because fifty foreign and British NATO warships were going in on Tuesday, and recommended that I 'slow down and wait outside till Wednesday'. That was certainly the easy way but I hate being in a crowded sea area at night, alone, when I need sleep, and I now had only one navigation light. *Gipsy Moth* seemed to have picked up Sheila's message because she decided to put on a spurt to arrive ahead of the warships. At 0700 on Sunday 9 May she had 285 miles to go and had averaged 158 mpd for the past sixteen hours, so she intended to arrive early on Tuesday. She was making 9·5 knots fluctuating to 10·5 with no fuss or difficulty in a wind S by W, 27·5 knots. The rig seemed to suit her very well – main stays'l and mizen with the tops'l. 'The tops'l is setting beautifully and it seems the mizen-stays'l and big jib only spoil its effectiveness with the wind on the quarter.' Later I dropped the mizen and then lowered the tops'l about 10 ft down the mast, after which I changed down the windvane. That seemed to work well and may prove a good rig for running when one does not want to pole out. The pressure on the sails is farther forward and I think it is much easier on the self-steering.

Clearing up continued all the way to Plymouth. A lot of the work would have to await the attention of the boatyard. For example, the floorboards all had rounded edges where they had been battering each other in the cabin surf, and a lot of fitting and painting would be needed. But I found my razor at last, in the bilge under the heads floor. My hairbrushes also turned up, thickly matted with filth and never usable again. The third and fourth drawers up in the fixed chest of drawers in the cabin were full of photographs, newspaper clippings and ship's papers, such as my passport, *Gipsy Moth*'s registration certificate, the radio licence, the visitors' book full of addresses, and many unacknowledged telegrams and letters. All went under the water and were mostly pulp. Perhaps those many people who helped me before and during the voyage, and those who sent me letters and telegrams, all of whose names I faithfully recorded, will accept this account of *Gipsy Moth*'s knockdown as my reason and apology for not writing to thank them for their kindness.

At 2200 on that Sunday 9 May, *Gipsy Moth* was running into the Channel nearly blind, with visibility down to a mile through light fog and no fix for 217 miles. It was not until 1625 the following day that I got a sight of a hazy sun through the fog. This put *Gipsy Moth* on a position line which gave the distance off Plymouth but no indication whether she was heading north or south of the Lizard.

Gradually the D/F bearings of the Lizard changed from NNE to N by E, and although I was having trouble with the

D/F loop and reckoned it to be giving readings 20° in error, this indicated that *Gipsy Moth* was moving to the south of the Lizard.

Tuesday 11 May, 0300: 'I awoke to stillness – I mean no steamers around and the Lizard siren sounding a mournful, fear-inspiring long and short, seemingly near. I found the heading had gone to 30°, so got agitated in case *Gipsy Moth* had turned and made for the rocks as soon as I fell asleep. However, I reckoned the mournful moaning blasts came from the NW so that if I could keep going eastwards I should be all right. And I need not have worried about the silence; because now the air is again throbbing with steamer engine noise and several are around *Gipsy Moth.* I actually saw some steamer lights for a few seconds so the fog must have thinned. To hell with fog – and calms – and especially the two together. *Gipsy Moth* has only done eight miles in the past three hours. I reckon she is at present right in the middle of the westbound steamer lane and just a few miles south-east of the Lizard. Spending a night here becalmed in fog is not my ideal location for peace of mind.' But with the dawn the fog gradually lifted and it was a fine, sunny, calm day with a light breeze. All day *Gipsy Moth* ghosted along at 1·5–2·5 knots. At noon she had only 24 miles to go.

The breeze strengthened and as I passed Rame Head it was too strong for the big windvane and I had to change it for a smaller one. I passed the great breakwater across Plymouth Sound at nightfall and my beloveds, Sheila and Giles, came out to meet me in the Flag Officer's launch, lent to Terence Shaw by Admiral McKaig. Soon after midnight we were all eating scrambled eggs in the Royal Western Yacht Club while I was telling my tale.

Gipsy Moth was home again after sailing 18,581 miles in twenty weeks and four days elapsed time. I had spent five days in Bissau, twelve days in El Bluff, and seven days in Horta, so that the total sailing time was 120 days, which gave an average distance logged per day of 154·8 miles, and per week of 1,083·9 miles.

VI

Frank Dye

Frank Dye is a quiet and unassuming man who has for many years entertained readers of British yachting magazines with accounts of his somewhat remarkable feats in open boats. With his wife, Margaret, and sometimes other hardy friends, he has set off on many voyages in his favourite craft, the *Wayfarer* type of open sailing dinghy, designed by Ian Proctor. Although basically a large dinghy the *Wayfarer* is built for strength and its designer fully intended that it should be able to cross oceans as well as hug coasts – all the same even Ian Proctor has been amazed at some of Frank Dye's achievements. In his 'ocean going' *Wayfarer* he has sailed to such faraway places as Iceland and Norway – not, as might be imagined, without incident. In his latest book, *Ocean Cruising Wayfarer*, Frank Dye (assisted in his writing by his wife) manages to give a gripping account of open-boat sailing, though perhaps sometimes underplaying things rather a lot (apparently when he finally reached Norway after crossing a very inhospitable North Sea he did allow himself the laconic comment, 'Upon reflection it did seem incredible that boat crew should have survived'). 'Force Nine! – What Will It Be Like?' epitomises Frank Dye's direct and personal style of writing as he brings to life the hardships experienced by himself and his crewmate, Bill. . . .

FORCE NINE! – WHAT WILL IT BE LIKE?

Frank Dye

The 1340 shipping forecast came over well. The wire aerial attached to the shrouds had made a big improvement. We turned in early and listened to the cricket scores. They were having fine weather in England, and we both wished that we could share some of it. The forecast started unpromisingly: 'Gale warnings are in operation in sea areas south-east Iceland, Faeroes, Fair Isle, Viking, Cromarty, Forties, Forth, Dogger, Fisher.' The general synopsis at 0600 GMT was as follows: 'A depression of centre pressure 975 about 100 miles [160·93 km] north of Lerwick is expected to move north-east up the Norwegian coast, but with a secondary low developing over the Skaggerak and moving east.'

Now came the shipping forecasts for the next 24 hours:

Viking and Forties Wind westerly, force 7 to gale force 8, veering north west and moderating overnight, to force 5 to 6. Showers, otherwise good visibility.
Fair Isle Wind north-west, gale, force 8, to severe gale, Force 9, moderating later in the day to force 6. Rain at times, otherwise good visibility.
Faeroes Wind northerly, severe gale, force 9, backing north-west. Force 5 by morning. Showers, otherwise good visibility.

We were very shaken. Force 9! I wondered what it would be like. Very bad indeed, I expected. I tried to break the news gently to Bill, but made a mess of it. He obviously thought the same as me: 'Shall we be alive to see the dawn?' Much to my surprise I discovered that I was not scared, even though the possibility of death was uppermost in my mind. My only regret was that I had caused Bill to risk his neck as well. In plotting our estimated position I tried to convince myself that we were in Forties, but already I knew that we were in Faeroes, and was reluctant to admit it, even to myself.

By 1430 the wind had increased very quickly. Dropping the

main, we continued running under genoa only. We were almost on a dead run, and the seas were rapidly increasing. The wind began to veer to the north-west, with gusts from force 6 to 7. We had to hold on to the genoa as long as possible, but with heavy cresting seas, it became necessary to keep a careful watch on the seas coming up astern, for a slight error would see us over. I considered replacing the genoa with the small jib, but it did not seem worth the effort required. All that we could now do was to hold on to the course for as long as possible, and check preparations for a possible force 9.

The forecaster seemed to have enjoyed telling us about it. We would have felt so much better if he had finished his report with 'Faeroes, force 9, you poor devils!' or some such terms of sympathy. At least he had the grace not to add his usual 'and good sailing gentlemen' at the end of the forecast!

By 1530 the force 7 was gusting up to force 8 NNW, and the wind was still climbing. The whine in the shrouds became more and more shrill and insistent, until I felt it would never stop. Bill rigged the drogue, whilst I dropped the jib. We dropped the mast carefully, lowering it into the crutches in the lulls between the breaking seas.

After roping the mast into the crutches and tying the cover over the boat, I told Bill to get his head down before he was sick. He was going to need all his strength and stamina before the morning, if we were to survive.

A full-blooded force 8 was blowing by 1630, and I suggested to Bill that he might like to have a look. His answer was a decided 'No'. My view was very impressive – seas long, high and steep, with wave crests cascading down their fronts, and foam everywhere. I sat on the stern locker feeling awed but, surprisingly enough, enjoying such a thrilling sight. I considered filming it, but decided that there was too much spray about.

At 1730, under the comfort of the boat cover, I began to write up the log. By now a full force 9 was shrieking outside. It was bitterly cold, and the wind cut into one's face like a knife; it was difficult to look to windward, and to breathe into it was almost as bad. Beneath screwed-up eyes I reckoned that the seas were at least 28 ft (8.53 m) high. Thinking of Maud who by then was at the Torshaven Festival and whom we had hoped to meet again in Norway, I commented to Bill: 'What rotten luck for the Torshaven Festival.'

Bill dozed, even though he must have been bitterly cold, while I carried on writing up my log. Outside, the drogue warp was creaking badly. What a great pity that the Norwich chandlers had been unable to supply us with that one-ton (1·02-tonne) nylon I had wanted. I was not sure that the 10 cwt (508·02 kg) Terylene was adequate for the job, especially after the chafing it had suffered on Rona. Almost immediately *Wanderer* drove back against the sea-anchor. It must have parted, for I felt her swing and heard a sea hissing down. That was all there was time to hear, for suddenly I was choking in a torrent of foaming water; there seemed to be tons of it, all dark green and frothing, pushing me down. It seemed like hours before I surfaced. I had swallowed a great deal of water, as I always panic under water, and immediately the thought filled my waterlogged brain: 'If this is drowning, I don't like it.'

Bill and I were both still in the boat, now both on the port side, and still under the cover, so *Wanderer* must have rolled completely over – possibly several times. The mast crutch had gone, but that seemed all. I was still clutching the log. We bailed like hell, but there was not so much water as I had expected; probably the cockpit cover had kept a lot out. We pulled in the sea-anchor warp and discovered that it had broken near the clip. I went forward to tie on a small running drogue – an unpleasant task, but a skipper's job in such conditions.

The seas were enormous, rearing 30 ft (9·14 m) above us, with heavy water collapsing from each crest. I told Bill to get out the oil, but we found it had little effect. Possibly only 50 gallons (227·3 litres) at a time could hope to kill such seas. I got out a haversack to make a temporary drogue; Bill emptied the other rucksack and, by cutting holes in it, threaded them on to the shaft of the grapnel. We were only just in time, as the running drogue had now gone. Bill surged the new one, trying to keep us head on to the seas. I paused for a few seconds to admire the wild scene, and then we decided that we must have a larger drogue, and quickly. Fortunately the mainsail was still rolled round the boom – that could be used as a drogue, if I put a lashing on one end so that the sail opened into a cone when pulled through the water. Bill suggested that we doubled the warps. What a good idea! We should have done that before.

Working under the cover, I felt fear – if we capsized, I drowned! By uncleating the end of the warp, doubling it and attaching it by a bowline to the mainsheet, which I had already tied securely along the boom, we made ready. It was a risky operation to go forward to lead the ropes through the fair lead, as we now had no life-lines.

Our mainsail drogue worked well. Bill surged it, while I scrambled forward again to bring in the haversack. Not a hope in hell if I get swept off the bows! We badly needed our life-lines. The weight of the grapnel anchor was causing our bags to sink too deep, pulling our bows down into the breaking crests; so I pulled it in, removed the grapnel, shackled a short chain through the holes in the haversack with an empty tin of Shell oil on a 6 ft (2 m) line as a float, and once overboard it performed beautifully.

We started a 15-minute watch system. Each in turn sat on the stern locker with the cockpit cover held round his waist, and pulled the dinghy into any crest that looked like becoming dangerous. It was very wet, very hard, work. Bill emptied the water with a bucket down to the floorboards during his watch and I crawled under the cockpit cover to pump out the rest. As I heard each wave roar down, I broke into a horrible sweat. It was an unpleasant, possibly fatal, position to be caught in if we capsized. Once the dinghy was pumped dry, I collected gloves from the under-deck bags and returned to the open air. The mast was dipping under the water as each wave caused the bow to lift, but it did not seem to be causing undue strain. I tried to doze, but it was quite impossible.

By 2015 it was Bill's watch and the seas were bad, at least 30 ft (9·14 m) and very heavy. Suddenly a real bad one roared down on us from the port side, and crashed in. Roaring right over us, it rolled us over. I had a fleeting memory of being thrown clean out of the stern, seeing Bill going under me, then the boat coming down on me. Down I went into the green depths with tremendous weight driving me downwards. More panic – down, down! Needing to breathe, I choked and began to drown.

We both surfaced clear of the boat and ropes, although Bill

had the drogue warps over his head and shoulders. He climbed over the dinghy stern, but I lacked the strength to do the same. So I hooked an arm and leg over one side and rolled in as *Wanderer* rolled towards me. The boat was completely full. Bill took the warps forward through the fair leads and began to surge the dinghy. He had to keep his head up at all costs. If he was seasick now, he would lose his strength and determination, and those were the only two things that would keep him alive in these conditions. So I bailed with the bucket and felt dreadful.

The mast had gone, the centre section of it shattered for about 5 ft (1·52 m) of its length and its top banging into the side of the boat, only held by the halyards and splintered wood. I was about to cut it adrift by severing the shrouds, when Bill suggested that we ought to keep it. 'We may want it tomorrow,' he suggested dryly. Just then I was more concerned about riding out the gale. Conditions were far worse than I had imagined. However, I undid the shrouds from the hound band and pushed the shattered wooden mess beneath the cover.

The seas became even worse, and much more confused with a heavy cross sea building up as the wind backed. I would have felt frightened had there been time to think. I wondered if we would be alive to see the morning, and felt surprised that I was not particularly worried at the thought we might not.

The cover was keeping most of the water out of the boat, for the seas seemed to wash straight over it and one merely had to lift the cover to let the water run back to where it belonged. It was only necessary to bail when a heavy sea came aboard – about every 10 minutes.

It was now quite impossible to look into the wind. It was screaming, and the tops of the waves were blown completely away, hitting one's body, and feeling like hail. Within our limited vision the whole sea seemed to be smoking. Entire waves were breaking in a wall of solid water with tremendous roars. Just to see such seas breaking away on the beam was frightening – 25 ft (7·62 m) of solid water, with another 12 ft (3·66 m) of overhanging crest above it. It was only a matter of time before we got one aboard. It was impossible for such a little boat to rise to it; even a five-tonner would have been driven under.

We continued to surge the warps in 10 minutes. It became difficult to see through my glasses. My cleaning handkerchief was saturated, so I kept wiping my gloved finger over the lens, which at least spread the salt evenly – sufficient for me to see anyway.

About 2100 hours we caught the inevitable. I just had time to shout to Bill. We both hauled in on the warps frantically, attempting to pull *Wanderer* through the crest. She rose gallantly, but was in an impossible position: she seemed to be rising at 60° and there was still a 15 ft (4·57 m) crest curling above us. Down it came and we were driven bodily under. With ears roaring under tremendous pressure, and swallowing water, I fought back to the surface, only to discover that *Wanderer* was lying bottom up. I had visualised this happening. Now we must find the answer quickly if we were to survive. The boat would be very stable in that position, especially with the rollers tied in the bilges.

I found myself at the stern, and pulled myself round to the same side as Bill, and we climbed aboard. It was a bit difficult with waterlogged clothes and boots full of water, but the bilge runner just gave us a toe hold, and we were able to jam our fingers in the centreboard slot. I noticed that the self-bailer was not sealing properly – no wonder the boat had leaked. We must have done the damage unloading her at Kinlochbervie. With the help of the next wave we were able to roll *Wanderer* over. We climbed in and found her full of water, right to the very top of the rear buoyancy, and waves continued to wash in. The drogue lines had jumped out of the fair lead and, telling Bill to keep his head up, I asked him to lead the warps forward. I could not find our buckets beneath the cover, but with Mrs Jespersen's fish bucket and our plastic potty we both began to bail. Three times waves washed straight over us and refilled the boat, then just as we had become almost buoyant, another wave filled us. I heard myself scream out: 'Oh God! Give us a chance; we haven't cleared the last lot yet!' He gave us that chance, and we took it. Bill hauled in on the warps, to swing *Wanderer* head on to the seas, and held the cover over us, and I bailed flat out. The port rear floorboard had moved forward, so I had a bailing well. There is a lot of water in a waterlogged Wayfarer, but eventually I won.

At 2345 I shouted: 'Bill, the boat is completely dry, I shall be damned annoyed if you fill it again.' That was the wrong thing to have said, because immediately a sea roared in from port and *Wanderer* was rolled over. Once again I remember being thrown clear, Bill going under me, and the hull coming over on top. Again came the ghastly descent into dark green water, feeling the horrible weight over me and choking back to the surface. *Wanderer* lay on her side this time. We climbed aboard to find only 3 in (7·62 cm) of water in her. Most extraordinary! She must have rolled very quickly. We were very tired, especially mentally, and there was a constant roar, the sting of spray and the strain of judging each wave. The clouds began to clear slightly to the north, but the wind was as strong as ever. If the wind did not die down before darkness fell we should be in real trouble, for we should no longer be able to see the dangerous crests in time to pull the dinghy round to meet them bows on!

It was still pitch black at 0030 hours on Wednesday, the following day. The wind was still at full strength, and the seas as bad, if not worse, with heavy confused cross seas roaring about. I was shivering violently above deck, so I went below and was warmer, but the mental strain was too much to bear, with the possibility of being trapped under the cover if we capsized. Bill also kept sheltering and then emerging – I assume for the same reason.

We were hungry, but could find no food. It started to rain, but it would need a torrent to kill the sea. By 0130 it was just light enough to see, and there seemed to be a slight reduction in the wind – now about force 8, and only occasionally gusting to 9. We were so cold that it took conscious thought to realise the difference in wind strength. The seas were still awe inspiring, and we were not yet out of trouble, but my brain was now ticking over and beginning to measure our chances. I now believed that we might survive – the boat was in good condition, and nothing essential was damaged; the drogues were working well, and showed every sign of lasting out; and the crew were both in good shape. I was amazed at Bill's stamina. He had not been sick during the storm, showed no signs of failing and was in better spirits than a few days ago.

The mast had shattered half-way along its length at the worst possible place, so that neither half was long enough to use on its own. The broken ends were badly splintered and we had no spare wood to repair the spar. The mainsail, which was acting as a temporary drogue, was recoverable, provided the warps did not part; and even if it did carry away or was torn, we could manage with the two jibs, supposing they were still with us. All our water was still aboard, for the lashing had held during the previous night. Our food position was doubtful, since the tins had been emptied on to the floorboards when the rucksacks had been utilised as drogues, and had now probably all gone overboard. Perishable food in the under-deck bags must be ruined, but fortunately our eggs were still in stock, clipped in plastic containers beneath the decks.

The clouds were breaking up in the northern half of the horizon, from the west round to the north-east, but that did not necessarily mean the end of the gale. There could be more to come. It was to be hoped not, for we needed warmth and sleep badly. I was not sure how many more capsizes we could survive – one, possibly two perhaps.

By dawn the wind was force 8 and definitely moderating. A few hours more of this and the seas would have subsided. It was still much too dangerous to leave the dinghy to her own devices, and we continued working the warps, swinging her to meet each breaking sea. It was bitterly cold, and we were both shivering violently. I tried sitting on the water containers under the cover thus getting my body under cover but keeping my head in the open, but the water ran up my legs and pocketed around my thighs. I worked the water down past my knees and into my boots, and felt warmer. I felt sick with the salt water I had swallowed, and when Bill passed me a water container, I drank deeply.

At 0430 hours it was full daylight. The seas were as high as ever, but the wind was no more than force 7. Mostly the seas were now breaking on the back face. Occasionally we shipped a green one, but fortunately they did not capsize us, I still could not relax and was desperately tired. An hour later the seas were still as bad, but the wind was dropping to force 6. Bill was still working like a trooper, his strength never failing. Suddenly I realised that the worst was over, and felt completely drained of energy. I was bemused and numb with the reaction. We badly needed food.

VII

Hammond Innes

Hammond Innes is better known as a best-selling novelist than for any connection with the sea – though in fact many of his books do have sea settings, notably *Wreckers Must Breathe*, *The Strode Adventurer*, *Lefkas Man* and, most especially, *The Wreck of the Mary Deare*. As it happens for most of his life Hammond Innes *has* had a great deal to do with the sea, sailing and racing, and owning several boats of his own, the best loved being the yacht *Mary Deare* in which he and his wife, over a period of many years, sailed all over the waters of Northern Europe and the Mediterranean. Hammond Innes has written numerous accounts of these voyages in yachting magazines, and later collected these pieces into a most entertaining volume, *Sea and Islands*. During many of these voyages he experienced in full the dangers of the sea: here, in an extract from his book, he looks back on an alarming event which took place during one of Britain's best-known yachting events, the North Sea Race....

DISMASTED

Hammond Innes

The North Sea Race has always been one of the most popular of the Royal Ocean Racing Club's events, attracting a big foreign entry. It is run early in the season, at Whitsun, and is usually reckoned to be tough. The number of boats entered has risen steadily and on this occasion eighty-two crossed the starting line. The course is Harwich to the West Hinder light vessel off the Belgian coast, thence north to the Smith's Knoll light vessel off Norfolk and so to the finishing line at the Hook of Holland – a big Z covering the southern part of the North Sea. Because of its finishing point this event is generally known as the Hook Race.

When we arrived in Harwich one late afternoon in May, the Dutch contingent, twenty strong, was already massed under Harwich Town and some of the British boats that had come up a fortnight before on the Southsea–Harwich race were lying to the buoys provided by HMS *Ganges*, the training establishment for ratings at Shotley on the other side of the estuary. We anchored just outside them. The wind was from the north, about 15 knots and very cold, suggesting a cold, wet beat most of the way.

We were racing this year with a complement of six, which is on the light side for a 16-ton ocean racer. Bob and Michael had already joined ship to help bring her round from the Deben estuary so that now there were four of us on board, including my wife, Dorothy, and myself. We had tea, changed into our shore-going rig and took a launch to the Naval pier. The sun was shining and it was warm ashore as we walked up to the *Ganges* Mess for the pre-race cocktail party. The big room was packed, a sprinkling of wives among the men, and crews pouring in by car from boats lying miles away up the East Coast estuaries. The talk was of boats and prospects, everybody relaxed, for the race starts near the top of high water and this was not until three-thirty the following afternoon. So confident was I that *Mary Deare* could cope with anything in the way of bad weather that my only concern was that we shouldn't miss the new herring. Whitsun was early that year. But at dinner a Dutchman at the next table assured me that the first of this delicacy had already been landed. 'Ja, ja. Is already kom. Is good, ja?' This with a wealth of demonstration as to the way it is eaten – head thrown back and the raw sliver held aloft by the tail.

Next morning we were up at six forty-five for the weather forecast: Wind northerly backing north-westerly, force 3–4. The burgees of the neighbouring yachts showed that it had already gone into the north-west, confirming once again that forecasts are more often an indication of what is actually happening than what is to come.

There was much to do that morning. Spinnaker, genoa and No. 2 jib to be stopped – that is, rolled along the line of the hoist and tied with rotten cotton so that the sail can be set in position and broken out at the moment required. The main standing rigging had to be tightened. I had been out two weeks before with full sail in a strong breeze; the forestay wires had been stretched and checking the line of the mast by looking up the track of the main-sail sides I had noted that the top of the mast above the upper spreaders was bending very slightly to leeward under the weight of the genoa when heeled in a strong breeze. Somebody had to be hoisted up the mast to tape the outermost edge of the upper and lower spreaders, a thing the yard had forgotten to do. There are screws here and if they are not covered by tape they rapidly produce chafe on the Terylene mainsail when running before the wind.

By ten-thirty the other two members of the crew – Cav and David – had joined ship. By eleven-thirty all work had been completed. Both forestays had been tightened two turns on the rigging screws and the upper shrouds that run from the chain plates amidships to the top of the mast had been tightened one turn. We retired below for a drink and a discussion of tactics.

The start at Harwich is easterly across the line to the Guard Buoy not much more than quarter of a mile away, thence southerly to the Beach End Buoy about two miles, easterly again for four miles to the Cork Sand Buoy and then south easterly to the West Hinder just over fifty miles. It looked like genoa across the line, hoist spinnaker at the Guard Buoy on starboard tack and a spinnaker gybe at the Beach End Buoy for the run down to the West Hinder on port tack. All of which really requires a practised crew that have worked together regularly, for the spinnaker is big, a nylon sail bellying out in front of the boat and carrying a great weight when full of wind. It is boomed out on one side (opposite side to the mainsail boom) and to gybe it the boom had to be detached from the spinnaker and transferred to the other side, all at the exact moment course was altered and the mainsail brought across. Our crew had never sailed together before as a team.

Further, we should be rounding the West Hinder light vessel at night. This would mean hoisting genoa and hauling down the spinnaker at the moment of rounding for the beat north, a tricky operation to be carried out in the dark. We had another drink and hoped it would all work out. A large lunch then of soup and cold chicken and salad. By the time we had finished, the smaller Class III boats were getting under way. Owing to the large entry, this class was being sent off in two waves at two-fifteen and two-thirty. Our own start – Class II – was timed for two forty-five.

We got the weather forecast at one-forty. It was the same except that it suggested that the wind would strengthen to force 5. We hauled up the anchor, stowed it below with the chain, turned into the wind under engine and hoisted the mainsail. I cut the engine then and the genoa was hoisted, but it had been wrongly stopped and had to be lowered. The wind was very light under the shelter of the land and I had drifted down-tide among the Class I boats, so I re-started the engine and motored towards the line as the starting gun for the first wave of Class III went. In a matter of moments, it seemed, they were round the Guard Buoy and going away under spinnaker, a brave, multi-coloured sight.

I switched the engine off and we jogged around under mainsail whilst the second wave of Class III went away. Our own class was manœuvring towards the line now as we waited for the ten minute gun. Time hung heavy, then the five minute gun. Dorothy started the stop watch and began the countdown. Four minutes, three minutes, two ... I had the genoa broken out. We were drifting up close to the line – too close, I thought, and gybed. In a 220-mile race I preferred to start a few seconds late rather than risk having to put about in the midst of nearly thirty boats because I had crossed the line ahead of the gun.

I was planning to manœuvre myself towards the starter's position close under Harwich pier, but I was blocked by another boat. By the time we were clear of it all the twenty-eight boats were moving down on the line. The gun went. Too far out across the estuary we had little wind and it took longer than I had expected for *Mary Deare* to gather speed. We crossed the line with the tail-end group, tension unrelieved, for the Guard Buoy was coming up and we were being pressed by a Belgian closing us on port side. It was a near thing. We rounded the buoy very close and broke out the blue and white spinnaker, the Belgian's bows a few yards from our stern. For a moment we had only half a spinnaker set, the rotten cotton of the stops holding in the light air. A couple of hard tugs and it bellied out and we were away down the estuary, closing with *Thalassa*, veteran of many Hook Races and, on handicap, rated second boat in our class. We were rated twenty-third. A gust and a slight shift of wind enabled us to cut under her stern and move away on the windward side of her, constantly adjusting the sheet ropes to stop the spinnaker collapsing. Behind us the big Class I boats, which had started a quarter of an hour behind us, were coming up fast. *Swerver*, a Dutch boat and the final winner of this class, rounded the Cork Sand Buoy just ahead of us.

Once round this buoy the alteration of course for the West Hinder light vessel made spinnaker work easier. After playing with the sheets for a time we got it properly set and then we were pulling into the smaller Class III boats that had started ahead of us. It was a wonderful sight in the bright sunlight. We were in the centre of a great fleet of yachts all with their spinnakers set, all going well. They looked bright as flowers in the sunlight, every sort of colour, and the sea sparkling. But when I finally relinquished the helm to the watch on duty and got down to my navigating, I found that the glass had dropped from 1,020 to 1,012 millibars. It was a biggish drop and boded no good. The shipping forecast confirmed it. The wind was already strengthening out of the nor'nor'west.

We dined in comfort – Dorothy serving a Boeuf-en-Daube (prepared at home in advance) followed by cheeses and fruit, the boat rolling slightly and a powerful surge of water at the bows as she ploughed along at around seven knots. We had passed through a large number of the smaller boats and for a time sailed level with *Sposa II*, rated top boat in our class. As evening closed down we pulled away from her. Some of the Class I boats were still behind us and away to the north we could see *Thalassa*'s green spinnaker. In a lull, *Jabula*, one of the fastest and best-sailed of the smaller boats, began to close up on us. But then the wind strengthened again and we pulled steadily away from her.

Darkness came. We switched on port and starboard navigation lights, stern light and masthead light, and those not on watch went to their bunks for the four-hour run to the West Hinder. About eleven I got up to check navigation. The beam of the Noord Hinder light vessel loomed to the north. For a time the actual light was visible. At half-hour intervals I was getting the radio beacon of the West Hinder loud and clear on my radio direction finder. Position right where it should be – over the bows.

Midnight, and I was up on deck, searching for the West Hinder's light. Not a sign of it. But all around us the firefly glow of the fleet, masthead lights and stern lights. Somebody up front had a great white beacon in the cockpit powerful enough to be the beam of a lightship ... all very confusing. It was like being in the centre of a huge fishing fleet – lights everywhere.

I went up for'ard and leaned my back against the mast, bracing myself to the surge and roll of the boat. Above me hung the great canopy of the spinnaker, full and taut with the weight of the wind. No sound up there, but from the bows a great noise of water as we creamed along with the surf of a breaking wave-top; and then suddenly the sound would drop away as we slid into a trough, only to start up again as the stern lifted and *Mary Deare* plunged forward. It was wonderfully exhilarating just to stand there and feel the boat so alive and driving furiously towards the Belgian coast.

But all I cared about at that moment was the West Hinder light. The boats ahead were spread out in a fan and we looked centrally placed. But with the loom of the Noord Hinder falling away to the port quarter, the West Hinder should have been visible. Stern lights of the leading boats, dipping in the waves, gave flashes that were hard to distinguish from those of a light vessel. Four every 30 seconds I was searching for. I am blessed with remarkably long sight, which has so far survived the close work of writing. I can usually see a rock or a buoy, the vague blur of land on the horizon, before any of my friends. But now the blink of the West Hinder eluded me.

Going back to the cockpit I looked astern and saw the white-capped tops of waves, saw the way the man at the tiller seemed to be lifted right up and then thrown back again. There was quite a sea running and I remembered with a tautening of nerves that a crew who had not sailed together before would have to drop that wind-filled spinnaker as we rounded the lightship, hoist the genoa, and at the same time we should have to haul in the mainsail. I didn't like the thought of it in the dark. So many things could go wrong, and the wind was force 5 now – 17–21 knots.

Bob was at the helm and we stood talking about it for a while, our eyes searching the horizon beyond the plunging compass light. David had gone for'ard with the glasses. His sweatered figure appeared in the red of the port navigation light. 'I think I can see it now. Away to starboard. You have a look.'

I crawled for'ard again and he pointed to a gap between the stern lights of two boats. I, too, thought I saw it. It meant we were too far north. But the tide was flooding southwards. A quick mental calculation of the probable distance off and I realised we were as well placed as we could have expected.

It was time we began to get organised for the 300° change of course. David took the helm and I told him to head for where we thought we'd seen the loom of the light. Bob and I clambered for'ard to grapple with the spinnaker net. This is a cat's cradle of strings hoisted for'ard of the mast to prevent that most frightening of all spinnaker misdemeanours, the wrapping of the sail around the forestays. Once a spinnaker spills its wind and begins to wrap, it goes on winding round and round, sewing you up in such a tangle that the only answer may be to hoist a man to the top of the mast. It was something that didn't bear thinking about, in the dark and with a sea running.

Back in the cockpit I found David sailing with the wind dead aft and still not quite headed for the loom of the West Hinder. I watched for a moment, and then we both saw, not the loom, but the light itself. It was nearer than I had expected. Two miles, perhaps three – and still on the starboard bow. There were three courses open to me; to hold on and when we were just north of the lightship drop the spinnaker and run down on to it under the genoa, to gybe the spinnaker right away, or to continue as we were, but sail the boat 'by the lee' – in other words, with the wind on the wrong side. This last meant taking a risk, for if the wind got behind the mainsail the whole boat would become unmanageable.

No question which was the right thing to do, but it was dangerous and obviously I was the person who should take the risk with my own boat. I relieved David at the helm and began half an hour's very concentrated steering, my eyes fixed on the leech (the rear edge) of the mainsail, watching for the slightest back-lift, my whole mind concentrated on that and the feel of the wind at the back of my right ear as I stood four-square to the stern, sensing every slight shift of wind direction.

I heard David and Bob discussing how best to handle the spinnaker on the turn – heard them only vaguely, for every now and then the leech of the mainsail lifted on a surge and all my nerves were bent on bringing the boat safely down on the tide to arrive just south of that slow-flashing glimmer of light. The lead boats were rounding it now, the big Class I boys. I could see them pulling away, coming up towards us to cross our bows. Our closer rivals were moving in from left and right, closing us fast. I could see more than the lightship's lantern now. I could see her riding light, could see the whole ship.

'Is it all right with you if we hoist the genoa first?' This from David.

'Yes, of course.' It would act like the net, stopping any chance of the spinnaker wrapping.

'We'd like to take the boom off first. All right if we leave the spinnaker loose-footed? It'll only be for a moment.'

'Yes.' What else could I say? The light vessel was coming

up very fast now and we were still to the north of it. This was no time to argue with the foredeck about the best way to handle that monstrous wind-bellied pile of nylon. I was sailing more and more by the lee, edging south with every tiniest shift of wind, willing myself and the wind and the seas to get *Mary Deare* the right side of that anchored iron hulk that was now sweeping the sails with a brilliant white light.

The watch below were coming up on deck, bringing with them the heavy orange bulk of the genoa sail bag. They dragged it for'ard along the plunging deck, passing out of my line of vision. I was aware of activity up in the bows, but I had no eyes for anything but the lightship and the mainsail. Twice the wind caught the back of the sail and only the boom guy – the thin wire brace running from the end of the boom to a block and tackle in the bows – prevented the boom from slamming across in an unintentional gybe. Each time I just caught the boat before she became unmanageable.

The light vessel was looming over the bows now, her beam beginning to sweep above our sails. Out of the tail of my eye I saw a big boat closing me on the port side, saw her butcher's-striped spinnaker belly further and further out ahead ... something wrong there; the halyard must have slipped. She seemed to be coming down on us. A quick glance and I saw they were in real trouble. The spinnaker was falling away towards the bows, the stripes billowing out and smothering the for'ard part of the boat; it was all picked out in the swinging beam of the light, in photographic flashes.

'Speed it up, if you can, Bob,' I called. 'There isn't much time.' The light vessel was right over our bows, the tide sweeping us across it, and the boat with its spinnaker trailing was coming in on us, forcing me to turn away from her. The wind hit the back of the mainsail. I swung *Mary Deare* back and for a moment we were headed for the other boat. But we were just clear of the light vessel and the genoa was up, the spinnaker boom on the deck. 'Have you let go the boom guy?' I called. I thought the answer was Yes, but it was lost in the spill of a wave and the surge of the boat. The spinnaker was free on the port side. They were hauling it in under the lee of the main. As it came down I told Cav to haul in on the main. The big boat was rounding-to right alongside the light vessel, her decks alive with figures heaving the trailing spinnaker back on board.

We were clear and I rounded-to myself, neck-and-neck with another boat, squeezed in by it as it closed from starboard. 'Haul that mainsheet in,' I yelled. Cav gave a great heave, all his weight on it. There was a snap and the trailing end of a wire came curling into the cockpit. The boom guy had not been let go. But we were round, with the genoa and main hardened in, the spinnaker down and the boat driving. Close alongside a white hull wallowed – *Kiff* rated only four above us. But we were pulling away, and clear of the lee of the light vessel, we gathered speed, conscious of the boat heavily heeled, conscious, too, of the weight of the wind and the size of the sea.

Gradually things were sorted out, the spinnaker gear all stowed, the decks tidied by the safety-harnessed figures that crawled and clutched their way in the rearing ghostly gleam of the navigation light.

'About fifteenth boat, I think.' David, who when he wasn't underwriting was doing parachute drops or Marine Commando work in small canoes or frogman's suit, was fiercely competitive. 'I counted them. About fifteenth round the Hinder, wouldn't you say, Bob?' His voice sounded excited as well it might, for we were rated 42nd in the fleet.

'About that.' As always Bob's voice was quiet, noncommittal.

I handed over the helm to Cav and Michael. Cav, who is a painter, still had the picture of our rounding the light vessel clear and vivid in his mind. It was fixed in his memory, as it was fixed in mine – a mental picture so sharp that it would stay with us until it could be reproduced on canvas and in words. 'Fantastic,' he said. 'Absolutely fantastic. It was like Piccadilly Circus – all those boats converging and the swinging beam of that light and the spinnaker coming down in a tangle over that poor devil's bows. Fantastic.' He was still burbling excitedly about it when I went below and got down to my charting.

The course was north, but the best we could do was about 20°. That would take us up past the Noord Hinder and away on a long leg that would never meet Smith's Knoll. Some time in the morning we should have to go about. But for a few hours we could stay on this tack and get some sleep. I pushed open the hatch. 'Don't pinch her,' I said. 'Keep her sailing all the time even if you do see boats up to windward of you.' Michael was a very good dinghy helmsman who had sailed with us to Spain the previous year. I knew he could be relied upon to keep the boat going really hard. I undressed to my underwear and slipped into my sleeping bag in the quarter berth, which is just below the main hatch.

Sleep was impossible, but I dozed, pressed into the side of the bunk by the angle of heel, hearing the water thundering past the steel hull close beside my left ear, my body riding with the plunges, feeling the slams as she dived into the troughs. The slams got worse and I thought: 'We must be running straight up the Hinder bank – these are the overfalls.' I thought of the rigging, hoping I'd tuned it right, remembering the two turns I'd taken on the forestay, the turn on the main upper shrouds. But she was a tough boat, built as a cruiser to go round the world, down round the Horn if I wanted to – the designer's words, not mine.

I suppose I slept. I remember seeing Cav in his oilskins. He seemed to be clambering along the upper side of the doghouse above the galley. He was peering out of the port doghouse window and his face, with the tousled iron-grey hair, was lit intermittently by light. A storm? Lightning? Or was it the sun coming up? The first grey light of dawn was showing. No, of course – it must be the swinging beam of the Noord Hinder. 'Is that the North Hinder, Cav?'

He turned to me and nodded. 'Abeam now and quite clear.'

'Enter it in the log book, will you – time and mileage run by the log.' I closed my eyes. The movement was very trying. Ninety miles from the West Hinder to Smith's Knoll. Beating like this would add another – how many? – thirty, forty miles? It wasn't going to be pleasant. I could feel the cold through two layers of blanket and a down sleeping bag. We'd be feeling very battered and tired by the time we rounded the next mark and started the downhill run to the Hook. But it would be daylight all the way and we had a good crew. It's the crews that crack usually, not the boats. Certainly not *Mary Deare*.

The watch changed. Cav and Michael came below. 'We've

pulled up on several more.' Michael was struggling out of his oilskins.

'How many can you see now?'

'One or two,' Cav said. 'Up to windward of us. Another astern and down wind. *Mary Deare*'s going very well – just her weather.' He had started his sailing life way back on the big 'J' Class boats. The time was just after four. 'Dawn beginning to break,' he added. 'Nasty-looking sea.'

I lay and listened to the slight change in the boat that follows a new hand on the helm. How long ought we to continue on this tack? Should we make a long leg of it and then one across to the Outer Gabbard lightship and one up to Smith's Knoll? Or should we take short tacks, back and forth up the direct line between the West Hinder and Smith's Knoll? I thought three long tacks. It would be easier on navigation. I was beginning to worry about that. It's hard to concentrate on figures when the world is standing on its head, and I'm not fond of figures. Some of these liner boys would be horrified if they had to navigate the way we have to – wet and cold on a chart that's never still.

And then I was listening to the slams as she hit the seas. For a time they had been much less, as though the wind had lessened. But I knew the easing of the motion had been due to the fact that we had cleared the Hinder bank and the seas had become more regular. But now the tide had turned. It was running north. Wind against tide – the seas were getting steeper, breaking more often. I clambered out of my bunk, pushed open the hatch doors. Bob was at the helm. I can see him now – a tall, military-looking figure in yellow oilskins, his glasses misted with spray, his head bare and his neck muffled in a towel. 'Is she getting heavy on the helm?'

'Carrying a bit of weather helm, but nothing excessive. She's going very well.'

'You don't think she'd sail better if we changed to Number Two jib?'

'No, she's all right at the moment. Might be worth considering later if the wind gets up any more. But not to worry now.'

I went back to my bunk, lying there and feeling with every nerve the movement of the boat, trying to make up my mind whether to order the change. I wasn't thinking of the boat being too heavily pressed by the weight of canvas or that she was in danger. That never occurred to me. And the way we were going I was quite prepared to blow out the genoa if it would win us the race. No, all I was thinking about was whether she would go faster under the Number Two. It is a fact that in heavyish weather boats often lose time by hanging on to big canvas too long. *Mary Deare* I knew from experience slowed up as soon as the lee rail was under and the deck awash. I had proved this time and again, and the signal was invariably a heaviness on the helm.

About a quarter of an hour later my nerves came suddenly alert to the heavy slam of a wave and what I thought was an ugly additional sound. Did I imagine this, or was it premonition? I don't know. All I can remember is that I was wide awake and every nerve tense to the movement of the boat. I began to want very much to order the change down. I tried to balance my knowledge of the feel of the boat below against Bob's experience. He was at the helm and I was well aware that what sounds like heavy weather down below is often an exhilarating sail for those in the cockpit. And so I hung between sleeping and waking again, listening, waiting – discouraged as much as anything by the effort it was going to cost to struggle into my oilskins and go for'ard into the wet and the wind to change the sail. I was only just recovering from a bout of 'flu.

Slam! And another sound. A sound like a sharp crack, merged with the slam. And then a sudden quietness. No rushing of water, no surging roar of speed, and the boat rolling.

The hatch banged open. 'That's your mast gone.' It was David's voice – quiet, but very clear and pitched a shade high.

'Are you serious?' But after that first stupid question I didn't say anything. There wasn't anything to say. The mast had gone, and that was that. I knew it had gone by the feel of the boat. I dived out of my bunk to rush on deck. Cav was there, too. Michael followed. I'd no oilskins on, no shoes. I hesitated and then got my oilskins. The mast gone, there was no desperate hurry. We couldn't put it back on again. It wasn't something you could deal with in a hurry. I remember lacing up my shoes, knowing I would need a firm foothold on that rolling deck. I told the others to get their things on. And all the time I was thinking – 'This must be my fault; I got the forestays or the shrouds too tight.' And yet I didn't see how that could have dismasted us.

Up on the deck the grey light of day showed steep, ugly seas – all grey. It was five o'clock in the morning and the Noord Hinder was way astern. Bob was already up for'ard, heaving in the genoa, which had fallen over the side. The mast had gone at the upper cross-trees. The topmast section was suspended from the splintered remains by a wire halyard and was banging to and fro against the starboard shrouds. As far as the lower cross-trees the mast was splintered, the mainsail track torn away; below that the mast was intact, the lower shrouds still standing. At least we had something on which to rig a jury sail.

I was thinking about this problem as I went for'ard. The genoa was inboard by then. We got the main boom sheeted hard in, pulled the trailing mainsail in over the guardrails. Dorothy started to come on deck. 'Tie-ers, please,' Michael called. She never did get on deck, poor girl, but was forced to remain below in that rolling madhouse whilst the hatch kept banging open in her face as one or other of the crew demanded this or that – a pair of pliers, the genoa bag, a rope to use as lashing. And then things began to be bundled below for her to sort out.

I remember, after the mainsail was partly lashed, somebody called out, 'Have you got heavy duty wire clippers on board?' These are recommended equipment for ocean racing and I had toyed with the idea of getting a pair that year, for the lifeboat had had to go out to two boats during the Southsea–Harwich race, one having been dismasted. But to be of any use they have to be really massive things and anyway I had thought that though others might be dismasted, it wouldn't happen to *Mary Deare* with her stalwart and relatively short spar.

Now I doubt whether I shall ever carry such a tool. Had I had a pair on board we would undoubtedly have sheared through the wire halyard from which the topmast was suspended, probably some of the standing rigging, too. We might well have lost the topmast section then and with that gone the evidence of what had caused the dismasting would have been lost. It might even have been put down to the rigging having parted.

'No,' I said. 'We'll just lash it.'

It took time to lash that banging lump of mast with all its trailing wires. By then boats were piling past us, all the yachts we'd left behind us, the hard sailing wasted. It was a bitter moment. An oilskin-clad figure in the cockpit of one boat added insult to injury by taking a photograph of us. And a little later Mike called out that there was another boat in trouble. But she was only reefing and changing to a smaller headsail. She went on her way and about this time I saw a batten lying on the deck. It started me salvaging what I could, thinking ahead to the time when I'd have to cope with setting all this to rights. It was then, I think, that I made up my mind to head for home, not down-wind for a Belgian port.

We saved all the battens – those plastic stiffeners that hold out the back edge of the mainsail. I even rescued the burgee flag and its staff. The signal halyards were undamaged. We cut the slides from the mainsail to free it from the topmast section and bundled it down below to Dorothy, who somehow managed all alone to stow the huge pile of wet sail up for'ard out of the way.

In forty-five minutes exactly everything was lashed and stowed, the decks cleared and I had started the engine. We headed east with the seas on the starboard bow.

That I should head eastward under engine for the English coast may seem the most natural thing in the world to anyone who does not understand about ocean racers. In fact, *Mary Deare* was one of the very few boats in the fleet that could have undertaken this sixty-mile voyage against wind and sea. Most ocean racers are equipped with auxiliary engines. Those without are penalised on handicap, for the original idea was that the races should be between cruising boats. Now, however, engines tend to be small in relation to the size of the boat, designed to do little more than get the ship in and out of port. Moreover, when racing, most of them carry the minimum of fuel to reduce weight. This means a small range under power and the engine itself often incapable of pushing the boat satisfactorily against the wind, certainly not against a biggish sea as well. Doubtless for this reason the other

English boat to be dismasted turned down-wind and put in to Zeebrugge in Belgium.

Mary Deare, however, was designed very much as a crusier, which is why she rates below much smaller boats. In the original design discussion I had stipulated a Coventry Victor horizontal twin-cylinder diesel because this engine had the best thrust-weight ratio and I was determined that the engine should be powerful enough to earn the space it took up. To some extent the boat was designed round it and the tank, which was fashioned in one piece with the steel well of the cockpit, had a capacity of some 45 gallons of fuel. The manufacturers claimed a consumption of only half a gallon per hour, which should give us a range of 500 miles under power.

I remember before the race I had discussed with the boatyard the possibility of removing most of the fuel to reduce the weight aft. They always fill the tank at the end of each season to preserve it during the winter lay-up. But once filled it is extremely difficult to drain and I was very glad now that the boatyard had said it was impossible. I had run the engine for perhaps four hours so far during the season. If the yard had really filled it up at the end of the previous season then I had a virtually full tank. I just crossed my fingers and hoped, and nothing would induce me to dip to find out. To run for the Belgian coast meant shipping a new mast out with risk of damage and it would then have to be rigged by a strange and perhaps unsatisfactory yard. We were due to leave three weeks later for Sweden and I was determined to get the boat across to England.

Only one of the crew suggested that it might be better to turn down-wind and run for it, and I was relieved to hear Bob's quiet voice say, 'Skipper's right. I'd rather be out in open water if the engine's going to pack up and the wind goes on rising. Better that than a lee shore.' And so we plugged on, the engine note not varying. But progress was slow. We thought perhaps 2½ knots. The seas were unpleasant in the squalls and it was bitterly cold. The boat rolled violently, the shattered remains of the mast swaying wildly. Sixty-odd miles at 2½ knots. 'It's going to be a slow business,' Bob said, sitting at the helm with his towel round his neck, his hair streaming water. We should go a bit faster when we got into shallower water and came under the lee of the English coast – about 20 hours altogether we reckoned.

Sickness caught up with some of the crew in the wild unbalanced movement and I sat at the helm hour after hour, praying that the tank really was full, that the engine really would only consume half a gallon an hour, that the fuel lines wouldn't choke or the injector nozzles carbon up, things that require a good engineer to put right. It was like that time two years before when Robert Clark, the designer, and myself, with a Dutch journalist, had motored the empty hull across from the builder's yard in Holland for completion in England. We had gone out into a gale first time with a qualified engineer on board and had had to put back to the Hook of Holland. The engineer was sick and had to be sent home and when I told Robert I'd always sworn I wouldn't do the trip without an engineer on board, he had replied, 'You don't refuse to go out under sail unless you have a spar-maker on board for fear your mast may break – why insist on an engineer in case your engine fails?'

I thought of that remark now. We'd broken the mast and there was nothing that a spar-maker could have done that we hadn't done. Now it was up to the engine and I didn't think an engineer could have done much if it broke down, rolling as we were. The rolling, which was very violent, affected us all, and when we weren't on deck steering, we clung to our bunks as the only safe place. God knows how my wife had managed to produce hot drinks immediately after we'd cleaned up the mess and salvaged all the gear.

Some time during the morning we sighted a yacht headed north under sail. She was a long way away, but watching her, I envied her her tall mast and her sails. Around midday a ship ploughed across the horizon to the south. She looked like the Harwich train ferry, but I couldn't be sure. It is very difficult to be sure of the course of a ship passing you at the limits of visibility, but I thought she was headed a little south of our own course. If so, we were to the north of the Galloper light vessel, which I wished to sight before we closed the East Coast banks.

Twice Cav and I saw what looked like a light vessel to the south of us. But each time it turned out to be a fishing boat with a steadying sail. And then suddenly there it was –

definitely a lightship. It couldn't have been anything else but the Galloper; nevertheless, I turned south and closed it until we could see the name painted white in huge letters across her red hull.

The time was then just after three in the afternoon. We had thirty miles still to go. We did this in $5\frac{1}{2}$ hours, and in the grey light of evening entered Harwich estuary. We dropped anchor in the Orwell River, close under HMS *Ganges*. I switched the engine off and all was suddenly peace with the curlews piping on the mud banks and a bitter cold wind driving up the estuary. The time was 8.30 p.m.

Below in the warmth of the saloon, already neat and tidy again, with a cloth on the table and the bottles and glasses out, we drank a toast to the sturdy little engine that had brought us so uncomplainingly through a dirty sea more than sixty miles from the scene of our disaster in just over fourteen hours. We were thinking of the rest of the fleet then, some of them still beating up to Smith's Knoll. 'They'll be tired and cold,' we said. 'Wet, too. They'll have a bitter night of it.' So we tried to console ourselves.

Fortified by a few drinks I surreptitiously got the dipstick and went up into the cockpit. But David had seen me go. 'I wonder how much fuel we *have* got left?'

I gave him the dipstick and unscrewed the top of the dip tube. The steel rod was inserted and when he drew it out he stared at it in amazement. 'It's hard to believe,' he said. 'But you've still got three-quarters of a tank left.'

Down below the post-mortem had already begun. Why had the mast broken? Only Cav with a painter's eye for detail came near to the truth – a constructional weakness. This we established a few days later at Whisstock's yard when, with the designer, the spar-builder, Claude Whisstock, Bob and myself all present, we took a saw to the salvaged topmast section. This revealed that there was also a bad crack on the starboard side – the side that would have been free of pressure during the race. In other words, the process of disintegration had started either earlier that season or the previous year. Robert Clark is not only one of the most brilliant yacht designers, but also one of the most experimental, and in *Mary Deare*, one of the first ocean racers whose crew were relieved of the chore of setting up backstay runners every time she was put about, he had compensated for their absence by giving her a mast that was not normal, almost round section, but very elongated fore and aft; as somebody said when it was building, it looked like a 'plank on edge'. This type of mast is commonplace now, but at the time it posed a problem for the builder. Most designers specify solid sections by way of the cross-trees to strengthen a hollow spar at this vital point, but to achieve lightness Robert Clark's masts were usually hollow throughout. In the absence of specific instructions to the contrary, *Mary Deare*'s had been constructed this way. The effect of this was that the thrust of the cross-trees – the rigging spreaders – had not been transmitted to the mast as a whole, which would have been the case in the then conventional round mast, but was concentrated solely on the flat side – concentrated, therefore, on $1\frac{1}{4}$ inch thickness of planking. The result had been almost inevitable. As the spar-builder said, it was like pressing on the centre of an empty match box. But knowing the cause of it was little consolation. We had finished fifth in our class the previous year; this time, rated 42nd in the whole fleet and lying perhaps better than 15th, our chances on corrected time had looked as good as they would ever be for a heavy boat like *Mary Deare*. Nor was it any consolation to know that 36 other boats – almost half the fleet – had been forced to give up for one reason or another. And now there was all the work of getting a new mast built and stepped in time to meet our deadline for Sweden.

VIII

David Lewis

David Lewis, a New Zealander of Welsh and Irish descent, ran a busy medical practice in London for 18 years – and for most of that time secretly dreamed of sailing round the world. Unlike many others he made his dreams come true – gave up his practice, gained sailing experience, took part in the first single-handed Transatlantic race, and then built his own catamaran, *Rehu Moana*, in which, with his wife and two small daughters, he duly sailed round the world. An account of all this is to be found in two very readable books, *Daughters of the Wind* and *Children of Three Oceans*. During these voyages Dr Lewis became the first navigator in modern times to make a Pacific crossing (2,500 miles from Tahiti to New Zealand) without instruments, following a legendary Maori course and using only the sun and stars to steer by. His landfall was only 26 miles in error! In 1968–69, under a research fellowship of the Australian National University, he spent 9 months in *Isbjorn*, a 39-foot auxiliary gaff ketch, investigating surviving navigation methods in the Western Pacific. More recently, becoming fascinated with the idea of sailing alone to Antarctica, Dr Lewis acquired a 32-foot long steel sloop, *Ice Bird*, and set off on the momentous voyage recorded in the book of that name. The following extract gives a vivid impression of what it really means in a small boat being 'beset by ice'....

BESET BY ICE

David Lewis

Morning. 12 December.

'Wake up you degenerate old man, it's a quarter of five already.'

An obscene grumble from me.

'Now, that's physically impossible for me to do. Here, drink this.' Jim guided a mug of scalding coffee into my hand as I groaned and sat up, noting with a jaundiced eye that the sun was shining as it had been for most of the night. Since I was already wearing nylon briefs and jeans, socks, vest, shirt and heavy wool jersey, dressing consisted merely in pulling on a pair of waterproof trousers, insulated boots, parka, fur hat and gloves (thick industrial rubber ones worn over a thin woollen pair). Miserably tired, I stumbled up the three steps of the companionway ladder.

A light northerly breeze was ruffling the surface of the bay; and Bismarck Strait outside, except for scattered bergy debris, was ice free. There came the faintest stirring of excitement. So far my luck was holding; the first part at least of the road south was open and the wind was fair.

Still alongside *Hero* I hoisted the mainsail with its unwieldy gaff, then the genoa. Willing hands helped me cast off. Cameras clicked. My stomach gave a sudden lurch of emptiness at parting from such loyal friends, who expressed their own feelings after the manner of men everywhere.

'Piss off Limey and don't come back.'

'Just call me up Yank when your horrible floating coffin breaks down and I'll take you in tow.'

Ice Bird drew away. The other side of the channel loomed; it was time to come about. Tiller hard over, weather headsail sheet cast off, a hasty grab for the winch handle to trim the flapping genoa and the wavelets were rippling along the yacht's side as she gathered way on the new tack. Brash ice crunched and tinkled under the forefoot. A glance astern showed that *Hero* and Palmer Base had already dwindled. No time for nostalgia; the skerries, ice-capped islands and grounded bergs strewing the next part of the route demanded every bit of my attention. The moment was hardly opportune to connect up the as yet untried self-steering gear, since the many obstructions necessitated constant changes of course and the wind was fickle. In fact common prudence would suggest I unship the vane's lever arm, which projects down into the water, lest it be damaged by ice – but I did not think of this at the time.

Preoccupied as I was with trying to get the best out of the yacht's makeshift gunter rig and of navigating unknown and difficult waters, all at a time when I had been abruptly thrown back on my own resources, I felt exhilarated to have at last the chance of learning at first hand what I had studied in theory for so long – the arts of an ice skipper. *Ice Bird* had been re-born. In only one month last season and a month and three days this spring, she had been transformed from a near-wreck into a ship fit for that exploration of the Antarctic coasts that had all along been my aim. We, *Ice Bird* and I, were once again an efficient team.

The start was auspicious. The 'Banana Belt', so named by the cynical British, was so far living up to its reputation for good weather. Easily identifiable landmarks made position fixing easy. I was steering towards Cape Renard twenty miles away, a sheer red rock tower capped rakishly by a tip-tilted glacier. It signposted Le Maire Channel. Looking back I could see how the almost equally spectacular Gerlache Strait was beginning to open out between the glaciated peaks of Anvers Island and the stupendous continental escarpment. Danco Coast is the name given to the more northerly portion of the mainland peninsula; the southern part, towards which we were now heading, is Grahamland.

Before long the motor had to be pressed into service, for the wind fell lighter and the way grew ever more tortuous. Icebergs are easily avoided, always provided you can see them, I mused, circling one stranded monster. Pack ice was another thing altogether, since it could obliterate every bit of navigable water. Moreover wind and current pressure could buckle twenty-foot thick floes like cardboard or cause them to override and raft over each other.

This seems as suitable a place as any to enlarge further on the varieties of ice found at sea. Icebergs and their smaller cousins, growlers and bergy bits originate, of course, on land. With something like three-quarters of its bulk submerged, a berg drifts slowly northwards whenever the summer thaw releases it from imprisonment in the pack, gradually weathering into fairy-castle shapes or turning turtle as its stability is undermined by the waves and ultimately melting in warmer seas. Or else it may ground, commonly on the hundred fathom line, which is six-hundred feet down. Here its voyage ends unless it breaks up. Immovably stranded, its two-hundred-foot cliffs erode through the years into pinnacles and purple caverns of ever more fantastic beauty, until in the end the pale sun wins its predestined victory.

Pack ice, as mentioned earlier, is formed by the surface of the sea freezing. Fortunately for me, the floes that I encountered were generally old and near to melting and were generally only four to six feet thick.

Pack appeared likely to be the immediate problem. By 11.30 a.m. we were approaching Le Maire Channel. Under motor alone, for the rock and ice cliffs that towered close aboard had cut off every breath of wind, we weaved in and out between the lines of floes that almost but never quite choked the approach to the defile. The tidal current was perceptible. Were we going to encounter pressure where there was no room for manœuvre? I stood tense at the tiller, envying the relaxed Weddell seals dozing on the floes and the Gentoo penguins preoccupied at their fishing. Every now and then the motor would miss a beat and my heart seemed to stop with it. This maritime canyon was no place for a breakdown.

I jerked my head up, startled at a sudden rumbling roar from above. Staring up the mounting succession of ice fall, cirque and snowfield, my eyes at length found the snow cloud that marked where a hundred ton serac had just tumbled into ruin. The strait, narrow enough at the best of times, became effectively constricted to a mere ribbon as the only lead narrowed. Worse still, the open water channel began to trend right under the left-hand ice cliffs, which were now fully exposed to the disintegrating effects of the midday sun. I had no idea of the extent of the avalanche danger, but the question was academic since there was no other route. I had to try this way. It seemed an age that we nosed along, the rattle of the exhaust booming back from the ice cliffs, the while I apprehensively divided my attention between the half-tide rocks and looming seracs to port and the sinuous ice edge opposite.

At last *Ice Bird* chugged round a corner (the engine's beat had now steadied, thank goodness) and crunched through a line of brash out into the sunlight. This was a place where the passage widened out to receive a heavily crevassed mainland glacier. The time was 1.30 p.m., two hours since passing Cape Renard. We had come almost to the start of the real narrows, the four-mile-long Le Maire Channel proper.

At this point I noticed that the plywood wind-vane was gone. Clearly I had failed properly to screw home the securing bolt. Ignoring the unworthy thought that there were still three spare vanes aboard, I turned back along our wake and was lucky enough soon to retrieve the inconspicuous varnished board.

Back on course, we soon reached the bend that had so far hidden from us the throat of the pass. A berg which, judging from its water-smoothed surface and vertical tide marks, had but recently turned over on to its side, had cleared an open space in its fall. We crept past it, rounded the corner and there ahead stretched the narrows – no more than half a mile across, flanked by three-thousand-foot walls. That first glance conveyed the absurd impression of there not being room enough for *Ice Bird* to pass. Yet, as I well knew, even large icebreakers used the channel.

The deeper we penetrated the more I marvelled at the wild beauty of this place. Sun-warmed rock buttresses ribbed the dazzling snowfields of the eastern wall but, on Wandle Peak opposite, the westering sun had already cast the hanging glaciers into purple shadow. Ice floes slowly gyrated with the current. The 'ark ark' of porpoising penguins and the engine's staccato echo were the only sounds to break the silence. Then came the thunder of a nearby ice avalanche. I watched the water boil as the great blocks rained down, and saw the pack heave up alarmingly. No need to worry: the spreading undulations were so quickly damped down by the ice cover that no more than a few gentle ripples reached as far as *Ice Bird.*

I will not attempt to enlarge further upon this unforgettable scene or the effect it had upon me. In any case Le Maire Channel crops up again later in this story, even if in rather different circumstances, so I will content myself with recording that the pack was kind, no denser than 6/10. In two and a half hours of rather circuitous motoring we traversed Le Maire Channel and emerged into the open around four in the afternoon. I heaved a sigh of relief. Surely the way would be easier now that there was more room to manœuvre! The rest of the route to Argy lay along Penola Strait between the sheer Grahamland coast to the east (on the left hand) and a screen of islands and rocks some four miles out to seaward. The largest of these, Hovgaard and Petermann, with their attendant skerries, stretched south for about ten miles. The small low Argentine Islands, where the British base was situated, began five miles south of Petermann.

I was soon disillusioned. The pack became progressively more dense and it even appeared to be moving in behind to block off the way we had come. In preparation for the backing and butting aside of the ice that seemed to be in prospect I shut off the motor so that I could, rather belatedly, disconnect the vulnerable self-steering lever arm and refuel. After the abrupt cessation of engine noise the stillness seemed unnatural. *Ice Bird* floated motionless in the centre of a mirror-smooth polynia – a patch of clear water in the pack.

There had been 26 US gallons of petrol aboard that morning, 20 of them in four five-gallon jerrycans lashed to the rails forward. Eight hours under power had used up six gallons. Lugging one of the jerrycans aft and emptying it into the fuel tank through the filler pipe on deck, I could not help comparing the ease of this operation, now that the waves had been damped down by the ice, with its awkwardness in a seaway. Twenty gallons of fuel remained in hand, more than enough to take me to Argy, I thought, as I pressed the starter button and the motor stuttered into life.

The only possible way past Hovgaard Island was along the shore lead, the tenuous tidal gap separating the fast ice frozen to the shore from the free drifting pack farther out. The prospect of traversing it was far from inviting. Ugly looking boulders everywhere projected through the fast ice and it was a reasonable deduction that other rocks lurked close beneath the surface outside the ice margin. Nevertheless, all went well until *Ice Bird* ran out from the shelter of the southern tip of the big island and, without warning, we found ourselves in real peril.

Jagged skerries were suddenly all around us and the pack was innocuous and quiet no longer. A heavy swell from the open sea was causing the ice floes to collide and buckle, battering them against the rocks and swirling them in the savage backwash. The little yacht lacked the power to make any impression on pack such as this. She was surged helplessly back and forth, bringing up repeatedly against the bigger floes with stunning force. For the moment she was completely out of control. I could only pray she would not be dashed against one of those grim islets, to be pinned down and, in all probability, pounded to pieces.

But the same swell that threatened *Ice Bird*'s imminent destruction was to prove her salvation. As the floes cannoned together in one place leads opened up temporarily in another. Two floes ahead parted. I slammed open the throttle; a floe dealt the hull a tremendous buffet; then we were moving – out from that fearful place. More by luck than good judgement I managed to zigzag along one lead after another until we reached deep water and quiet pack in the lee of Petermann Island.

Once again there was no alternative but to follow a shore lead. Three miles down the coast the island's precipitous cliffs gave way to gentler slopes and there, unexpectedly, stood a solid looking little building. I studied the chart more closely. Yes, there it was, marked 'Refuge Hut'. I hoped devoutly not to need it but its presence was comforting none the less.

I was determined to avoid at all costs the potentially dangerous southern tip of Petermann Island and so started to work across in the general direction of the mainland Coast through a series of narrow leads. We were well out into Penola Strait by the time Petermann Island had fallen astern. This would have been all very well because, save for some scattered bergs and a few skerries several miles away, the strait was free from obstruction. Unhappily the pack was now so close – eight- or nine-tenths ice cover, I judged – as to be all but unnavigable. The very few leads that remained all tended eastward towards the tumbling mainland glaciers that spilled down from the continental ice cap and led away from the hummocked Argentine Islands, now in tantalisingly plain view. And even these last leads were closing fast.

I was unaware until many weeks later that the Argy base personnel had spotted *Ice Bird* through their binoculars. Nor could I know that they had just radioed to Palmer that the previous day's wide leads had closed up again. Not even a strengthened expeditions ship, they warned, could hope to reach Argy. I had reached much the same conclusion.

By 6 p.m. we were virtually beset but I wasted another two hours and much fuel in fruitlessly charging floes that the weight of the yacht's overriding bow could never hope to force aside – because they were packed so tightly that there was no place for them to go. There being no point in trying any longer, I shut the engine off at 8 p.m.

The petrol tank was nearly empty again, the last few hours at full throttle in close pack having been prodigal of fuel. Eleven gallons all told had been consumed in that day's eleven hours' motoring. There were fifteen gallons left. I refilled the tank, attended to such routine maintenance as tightening the stern gland and took bearings to fix our position. Time for a last look round. There was still no wind and it was very warm, a remarkable +7°C., that I was not to experience again for more than two months. The sky remained cloudless, though a faint haze shimmered over the ice. Westward and southward, glistening under the low sun, gently heaving hummocked pack and its captive bergs stretched away into infinity.

Next day I woke periodically only to go back to sleep again, for there was not only that first day's weariness to make good but, more important, all the tiredness that had accumulated during the exhausting refit at Palmer. Between 8.30, when I woke up first and noted that the yacht was still close beset with some pressure and was nearer the glaciated mainland coast, and 2 p.m., the log contains only one word (entered later): 'slept'. The ice pressure had eased by two o'clock. Narrow lanes of water were visible between the floes. The decision, whether to tackle the 9/10 pack or remain where we were and save fuel, was solved by the view from aloft.

There were no patches of clear water. Within the hour the pack had closed in again.

Nevertheless there had been one important observation. The floes had loosened at high tide. From now on I must adjust my strategy accordingly. As a first step I must be ready to get under way by three o'clock next morning, which I judged would be just about the time of high water.

This having been decided, there was nothing more constructive to be done than to go to sleep again. Hunger awakened me at seven-thirty, when I ate a similar supper to the night before. Then, feeling a little demoralised by my helplessness and the enforced inactivity, I retired to my bunk once more.

I was up and about according to plan by three next morning, 14 December. I had slept, with only short breaks, for the major part of thirty hours. It was calm and sunny, with a temperature of −2°C. To my delight I saw that the floes were spaced much wider apart than the previous afternoon. The intervening water was itself lightly frozen over but the new ice, being barely half an inch thick, presented no problems. I got the motor going at once and, with high hopes, began picking a way towards Argentine Islands. Fifteen minutes later the engine stopped abruptly.

I am no favourite with motors since I lack the natural mechanical aptitude necessary for getting on really good terms with them. Nor had I had much occasion to delve into *Ice Bird*'s engine, Jim having been the one who got it going at Palmer. Now I was really on my own. With the help of the instruction manual I soon traced the fault to a block in the fuel line, but taking down and reassembling the carburettor in that cramped space without dropping some vital part into the bilge, was not so easy. The job, therefore, took me some time and, before the engine could be got running, the pack had closed in once more. There was yet more trouble. The end of the throttle cable had broken off. It slipped out repeatedly when I tried to replace it so in the end I had to be content with an engine that ran at a third throttle and whose speed could not be varied. Still, at least it *was* going.

Paradoxically, I began to feel much more confident now than at any time since leaving Palmer. Here was something that I found particularly difficult and had tackled on my own more or less successfully. I had 'earned my keep'.

Heightened morale encouraged me to get on with things I had been neglecting. After a general tidying up of the cabin I decided that this was an excellent opportunity to ease my conscience with the *National Geographic* by taking 'indoor' photographs. The absence of movement, so unprecedented at sea, and the strong light provided conditions too good to miss. All along I had been taking pictures in the cockpit with a Nikonis waterproof camera, loaded with Kodachrome II, clamped to the stern rail. A string which I constantly kept tripping over worked the shutter. The result was a high proportion of pictures of my own rear.

Hopefully the cabin shots would be a little more varied. The Nikkormat had a delayed action shutter release, which would be an improvement on the string. I clamped one to the forward cabin bulkhead. It had been loaded with High Speed Ektachrome pushed to 400 ASA to obviate the need for flash, a practice I adhered to subsequently with apparently good results. I proceeded to immortalise myself shaving, writing up the log, plotting bearings on the chart and making my first hot meal and drink on the Japanese wick stove – even though this involved no more than heating water and a can of stew. The kettle proved to be leaking, so I cursed and tossed it overboard, forgetting for the moment that the sea outside was solid. It bounced along in the direction of two very startled Adélie penguins who squawked in alarm and fled.

This incident gave me the idea of taking pictures of the trapped *Ice Bird* from alongside. An ice-axe driven into the snow provided a useful camera stand for the other Nikkormat. There followed an enjoyable twenty minutes of actuating the delayed release and then plunging across to the yacht so as to be posing nonchalantly alongside when the shutter finally clicked.

High tide that afternoon saw some loosening of the pack but so little that, after an hour's effort, we were no more than a quarter of a mile in a straight line from our starting point. Our situation had actually worsened for we were right in the track of a line of bergs that appeared to be ploughing southward through the pack. Bearings on the land showed later that it was the bergs that were stationary and probably grounded while the pack was moving northward. But which was in motion was irrelevant to our predicament. We had to get out of the way. Twenty minutes' pushing and squirming through gaps carried the yacht the necessary five hundred yards to safety.

Only just in time, Without warning the pack snapped shut like a vice round *Ice Bird.* From time to time the whole mass would begin to surge violently to and fro. Perhaps a distant berg had overturned. But after a minute all would become still again. It began to snow. It was then that I blessed the designer for the yacht's wedge shaped underwater cross-section because, as the pressure increased, she was squeezed bodily upwards. Her steel frame merely groaned and creaked a little but the stout craft was clearly in no danger at all.

The lack of a functioning radio transmitter was annoying: this was because I feared that my failure to reach Argy might be causing needless anxiety, rather than because of *Ice Bird*'s being beset. Certainly she was amply enough supplied, carrying as she did a good six months' food, even if variety were limited, and thirty-nine gallons of water (and this old pack had long since become fresh water ice). There was meths enough – four gallons – to heat up a hundred Primus stoves. I had exchanged what survived of my original paperbacks at Palmer. So light reading matter was no problem. The only item that was short was kerosene, a mere quart. Palmer had inadvertently used up the rest. Still, cold food would be no novelty. In fact, of course, the unusually persistent summer pack had to disperse soon – in a matter of weeks at most.

There was no immediate risk of the yacht's being damaged in the ice, much less wrecked or crushed. Nevertheless, such unpleasant possibilities did exist and it would have been irresponsible not to have thought out in advance ways of surviving the loss of my ship in the continental pack ice.

These emergency plans hinged on the fact that Antarctic Peninsula bases are not very far apart. The ultra light *Condom* could easily be carried, either inflated or folded up in a ruck-sack, over ice floes or across land and could be used to cross considerable stretches of coastal water in fine weather. Thanks to that not altogether purposeless overnight glacier trip from Palmer, I knew that my sleeping bag was more than adequate in the open. Add an ice axe, a knife, emergency food and, above all, the patience to wait for really calm conditions, and only incompetence or very bad luck could prevent my reaching safety under my own steam. At the present moment, of course, there was that most convenient refuge hut on Petermann Island.

The other dire contingency, foundering in mid-ocean through storm or collision with an iceberg, was less well covered. In fact I had no plan at all. The circular rubber raft, which I had sent back to England from Palmer as too cumbersome, would in any case have been useless. It was only capable of blowing along helplessly until its fabric perished – long after my own demise. In the Appendix, I have enlarged on the need for a steerable raft for ocean yachtsmen but, so far as I was concerned, *Ice Bird* must continue as her own lifeboat in the open ocean – and we must studiously avoid bergs.

These days beset in the pack seemed to flow into one another, the blurring of time in the absence of normal seagoing routine being accentuated by the continuous daylight. Despite the steel plates protecting the cabin windows and cutting off two-thirds of the light I could still read down below at any time of the night. The hours of high water, with the consequent loosening of the ice, became the significant twelve-and-a-half-hour markers. Thus, only my wrist watch and the log entries indicated that another day had come when I started the motor at 1 a.m. on 15 December.

It was colder now, −4°C. and snowing heavily. New ice had formed between the floes. High time to replace my thin jeans with warm Japanese quilted undertrousers. Once more the patient zigzag south-westward towards Argentine Islands was resumed. The penguins were still asleep at this hour, either erect with head beneath flipper or prone. At the yacht's noisy approach they would wake in a panic and dash off, leaning forward with flippers held stiffly out behind, to plop head foremost into the nearest lead. Once a seal poked its head up close alongside, choked in surprise and coughed up a stream of water, then hastily dived.

When the eventual closing in of the pack put an end to the morning's endeavours, another half jerrycan of fuel had been used up. Apart from what was left in the tank, only ten gallons remained in reserve. To set against this we were now, I estimated, in 65° 22′ S., so there *had* been fair progress.

Argentine Islands were only four or five miles off. (This modest success had been duly noted by the British watchers on their hilltop, with the unfortunate sequel that, when RRS *Bransfield* relieved them a fortnight later, she generously steamed another ten miles down Penola Strait to see if the yacht had been carried farther in the direction she had last been seen heading.)

The pack failed to loosen at all that afternoon. The temperature remained below freezing. Snow began to fall again and continued heavily all night. Nevertheless, I was pleased at our progress and looked forward with anticipation to the morrow. I could not know that 65° 22′ S. was to be *Ice Bird*'s southern limit.

Shortly after eight next morning, 16 December, the snow clouds rolled away and the sun broke through, rapidly melting the accumulated snow on deck. The ship was still heavily beset. But it was not this that caused my consternation. The familiar Penola Strait landmarks had vanished. It took a moment to recognise the island to seaward as Hovgaard and to realise that the whole pack must have drifted quite a few miles north-eastward during the night. Not only had the last three days' painful efforts been wiped out, but we had lost as much ground again as had so laboriously been won. The steadily changing bearings of the land confirmed that the drift was still continuing.

There was only one possible decision. As the log stated:

In view of the drift of pack, am abandoning Argentine Islands objective.

Will try to return north along Le Maire and on to Almirante Brown. [The Argentinian station at Paradise Bay on the mainland side of Gerlache Strait.] Worries pack, motor, petrol.

With such an inauspicious start opened a most memorable day.

For the moment initiative lay with the pack. *Ice Bird* was fast beset and nothing I could do would move her an inch in any direction. The small leads, in defiance of the bright sunshine, were still frozen over. Everything glittered and sparkled. What a picture the bright yellow yacht must make, I thought, against the shadowed blue ice of the Grahamland escarpment! Dropping down on to the ice with a camera, I began casting about, hopping from one floe to the next, in an effort to obtain the best vantage point. Yes, there was an ideal floe – even if the lead was a trifle wide. I crouched down and jumped.

Good, I had made it easily! I got to my feet jauntily and looked back. The lead was already a good ten feet across and was widening rapidly. The momentum of my leap had been transmitted to the floe with a vengeance. Now I watched in dismay as *Ice Bird* receded beyond a growing expanse of water. Recollection of the effects of immersion in sub-zero sea water were not reassuring. How to get back? With an effort I held down incipient panic and studied the situation more carefully.

My floe had by now come to rest against the opposite side of the newly formed polynia. Would any of the adjacent pans bear my weight? Not worth the risk, they all looked rotten. Therefore my floe must somehow be induced to go back. There being nothing to paddle with, I lay down gingerly on my back near the edge of the floe, put both feet against its dubious neighbour, glanced round to confirm that the angles were right and shoved off hard. The floe slid forward sluggishly, gyrated and came to rest at the edge of the polynia again but, this time, a little nearer *Ice Bird*. Heartened, I got up and took the photograph that had led to all the trouble, lay down again and repeated the manœuvre. After the third push the floe floated up to the yellow hull. I grasped the stern rail as if it had been my salvation (as indeed it was) and clambered thankfully aboard.

Almost imperceptibly the pack kept on drifting northward. For half an hour it was racked with violent sheering and rotatory movements, but when these ceased, as suddenly and mysteriously as they had begun, it had opened out a little. A faint southerly breeze began to stir, so hoisting the genoa seemed worthwhile. Then it was the motor's turn but this ran so erratically as to have to be shut off almost at once. With a sigh of resignation I got down to the job of stripping and cleaning the fuel line, fluently cursing the dollops of melting snow that periodically plopped down from the boom to splatter over the disassembled engine.

Meanwhile *Ice Bird*, with the genoa still set, was drifting through the interstices in the 9/10 pack. Every now and then I would scramble up from below decks, push away the currently obstructing floe with a boathook and direct the yacht's bow into a crack between pans that she could gradually force open by the gentle tug of her headsail. The engine adjustments took all of one and a half hours, so it was noon before all was done. The effort had been more than worthwhile, because I had at last succeeded in re-introducing the throttle cable into the carburettor. An immediate ten-minute trial confirmed that the power was indeed much increased. Mightily relieved, I switched off and sat down to a lunch of corned beef, ship's biscuits and coffee.

By one o'clock I was back on deck surveying the situation. It had not altered materially. We were still in Girard Bay between Hovgaard Island and the continental shore, though now the entrance to Le Maire Channel was open ahead. The glittering floes revolved slowly in the sunshine, gradually opening up short and narrow leads. Surely these could be utilised, given sufficient patience. But how? Certainly not by wasting precious fuel and taking the risk of straining the temperamental motor for the meagre results possible in such a near-unnavigable pack.

The obvious answer was to get out and push. I stripped off my quilted anorak and clambered down on to the snow-covered ice.

Two o'clock came and passed and I was still pushing. Sometimes I had to put my shoulder to the transom, or else I would grip one of the stanchions and haul from alongside. Yet again, the bow would have to be guided into an opening. Often it was easier to pole from on deck with the boathook. Transient puffs of wind bellied out the genoa to add their quota. We seemed not to be getting anywhere until I noticed that a group of frozen-in berglets, which had been some distance ahead, had fallen a long way astern.

This original form of yacht propulsion deserved to be immortalised, I decided rather smugly, and began to record samples of my efforts with a camera propped up on an upturned bucket out on the floes. I was re-setting the shutter after having taken a shot when an ominous plop sounded back at the yacht. The boathook, which had been leaning up against the bow, had disappeared and a new lead of uninviting dark water had opened between me and the vessel. Here was the morning's predicament all over again. The experience gained earlier enabled me to regain *Ice Bird* by the same method as before, but now I was cured of any penchant for further overside photography. I resolved to cling closer than a leech to the yacht in future.

For all these good intentions, it was not long before I had an even worse fright. While pushing hunched over from astern, the floe on which I was standing split and slid away, so suddenly that I was barely able to retain my balance on its rocking remnant. Working my precarious way from floe to floe towards safety was anything but easy and the experience forcibly brought home to me how rotten much of the ice had become. I must be far more careful and must strictly confine myself from now on to poling (with a dinghy oar in lieu of the lost boathook) from the security of the foredeck.

A fresh series of rotatory movements without any discernible set pattern now began to take place, first in one section of the pack then in another. Ice avalanches were coming off the cliffs ahead and I devoutly hoped that no unpredictable vortex would set us over beneath them. Fortunately none did so. *Ice Bird* re-entered Le Maire, from which she had emerged with such high hopes exactly four days and a half-hour earlier, in mid-channel at 4.30 p.m. The pack's density was much more variable and, once inside the pass, its drift speeded up. I was still fending off and pushing with *Condom*'s little oar, assisted by occasional zephyrs.

Worries – about being trapped against some obstruction and ground down by the irresistible pack or bombarded by ice avalanches – now faded. The pack swept steadily on, while tiny waves began to ripple along the hull as the wind wafted us across the increasingly frequent polynias. Once again I fell under the spell of Le Maire's grandeur. The camera began clicking again, only this time from the cockpit. But I soon despaired of capturing anything like a true image of those soaring precipices. As to the busily waddling and diving penguins and the somnolent seals, the former moved too fast to catch at the right moment, while the latter seemed always to be in the wrong place or too far away. Moreover, camera work was continually interrupted by the need to steer or pole off. Still the time passed enjoyably enough and it seemed but a moment before it was half-past six and we were rounding the final bend in Le Maire Channel proper, in much looser pack.

The motor could with advantage be started and, half an hour later, I hoisted the mainsail to make full use of the stiffening breeze. The ice became progressively more scattered as the mountain walls fell back on either hand, until at 8 p.m., Cape Renard came abeam to starboard and we sailed out into the open waters of Bismarck Strait and finally left behind the main body of the pack.

Since the wind, if still light, was fair the motor could now be shut off. With the sun shining as brightly as ever I hove-to to replenish the petrol tank and lay out ten fathoms of anchor cable, in somewhat premature preparation for arriving at Almirante Brown, still twenty-five miles to the north. When we got under way again I continued steering from the cockpit at first but later, as the temperature dropped, retired to the shelter of the companionway, where I propped myself up against the hatch coaming, holding the tiller lines with mittened hands. What water had splashed into the cockpit or on to the side decks froze solid. There was still too much ice about to risk trying out the as yet unfamiliar self-steering gear. I grew increasingly weary.

Alertness was essential, however. The hollow boom of swells rolling into caverns worn in the icebergs along our track spelled out a clear warning, if any were needed. More menacing even than the bergs were the growlers, whose bottle-green wave-worn silhouettes were only barely distinguishable as they wallowed awash like submerging whales. Fortunately the grumbling, gurgling noise that they made as they rolled to and fro was audible a good way off from a sailing boat. Was this the origin of their name, I wondered? Bergy bits, being much higher out of the water than growlers, were easier to see. All those with level standing room were peopled with sleeping penguins, stacked side by side like ninepins, who woke and craned their necks to watch us pass.

Soon after midnight the fifteen-mile wide Bismarck Strait was behind us and we entered the northward-trending Gerlache Strait, keeping well over towards the eastern or Danco Coast side. I hove-to again then, for coffee and biscuits and in order to study the chart in the shelter of the cabin.

Landmarks had become hard to distinguish despite the continuing full daylight, because the cold white light cast no shadows once the sun had set. It might be difficult to locate Canal Lautaro, the channel into Paradise Bay, and I needed to memorise all the prominent features.

In the event, Bank Island separated itself from its background three hours later and revealed the sought-for sound. I hauled in the main sheet, put the helm over and gybed the mainsail; then, steering rather erratically by pressing my bottom against the tiller, I brought the genoa across and ran in through the entrance. No sooner were we inside than the wind died and the motor had to be started.

I had expected to be able to spot the base at once, but a full hour passed before I managed to pick out its radio masts, so dwarfed were they by the vastness of the continental massif behind. A good many Antarctic bases, among them Palmer, are located for convenience on off-lying islands. The Argentinian scientific station Almirante Brown, on the contrary, stands on the Antarctic mainland itself. This was an added point of interest for me because, although I had sailed literally within feet of the continental coast in Le Maire Channel, I had not yet actually landed upon it.

It was five in the morning before I reached the station, having come thirty-six miles since beginning to break out of the pack the previous day. I thankfully throttled back the engine and let *Ice Bird* coast past the sleeping base, while I wondered if there were anywhere to tie up or whether to anchor instead. A bearded figure appeared and waved. I swung the tiller hard over and headed in towards the tiny jetty where he was standing. He called out, but I could not distinguish the words above the noise of the engine. His meaning was soon enough to be made clear.

Unforgivably, I neglected to look over the side to check that it was deep enough for the yacht's six-foot draft. Had I done so it would have been immediately obvious (the water being clear) that the bottom was shoaling fast. There came a grinding crunch under the keel, a series of bumps, and *Ice Bird* stopped abruptly. After surviving all the dangers of the pack, she had been run hard aground.

IX

Robin Knox-Johnston

'Going round the world non-stop – that's about all there's left to do now, isn't it?' Seldom can a casual remark have led to such a remarkable and fateful result – it was made one day by the father of Robin Knox-Johnston to his son and (to cut a very long story short) as a result that brave and determined young man enshrined his name forever in the history books by, indeed, becoming the first man to sail round the world non-stop. This historic voyage was made in *Suhaili*, a 44-foot Bermudan Ketch originally built in India 'as a family cruiser suitable for ocean sailing'. As Knox-Johnston relates in his engagingly modest autobiography, *A World of My Own*, it was not his original intention to try a world voyage in *Suhaili*, which frankly he considered too small for the job. Only when he failed to raise enough money to finance a larger boat did he fall back on the familiar, and by now well-trusted, old ketch. In this sturdy, if not apparently very exciting, boat Knox-Johnston set off in what had now become *The Sunday Times* Round the World Race – along with a handful of other competitors, including Bernard Moitessier, Bill King, John Ridgway, Chay Blyth, the unlucky Nigel Tetley and the ill-fated and doomed Donald Crowhurst. One by one the others faltered and fell out – though poor Tetley was within a few hundred miles of home when his trimaran broke up – and it was left to the modest and comparatively unknown Knox-Johnston to finally complete his encirclement of the globe in 313 days – having sailed approximately 30,123 nautical miles. In the episode reprinted here the reader is given a glimpse of the quiet sense of achievement with which Robin Knox-Johnston sailed on his last lap from the Equator to Falmouth, finally sailing across the 'finishing line' between Pendennis Head and St Anthony Head at 3.25 p.m., Tuesday, 22 April 1969.

THE HOMECOMING

Robin Knox-Johnston

We ran into the South-East Trades in latitude 24° South and twelve days later shot across the Equator, having averaged nearly 120 miles each day. It did not take me long nowadays to get *Suhaili* balanced and I found some spare time on my hands with which to prepare her, and me, for our confrontation with civilisation. I gave myself a haircut and trimmed my beard, and then trimmed the weed off *Suhaili*'s hull. I also gave the upperworks a scrub down. All the ropework was checked and where necessary new servings of marline put over splices and given a good coating of Stockholm Tar. I had time, as well, to check the sails and stitch up the split mainsail, usually working below but sometimes dragging the sail into the cockpit and working there despite the spray that frequently came over.

We were getting close to the shipping lanes again and I started to worry about seeing a ship to report us. I had seen only one ship, a Japanese bulk carrier, since leaving New Zealand. She was heading towards Rio from the Cape of Good Hope but had been too far away for me to be able to attract attention. Keeping a lookout for shipping was all very well when I was awake or in daylight, but after I had turned in at night I had to rely upon a rather weak oil lantern to avoid being run down.

This lantern disappeared one night from its accustomed position hanging from the pushpit aft, and I was left with the choice of rigging up an electric light or leaving the paraffin pressure-lamp going all night. I just did not have the petrol left to keep the batteries charged sufficiently for an electric light, whereas with 15 gallons of paraffin remaining, the pressure lamp using one pint a night could easily be left going without straining my resources. I started off by leaving it wedged in the lifebuoy on the top of the main hatch and pointing up towards the mainsail which, when illuminated like this, seems to show up fairly well. But one night of this was enough to show me that if I wanted to keep the lamp I would have to put it in a less exposed position. The cockpit wouldn't do as spray was constantly coming over, so I finished up with the lamp fastened in the vice on the saloon table and shining up through the skylight. This reduced the actual light showing from the boat by three-quarters, but it was the best I could do. It also made the cabin very hot, which made dropping off to sleep difficult, but unless we wanted to be run down, we had to show some sort of light.

As we approached the Equator the steady Trade Winds began to be broken:

March 5th, 1969 *Day 265*

The wind is beginning to fluctuate and we are getting some quite severe squalls. At one point this afternoon the weather looked so threatening that I handed the mainsail. It was as well that I did as when the squall hit we heeled right over and made about 5 knots under the other three sails alone. This evening we have run into a northerly choppy sea so we must be on the edge of the Doldrums, although we cross the mean limit of the S.E. Trades at the Equator at this time of the year and this, with luck, will be tomorrow.

Burning on deck by day and stuffy below for the first half of the night, but as we are moving, who cares?

I spent the day reading when not steering or trying to race the boat swimming. I was never exhausted before the stern came level with me, not because I am fit – I have little stamina now – but because we were moving well. Day's run to noon 118 miles . . .

The next day we crossed the Equator and the stomach pains that gave me my greatest scare of the whole voyage began:

March 6th, 1969 *Day 266*

I have had to work today with the wind south of east. She won't balance to steer north, so I steered. Quite nice but too hot for comfort. I don't know if it's the sun or unaccustomed labour, but I do not feel at all well this evening. I feel a bit sick and tired and I have a headache. I also have agonizing indigestion.

Tried the radio this evening but no one seems to be listening. Not much on the news.

Can't get to sleep.

Finished all the cigarettes at lunch today – it's a horrible habit anyway!

Having at last to give up smoking was more of a relief than anything. For some time I had been convinced that cigarettes were not doing me any good, but whilst I had them on board I did not have the willpower to give them up. Now I had no choice and surprisingly enough I did not miss them at all. But as soon as I got home and they became available, I started smoking again.

From a health point of view I would have to have stopped anyway. The indigestion developed until I had a permanent pain in the middle of my stomach. I got out my *Ship Captains' Medical Guide* and by the time I had finished looking up my symptoms and the possible causes, I was really alarmed. It appeared that I could have anything from appendicitis to stomach ulcers. I put myself on a diet of spaghetti cheese and rice puddings, which was most unsatisfying, but it did ease things a bit. I also started taking indigestion tablets, but the pain remained despite all this. Then its source appeared to shift and I got really scared. I took out the charts and measured off to the nearest decent-sized port, Belem, at the mouth of the Amazon, which was about a thousand miles away. That was at least ten days sailing, and in ten days if I did have appendicitis without any antibiotics on board to keep the thing in check, I would be dead. I cursed myself for leaving antibiotics off my medical list, and for not having my appendix out before I set sail, but it was too late for recriminations now. I decided to hold onto my course for home and just hope there was nothing seriously wrong. With any luck I might sight a ship and if that happened I could ask them to arrange a daily radio schedule in case the worst came to the worst.

I still feel guilty about this. If I had had appendicitis and had made a contact it would have meant great inconvenience to any shipping which diverted to pick me up. It would have been even worse if I had managed to make a radio contact and a search was necessary in order to find out where I was. The authorities go to a great deal of trouble for ships and yachts in distress. Apart from the expense, which is relatively unimportant, men's lives are put at risk in aircraft and boats to look for the man in trouble. Everyone who sets off in a small boat has this responsibility to the search and rescue organisations, that he should be ready for any emergency himself, and he should not set off unless he is capable and his boat fit for the job, as his negligence may be paid for by other men's lives. I have always felt strongly about this, and yet here I was, possibly in trouble which I could have coped with myself if my medical stores had been properly thought out. I did not feel very proud of myself.

On 9 March, after a couple of days of light breezes, the wind suddenly came up strongly from the north. This was the second time *Suhaili* and I had crossed the Equator from south to north and each time the Doldrums have proved untroublesome, largely, I think, because I went as far west as I could. The next evening I sighted a ship coming south. I let the lights get close and then started calling it with the Aldis. After five minutes without response, I lit a hand flare and then continued calling. Still no answer. I was beginning to think I had run into the *Flying Dutchman* and was about to give up when I realised that if I did have appendicitis this might be the last opportunity I would have to save my life, so I brought out a distress rocket and set it off.

The result was most spectacular; the whole sky was lit up by the blue flare which drifted slowly down on its parachute, burning brightly for about three minutes. I waited half a minute and then called the ship on the Aldis again. This time, after a minute or so, I got a flicker in acknowledgement and my hopes rose. I was all right, I could reassure my family with the news that I was still alive. Even more important for the present, I could ask for someone to keep in contact with me. I started calling the ship in the usual way used by Merchant Navies the world over but before I had even started sending *Suhaili*'s name he had lost interest. I lit another flare but received no response, although I continued to signal until his sternlight disappeared over the horizon. 'The lousy bastard', I wrote in my diary.

It really was quite unforgivable. There is a sacred tradition supported by law as regards distress at sea, that unless you endanger your own ship you will go to the assistance of a ship in distress. There was next to no sea running, the wind was between force 2 and 3, but this ship had completely ignored my flares and my signals, not even bothering to investigate what in any circumstances were unusual happenings. I only hope that if that ship is ever in trouble her signals are not treated as mine were – although I was not feeling so charitable at the time.

I saw a number of other ships in the ensuing days, two of which came really close, within half a mile, and not one of them answered my signals. This was a shattering revelation to me. I was trained as a merchant seaman to understand that keeping a lookout was the primary duty of the Officer of the Watch when at sea, and that if the Captain ever came on the bridge and saw a ship that you had not observed you were for the high jump. I remember once in the Arabian Sea being occupied working out a sight, during which time I watched ahead but not past the beam. The Captain came out onto the bridge just as a Pakistani destroyer, unseen by me, roared up from astern. I got the rocket of my life, and rightly so. It did not matter that in the circumstances the destroyer was bound to give way to us; something could have gone wrong, and I was on the bridge to keep a lookout for just that. It was a lesson I have never forgotten, and a few years later when I was Master of a coaster in South Africa I gave the second mate a bawling out for sitting in the wheelhouse chair whilst on watch because he could not keep a proper lookout from there. Now I was seeing the other side of the coin, and learning what it was like to be largely dependent on ships' lookouts. I came to the conclusion that you could not depend upon them at all, and that's not a comforting feeling for a singlehander.

After a few more days, the intense stomach pain began to ease off. I kept to my milky diet for a while longer and then cautiously went back to solids.

March 13th, 1969 *Day 273*

There has been no complaint from my stomach for a day or so now, so I think I can, in retrospect, diagnose my trouble as a combination of chronic indigestion and acute imagination, and it shows the dangers of giving a layman a medical book! I still have the indigestion and I'll be glad to get onto fresh food again, although apart from that there is nothing wrong with me. Five to six weeks to go with any luck.

I think now that the real trouble was the bully beef, which had started going off. The tins were sound but the considerable changes in temperature that they had experienced must have affected the contents. Anyway, I left bully beef out of my menus for three weeks and had little further trouble.

It took thirteen days to get through the North-East Trades. Once again there was little steering for me to do as *Suhaili* balanced herself well. Coming up from Cape Town before, we had been able to leave the tiller lashed and untended for sixteen days, only keeping a lookout from the hatchway, and we spent most of our time playing Canasta. It seemed harder work this time as I had to do all the sail tending on my own, but I had learned from my previous experience, and although I was pushed farther west than I would have wished, we made a quicker passage as I allowed the sheets to be slightly looser. The sea itself really posed a greater problem as there was a limit as to the amount of sail I could leave up without having *Suhaili* banged too heavily by the waves.

March 11th, 1969 *Day 271*

I awoke after an excellent night's sleep, full of good intentions. These mainly concerned the charger. However, the wind rising and a disgraceful sea getting up, I had to drop the idea. I really have not done too much today. I made what I consider to be an excellent fish pie – from flying fish I found lying on the deck this morning (I've mastered cheese sauces at last) – despite the boat's crazy motion, and I've done some scribbling, but that's about all.

It has not been an easy day though, on account of a confused sea on top of a heavy N.E. swell. It made me giddy watching it and this is very unusual. We've been ploughing under a great deal and the lower fathom of the jib is permanently wet. Despite this I have kept sail pressed on her, apart from a couple of turns on the mizzen for a short time, and the reward was 125 miles run to noon, which I am jubilant over. This is close-hauled and on a nasty sea. We covered 1½ degrees of latitude which is how I am measuring progress at present, and this is half a degree more than expected. I have changed charts and at last can see Britain. She is taking water a bit, but it is only to be expected when pushed like this. I'm not bothered as long as she doesn't strain herself. The worst bangs are, in fact, from beam seas breaking against the side, although on one or two occasions our motion has been like an elevator falling in its shaft without a brake to check the bang at the bottom.

The urge to smoke has not really bothered me. Quite often during the day I say I could do with a cigarette but it has not become an overpowering obsession. It's like steak; I can't have it at present and that's that.

On 17 March I celebrated my thirtieth birthday. The temptation to philosophise in my diary upon passing this milestone was irresistible:

March 17th, 1969 *Day 277*

Firstly all those sevens are obviously propitious, but I still doubt if we can get home by April 17th as I had hoped. I'm feeling very lethargic. Quite frankly I think I have been on my own long enough and am getting stale. I need something to break the monotony, and getting home is the best cure I can think of. After finding our noon position, the big time of the day is 2100 when I listen to the BBC News. I occasionally scribble a bit, thinking ahead to the book I shall have to buckle down to when I get home, and over the last few days I have described the business in the Foveaux Strait and off Otago. It won't do for the book as it stands, but it's still fresh in my mind now.

It does not depress me that this decade is past. I have enjoyed it and managed to do more than most people. Certainly I do not regret a day of it, although perhaps I would like to mark time at this stage for a few years. There seems to be so much left to do in life and I'm itching to get on with something new. This voyage is about played out as far as I'm concerned. Barring accidents we'll be home in a month and that will be an anti-climax for me, however the race has turned out.

It's rather depressing to think that in another ten years I shall be forty, which seems middle-aged from my present position; however, I can remember feeling the same about thirty, ten years ago. I think this is an ideal age actually, young and fit enough for sports, and yet with ten years of adult experience behind one. (I hope in ten years time I am as content.) Perhaps the most interesting thing that has occurred in the past ten years is the change of outlook of people. When I was twenty I had difficulty in identifying with people of thirty, and yet before I sailed I found I could identify more easily with people of twenty than those of forty. These are generalizations, but I wonder why this is. I suppose better education is the answer.

Now that I have got over my indigestion, apart from a recurrence today as a result of cooking a mixed grill for a celebration lunch, I feel well, but I have noticed that my fingers are becoming less sensitive. The other day when the deck bolt on the starboard runner sheared, I had to rig a tackle on the runner. I transferred a shackle pin from my left to right hand, and despite directions to the contrary, the pin slipped from the hand and fell overside. I was angry about this at the time as I am running short of shackles now and cannot afford to lose any more.

I called Dick [my brother in the Royal Signals in Germany]; we had arranged this schedule before I sailed; on 16 Mc/s at 1300 and 1400 G.M.T. as arranged, but could hear nothing except Latin American stations in reply.

Tried to set the Big Fellow today. Each time it twisted up into a ball, and on the last occasion managed to wrap itself round the forestay which took some sorting out. As usual it was torn when I took it in so that is that until I get some repairs done.

Usually on the run north in the North-East Trades, one finds the winds veering round towards the east the farther north one gets. For some reason the winds decided not to co-operate with me, or so it seemed at the time, and continued to blow from north of north-east. Then when they at last began to veer, they dropped strength; we had reached the Horse Latitudes. To put it mildly, this was frustrating. The Horse Latitudes usually commence about twenty to twenty-three degrees north of the Equator; we ran into them at 18° North, about level with the Cape Verde Islands. By this time I had come to consider any light winds from an awkward direction a personal insult, deliberately designed to hold me up, and the only way I could let off steam was by swimming until I exhausted myself and then trying to find an absorbing job to keep me occupied. It may seem incredible that I got out paint and grease and began to overhaul all the rigging screws, deliberately putting new servings on the threads and the splices, but I did it to stop the feeling of helplessness that would have built up otherwise.

March 23rd, 1969 *Day 283*

Oh God, this is hopeless. 67 miles to noon and we are still heading N.W., the best I can manage with a N.N.E. wind, a heavy northerly swell, and northerly, N.E. and easterly seas. I feel bloody dispirited. I can do no more than we are doing in these conditions.

Despite the good conditions yesterday we in fact made less northing than when we were all but becalmed. What the hell can I do? This is what gets me, the answer is absolutely nothing, but sit and hope for more average conditions.

Yet, as usual in the Variables, the weather could change suddenly:

March 25th, 1969 *Day 285*
Well, today beats everything. It got up to a full gale by lunchtime and I've spent most of my time reducing sail. I raced as long as I dared, feeling that if it's going to blow a gale from the S.S.E. I might as well take full advantage of it, but the seas were confused and I had to ease her to stop the pounding. By 2000 it was Force 9.

I don't mind gales in this weather; at least it's warm.

Our position at this time was approximately 24° North, 41° West and we were beginning to meet small clumps of Sargasso weed floating on the surface. When at school, collecting cigarette cards, I remember seeing on one of them a picture of a Spanish Galleon covered with long, trailing tentacles of weed in the Sargasso Sea. Columbus was the first to sight the Sea, and the seamen of the day were convinced that they were on the border of a vast malignant ocean of weed, that would trap their ships and keep them there until they starved or were killed by the primeval sea-monsters that lurked there. The thought of this picture fascinated me for years, and I visualised a vast number of nautical antiques just waiting to be collected by an enterprising adventurer.

The reality was disappointing. If you take a tea tray and drop five grains of rice onto it you will have an idea of the proportion of weed to water in the Sargasso Sea. The weed is broken off the coasts of the Caribbean by storms and is carried into the Sargasso Sea by the Gulf Stream. It propagates by fragmentation. It grows on the surface of the sea and only in a few tangled clumps does it go deeper than nine inches. The fascinating thing about the weed is the life it supports, most of which is normally found only along the sea coasts. I used to drag clumps of the weed aboard and shake out the small yellow crabs and shrimps that hide in the leaves, always hoping that I might find a Sargasso fish, a small, cleverly disguised fish found only amongst this weed. I have yet to find one, but on one occasion as I was picking over a lump of weed, an eel or snake about five inches long sprang clear and shot off very quickly with a jerky, sinuous movement. It had the same dull yellow colour as the weed, but moved too quickly for me to get a close look. I tried to find some reference to this creature in the books I carried with me, but there was no mention of it. As all sea snakes are venomous I was rather careful how I picked weed out of the water after that; I did not want to take any unnecessary risks even with what appeared to be a small edition of something. But I collected about sixteen crabs and rather more shrimps and periwinkles and put them with some of the weed in a perspex box aquarium that I made. The crabs' favourite food appeared to be tinned sardines, so from then on these figured prominently on my menus. I also tried bully beef but their opinion of it seemed to coincide with my own. The fatality rate was high amongst my passengers, and every day I had to pick out and bury a few corpses. The most robust crab hung on until four days from Falmouth, by which time I think the water had become a bit too cold – or he had become allergic to sardines.

The Variable winds in the Horse Latitudes nearly drove me round the bend. It was hopeless trying to leave the tiller untended as *Suhaili* would yaw and gybe so I had to steer the whole time, discontentedly watching pieces of weed drifting slowly past. When I grew tired in the evenings I would leave the tiller lashed, but I generally had to get up three or four times during the night to gybe back onto course, or as on this occasion:

March 29th, 1969 *Day 289*

Awoke for the news at 0200 G.M.T. Ike is dead. Well, he has been ill for a long time now and has been fading recently, but I still have a slight feeling of personal loss. I can still remember the excitement when we went back into France in 1944 and although, of course, Monty was 'our man', he had to share the honours with Ike. It is never pleasant for a proud nation to have to admit it is no longer the biggest power and to place its armies under a foreign leader; few men could have handled the situation with such tact and understanding.

The only break in the monotony of the days was when we

crossed a shipping lane, as apart from the hope of sighting a ship and getting a report through, the lane was usually well marked with rubbish such as bottles, dunnage, and even hatchboards, that littered the sea. Some of this rubbish is a real threat to a small boat. A hatchboard may weigh as much as a person and they are bound at either end with heavy metal bonds. If a boat hits one of these when travelling at speed the hull could easily be stove in. Even more menacing farther north are the pitprops that litter the sea lanes. *Suhaili* might have survived a collision with one of these but she is much more strongly built than the ordinary boat. A fibre-glass or plywood hull would not stand a chance.

On 2 April, at 2 p.m., when about six-hundred miles south-west of the Azores, we sighted a Norwegian cargo vessel ahead and immediately hoisted *Suhaili*'s signal letters and *MIK*, the International Code for 'Please report me by radio to Lloyd's, London'. As the ship came closer I got out the rifle and fired three shots into the air. When it was a mile away and through binoculars I could see no one on the bridge, I fired two more rounds. We passed about 150 yards apart, close enough for me to read the name and home port, Tonsberg, but it was not until we were abreast the bridge that the OOW appeared to take a lookout. By the time he had found his binoculars he had moved past and he did not bother to turn and answer my signal lamp. You can take as many precautions as you like, have the brightest lights and the biggest radar reflector ever made, but if the OOW is not doing his job, you've had it.

Four days later, after drifting with still only occasional bursts of wind from the south-west, we crossed another shipping lane; a busy one as there were ships in sight all afternoon. I spent the whole time trying to signal them but all ignored me until the BP tanker *Mobil Acme* appeared. I quote the conversation from my signal logbook:

Sent: British *Suhaili*. Round the world non-stop.
Received: Please repeat name.
Sent: Suhaili. Please report me to Lloyd's.
Received: Will do. Good luck.
Sent: E.T.A. Falmouth two weeks.
Received: R[oger].

I was jubilant. At last after four months I had managed to get a report through. I started to imagine the effect at home and at the *Sunday Mirror* when the news got through. I knew that my family would not have given up hope for me; I had pictured my father shifting a pin on the chart in the hall and telling everyone quite categorically where I was within a couple of days. I did not know then that Bruce had already been out in the Azores helping to organise a close lookout for me by the American, Canadian and Spanish Air Force units there, and by the local fishing fleets; although on occasions I heard aircraft, I did not see any until I was nearly in British waters.

Later that night I switched on the radio for the BBC News, thinking that there might be a mention which would confirm that I had been reported, but there was no comment. I began to think that perhaps the *Mobil Acme* had not reported me after all, although of course it was quite on the cards that Moitessier had already arrived and there was little interest in those who followed him.

In fact, the *Mobil Acme* must have cabled London immediately, as within two-and-a-half hours of the sighting, Lloyd's had phoned my family and told them that I had been sighted off the Azores. This was highly efficient work on everyone's part and brought an end to the anxious waiting at home. What pleased me was that I later heard that the *Mobil Acme* had added to their message to Lloyd's, 'Standard of signalling excellent'. This helped reassure people that I had not gone barmy and was also, from a professional point of view, a pretty compliment. I can say the same for the officer on the bridge of the *Mobil Acme* at the time, but then of course we probably went to the same signal school down London's Commercial Road.

We were due west of the Azores with 1,200 miles to go to Falmouth when we met the *Mobil Acme*. If the prevailing westerly winds held we should have had no trouble reaching Falmouth in two weeks. But that very night the wind swung round to the north and there it stayed for the next forty-eight hours, keeping us down to 89 and then 79 miles in the day's runs. The excitement of meeting the *Mobil Acme* and the thought that I was so close to home had led me into the yachtsman's trap of calculating an ETA based on the last good run, but the unfavourable winds and apparent silence of the BBC combined to bring about a feeling of anti-climax.

April 7th, 1969 *Day 298*

Up at 0400 when the wind arose from the S.W. I took a reef to ease her and help her reach, and went back to bed for a couple of hours. Steered all day.

I saw land to the S.E. during the early part of the morning. It faded as soon as the sun got high. This will be Corvo and Flores – 'where Sir Richard Grenville lay!' My sights put us 30 or so miles off at noon and I steered a course to pass well to the north. I'll visit the scene of the battle some other time.

The glass is dropping and as the wind is now S.W., we can expect a cold front and northerly winds shortly. I am heading *Suhaili* well north at present in order to gain sea room, as if we get a bad blow I'll have to run like last time we passed here, and I want as much room between me and the islands for this as possible. We're reefed down at present and running with a bias to port. Going comfortably at about 4 knots. I would steer her but I cannot see any stars and I have a shocking headache; anyway she is doing very well by herself at present.

This headache developed and I was sick the next day, probably due to food poisoning; anyway I did not eat anything for a day and felt better for my fast.

This good burst of south-westerly winds gave us a nice push homeward, but on 11 April, after three days and 359 miles, they eased.

Great, it's 2200. We are completely becalmed and there are ships all around so I dare not sleep – not that I could with the booms banging as they are. I feel completely licked. I don't think, even in the Variables, I have felt so low the whole voyage. Just sitting here, unable to do anything. There is some malignant being watching over me which takes a delight in playing with my hopes and frustrating my wishes.

This was heartbreaking; so close to home, as far as I knew unreported and unable to make radio contact to report myself, and now the winds had deserted me. But the next day, Saturday, 12 April, another sighting broke my solitude at last. From then on I found myself thinking of myself as a sailor rather than a sea creature. The spell which when I had rounded the Horn had made me want to sail on was finally broken. The sea was not now my environment but an obstacle between me and home. I suddenly wanted to see my own people and my own country – and the sooner the better.

I was sitting quietly in the cockpit repairing some flags when a ship came up over the horizon astern. I rushed to hoist my signal letters and got out the Aldis, but although she came close enough for me to read her name, *Mungo* of Le Havre, she motored by before I could finish signalling a message.

April 12th, 1969 *Day 303*

I took down the flags and began to do a few repairs when about five minutes later I looked up and saw the ship returning. This was very unusual and rather encouraging and when he started signalling my hopes rose. I received: 'What do you want?', and sent that 'I am non-stop round the world reported missing.' They asked what name and when I told them they began to wave so I knew I was recognized. I was by this time signalling with the fog horn and I sent R.T. 2182. This was acknowledged and I switched on the radio. For an agonizing minute the transmitter refused to work, but then we were through.

Now the news. Moitessier is apparently going round for a second time. I am thought to be 'Le Premier' and was reported missing some time ago. I asked him to send a message to Cliff Pearson [of the *Sunday Mirror*] for me and he agreed and when I told him to send the account to Marconi's he laughed and told me there would be no charge for this sort of message. I think at one point he doubted if I really was not a hoaxer and he asked my name and when I told him I heard him say 'Yes, that's right'. We spoke in a mixture of English and French. I was pretty excited at the thought of getting a message home at last and my English was scarcely coherent, so I don't know how he understood my French.

He asked me if I wanted a position and I told him I was in approximately 44° 30′ N, 22° 00′ W. He said I was exactly 44° 25′ N, 21° 58′ W. Any seaman will agree that as I had not yet got my Meridian Altitude I was pretty close. It's reassuring.

We chatted for a bit. I said I would be glad to get home and he said he could understand that!

At 1630 another French ship appeared, a tanker, *Marriotte*. She came over and gave three blasts which I acknowledged, so it looks as if the news is out. I'm sitting up for the BBC news at present.

That night, with the bit now well between my teeth, I kept the Big Fellow set, and although the wind died away to a whisper I stayed up with him, steering, and we made 98 miles to noon on Sunday, 13 April.

That evening, I switched on the radio for the BBC's 6 p.m. News and when it was over spun the dial through the frequencies as usual. I picked up the GPO High Frequency station at Baldock and decided to give him a shout. This had been a pretty fruitless exercise for three months, but my luck had changed at last and to my delight my call was immediately acknowledged. This was wonderful and after we had chatted for a bit the operator asked if I wanted to speak to anyone by phone. I asked for my home number. Mike answered and I'm told that he nearly went through the roof. Father was out, so I then spoke to Mother and Diana. The Chief Engineer in charge at Baldock, Mr Johnston, has since very kindly presented me with a tape of the conversation. It sounds a pretty exciting moment, as indeed it was, but the best news was that all the family were well. It is often forgotten that the worrying is not only confined to those left at home. I had had no news of my family for five months and I had had plenty of time to think of them.

Mike confirmed that Moitessier in *Joshua* had sailed on round the Cape of Good Hope and into the Indian Ocean, and I was able to discard the unworthy thought that the *Mungo* might have been misleading me and that Moitessier was right on my heels. Certainly I had expected him to be close and the Indian Ocean was the last place where I imagined he would be; as we now know, Moitessier eventually sailed on into the Pacific, where after 307 days at sea, he dropped anchor in Tahiti. So of the nine who had set out, only three of us were left, all British, which I thought to be a Good Thing.

Nigel Tetley in his trimaran *Victress* was off the coast of Brazil and Donald Crowhurst in *Teignmouth Electron*, the other trimaran, was thought to have just rounded the Horn. Mike also told me that Mother and Father and Diana would be coming out from the Scilly Isles in *The Queen of the Isles*, and that Ken, Bruce and Bill would be coming out in Guy Crossley-Meates's ex-air-sea-rescue launch, *Fathomer*, from Falmouth, where they had already installed themselves in the Marine Hotel. I only hoped that Bob and Di had remembered the specific details of my postcard booking from Australia and were keeping the best room for me! The rest of the family was already moving in on Falmouth, so it looked as if we were going to have quite a party.

Just the same, when I had finished writing up my diary, I got out the whisky bottle. Barring last minute accidents, *Suhaili* was going to be the first boat ever to sail round the world non-stop and I went on deck and poured a dram over her stern. As an afterthought I sacrificed another dram as a libation to Shony, one of the old British Gods of the Sea, before I took a good long swig myself. In the circumstances I thought he would have approved, but for the next two days my diary contains only 'Steered all day' and 'Steered all day, but it's getting very calm'.

On the following day, Wednesday, 16 April, I got through to Cliff Pearson at the *Sunday Mirror* and told him that I just might arrive in Falmouth on Sunday, 20 April, but as I was almost becalmed even while I spoke to him, it was very difficult to be more definite. Cliff told me that the Supporters Club in *Fathomer* intended to make contact on the Friday or at dawn on Saturday. He asked me to give any future positions in the code Bruce and I had worked out before I sailed and which had been approved by the GPO. The *Sunday Mirror*, as one of the sponsors for my voyage, naturally wanted as much exclusive copy on my return as they could get and they thoroughly deserved it. But already, Cliff told me, other newspaper boats were in the Scillies watching *Fathomer*'s every move. From my vantage point it all sounded good fun, and I wished I was a hound rather than the hare. I arranged to make a contact with Bruce on the Saturday morning and signed off.

With all these carefully laid plans on the boil, the wind dropped completely, and at the same time my long suffering battery charger gave up the ghost, which put me in a spot as my batteries were no longer taking a full charge and would not last for long. Once again I started to take the charger to pieces, but with the Big Fellow, staysail, main and mizzen set in the light airs, *Suhaili* needed my constant attention, and in the event I never was able to fix it. On Friday the batteries were further drained when I received a message via Land's End Radio from B.I. and spoke to George Martin of the *Sunday Mirror* in London.

April 18th, 1969 *Day 309*

George told me to watch out for a Beechcraft G-ASDO, which might be out looking for me. He also said *Fathomer* was being 'tagged' – real cloak and dagger stuff this – most enjoyable!

I am a little worried about my position as I did not get good sights today and I met a whole crowd of trawlers just before noon. These would, I think, be on the 100 fathoms line which, according to my sights, we were 30 miles short of at noon. There are some humps so maybe that's where they are, but I'd like to get stars tonight if the sky clears. 280 miles to Falmouth at noon....

It's 1830 and a most remarkable thing has happened. I was sitting on the containers reading *Timon of Athens* when I heard a scuffling in the starboard bunk and there, in the medical box, was a small grey bird with a slender pointed beak. It was the size of a wren. I have let it out.

That evening we were getting up amongst shipping and I could see navigation lights all round us so I did not like to sleep; I kept watch from the cockpit, fortifying myself with coffee laced with whisky. Shortly after midnight a well-lit ship that had been overtaking, slowed down astern of us and appeared to be taking up station half a mile away. At the same time I noticed a smaller boat which I had assumed to be fishermen coming in fast and taking up station. After watching both rather anxiously for some time. I decided to challenge the larger with the Aldis lamp. Back came the reply: '*Queen of the Isles*'. They closed in with flash bulbs popping and I was able to speak directly to Mother and Father for the first time for 309 days. It was a wonderful moment, but conversation was difficult in the rising wind and sea, and all too soon I had to give up trying to make myself heard and concentrate on reducing sail. The smaller boat closed soon afterwards and identified herself as *Fathomer*. They then stood off for the night, and with two watchdogs on guard I felt it safe to turn in.

When I awoke the next morning there was nothing in sight. My watchdogs had lost me. Visibility was down to two miles and the wind was up to force 7. At 0815 I switched on the radio and made immediate contact with Bruce; he asked me 'Where the hell' I was and I had to reply that I did not really know. I could almost hear him groan at this but there was nothing we could do about it. The sun was hidden and I could not get a sight. By 1000 the wind had risen to force 8 from the south-east and rather than strain *Suhaili* this close to home, I handed all sail, streamed the warp and hove-to. I spent the next two hours standing in the hatchway keeping a lookout for boats and hoping for a glimpse of the sun, which eventually rewarded me just before noon. I took a sight and worked out our latitude and radioed it out to Bruce. By this time all the newspapers were working together trying to locate us and it did not matter if anyone else knew my position.

I was tired and depressed. There was nothing I could do until the wind changed or eased and I turned in. This was the limit; to come this far and then get a contrary gale just when I could almost smell home, was too much. I did not sleep for long though. At 2.30 p.m. I drifted awake to the sound of a siren. I leapt out of my bunk, imagining some vessel bearing down on us, but the sound came from the *Queen of the Isles*. I waved to my parents and then looked around at the sea. Whether it was because I had had a rest or because there was a ship close up I don't know, but the wind and sea seemed to have eased, and rather shamefacedly I went about setting some sail and getting in the warp. *Fathomer* appeared just as I got under way again, riding the sloping seas incredibly comfortably for such a small boat. As she closed I picked out Ken, Bruce and Bill waving wildly on her foredeck, Bill, as usual, covered in cameras.

Apparently the three of them had been discussing the best way to handle this meeting. From my radio messages they assumed that I was still perfectly sane but they were a little concerned that after all these months of solitude I might be under some tension at the prospect of getting amongst people again, for they had a better idea than I did of the plans that were being made to greet me in Falmouth. They agreed not to say anything to me until I had spoken and they had had a chance to gauge my reactions. For my part I was waiting for them to speak first. The boats closed to within fifteen yards as we grinned owlishly at each other, and Ken later swore that

I then ruined a Moment in History when I at last shouted to him, 'I see you're still wearing that same bloody silly hat!' He promptly took it off and flung it into the Atlantic.

Fathomer and *Queen of the Isles* kept station with me all Saturday night. Following the gale the wind stayed stubbornly in the south-east, and as we would be pushed north towards the Bristol Channel if we stayed on the starboard tack, I went about and stood south. It seemed that the wind and weather were determined to give the lie to any ETA I gave Cliff Pearson in Falmouth, but as before I sailed I had given 14 April as the date round about which I expected to be home and I was only six days out in my reckoning now, I did not think he would complain if a couple more went astray.

At 7.15 on Sunday morning I tacked round and headed north-east towards Land's End, 150 miles away. After a large plate of porridge I took a sight and shouted my position to Captain Evans of the *Queen of the Isles*, who had done the same thing: although in shouting distance we agreed that in practice we were two miles apart. In the afternoon *Fathomer* shot off for the Scillies to refuel and bring out fresh bread, newspapers and cigarettes for the *Queen*. I had not had a cigarette for over six weeks, and although I certainly felt the better for it and had not really missed them, to talk of them in such casual terms had a far more disturbing effect upon me than I could have imagined. As I drank my after-lunch coffee, I felt an addict's craving coming over me.

With the *Queen of the Isles* acting as my temporary Nanny, I was looking forward to a last good night's sleep before I closed the land. *Suhaili*, with reefs in the main and mizzen to reduce the pounding, was sailing comfortably to the force 5 south-easterly winds, and with the prospect of some light rain during the night I turned in. I was too excited to sleep, which was just as well, because when I went on deck at 10.30 p.m. with a cup of cocoa, the horizon ahead was dotted with the lights of a French fishing-fleet. From seeing too few ships I was now seeing far too many. Navigating through a fishing fleet at any time is a tricky business, but to do it at night can be positively nerve-racking, particularly for a small boat under sail. By the very nature of their work, fishing boats are constantly changing course, and as fast as you work out the course to steer to avoid one vessel, the last one you observed has completely changed its mind and is bearing down on you with every intention of maintaining its legal right of way. Multiply this process by thirty or forty boats and the sea suddenly becomes a very small and dangerous place.

I went about and headed south to try to sail round the fleet, but when a couple of hours later I made up towards Land's End again, they were still square-dancing in my path. At this rate I could have gone on dodging about all night without making any progress at all, so I said 'To hell with it', held my course, and four exhausting hours later found myself in clear water at last. The *Queen of the Isles* had uncomplainingly sat on my tail throughout all these manœuvres, and although she received greater respect from the fishermen because of her size, she was as relieved as I to be clear of them.

At 5 a.m. on Monday, 21 April, the wind went round to the south-west, and leaving *Suhaili* running under reefed main, heading at last for the Lizard, I turned in.

I was up again in three hours. *Suhaili* had followed the wind as it backed slightly, so I had to gybe again to be sure of clearing Bishop's Rock off the Scillies, and Land's End. I also wanted to keep well clear of the strong tidal stream that runs between the two. At 1135 I picked up Bishop's Rock lighthouse, bearing 100° True, my first sight of home for 312 days. I suppose that seeing the slim silhouette of the Bishop on the horizon should have been an emotional moment. Over the centuries it has been the last and first sight of Britain for generations of seamen, but my recollection is that I noted the sighting in the log simply as a navigational mark. My emotions, more prosaically, were concerned with a pint of beer, a steak, a hot bath and clean white sheets.

Fathomer rejoined at 2 p.m. and took over from the *Queen of the Isles*. As if this were a signal the party started. A couple of helicopters clattered overhead with cameramen hanging crazily out of the open doors, and craft of all shapes and sizes joined us, one of them a tiny red skiboat from St Mary's. He probably had an easier time looking for me than I would have done looking for him, because most of the time he was completely hidden from me by the waves. A Coastal Command Shackleton appeared on the scene and made half a dozen low-level runs over the little convoy, scattering the helicopters out of its path like startled chickens.

Ahead of me I could see the grey shape of a minesweeper closing rapidly over the horizon. This was something I had been waiting for. HMS *Warsash*, an RNR ship, commanded by Lieutenant-Commander T. A. Bell, had been deputed by Rear-Admiral B. C. G. Place, VC, DSC, RN, Admiral Commanding Reserves, to escort me in. This was a wonderful choice of ship in view of my RNR connections, and when I saw her I would not have changed her for a dozen aircraft-carriers. She swept round to my stern keeping properly to leeward, flying *QKF*, the International code for 'Welcome'.

Tom Bell came right in, handling his ship beautifully. There was a cheer from the deck and as I acknowledged it I saw standing amongst the crew my three brothers. We exchanged the usual family ruderies and then *Warsash*, who like her sisters is not designed for slow speed work, pulled off to one side and thereafter kept station ahead of me until I began the run into Falmouth.

That night I advanced the ship's clock for the last time to bring us into British Standard Time. I was pretty well exhausted. I had had little sleep for the past few days, and I knew that the next day, if it was to be my last at sea, would be very tiring. Already my voice was hoarse from three days of shouting messages to other ships, and if one discounts my singing it had probably had as much work in that time as in the previous 308 days.

I turned in at 1000 with Wolf Rock and Tater Du lights in sight, getting up at 3 a.m. on Tuesday morning to gybe round towards the Lizard, which was well in view. By dawn I had passed through the overfalls off the Lizard (to the annoyance of my watchdogs) and with a good westerly was heading up under full sail towards the Manacles buoy. Falmouth was then eight miles away and I could clearly identify Pendennis Point and St Anthony Head, which mark the entrance to the harbour.

The convoy was growing hourly. Off the Manacles we were met by the Falmouth lifeboat and the tug *St Mawes*, both dressed overall and looking as smart as paint. The lifeboatmen were in their full rig of seaboots, oilskins and distinctive red 'cap comforters'. I took an immediate fancy to their headgear and after I got into Falmouth, John Mitchell, the mate of

Fathomer, presented me with his: it has now become one of my prized pieces of sailing gear.

The *St Mawes* was originally the *Arusha*, a BI tug stationed on the East African coast, and for this day the Company had chartered her and put her into her old livery, her black funnel with its distinguishing two white bands gleaming in the early morning sunshine. She bustled in flying an enormous Company house flag and I hoisted my own, together with the burgees of the Ocean Cruising Club and Benfleet Yacht Club, and for good measure I hoisted *Suhaili*'s signal letters *MHYU* on the port yardarm.

On board the *Arusha* I could see Captain Lattin and Captain Ben Rogers, who had been my first captain at sea on the *Chindwara*, and many other familiar faces. The Company had been my home since I left school, I had learned my seamanship in it, and they had given me every possible encouragement in preparing for my voyage. To be greeted like this was wonderful.

I was six miles – less than two hours – off Pendennis Point when at 9 a.m. the wind swung suddenly to the north-north-west and rose sharply. I was forced away to the east, reducing sail progressively as I went and the wind rose to force 7 and 8. This was when I got really angry. *Suhaili*'s inability to sail close to the wind isn't an unduly worrying factor at sea, but for close work like this it was infuriating.

As I drove to the north-east away from Falmouth and towards Dodman Point, the helicopters and light aircraft which had been fluttering around disappeared. I imagine that with the prospect of a full day's tacking before them, they wisely decided to refuel and leave me with my seaborne escort of yachts and small craft, which stuck gamely and wetly to me for the rest of the day.

At least the wind was offshore and by creeping in towards the land I was able to keep to smoother water and a higher speed. I threw in another tack towards Porthmellon Head and out again to Dodman. It was cold and wet, but nothing was going to stop us now. *Suhaili* and I had been away for 313 days and covered over 30,000 miles together; heaving-to at this stage was unthinkable. Off Dodman we wore round and began to tack towards St Anthony Head. We raced across the harbour entrance until I was clear for the run in. I wore round for what I thought would be the last time, easing the sheets to give us a fast and comfortable finish. As we neared Black Rock, which lies between Pendennis Point and St Anthony Head, there seemed little for me to do except wave to the bustling fleet of small boats that was closing in round us. On Pendennis Point I could see the sunlight reflecting on the lines of parked cars, and on the front, people were waving to us. We were nearly there, and that pint of beer was almost in my hand when the Harbour Master's launch came bursting through the mêlée and I was told that *The Sunday Times* had established the 'finishing line' between Pendennis Point and Black Rock. At that moment another competitor nearly dropped out. I had left Falmouth between Black Rock and St Anthony Head and saw no reason why I should not take the same route coming in, and I said so in terms that were unfortunately picked up by the BBC TV microphones at the time. Nevertheless, showing more forbearance than I usually do, I wore round to make another tack to the west. Half an hour later, at 3.25 p.m. I crossed the finishing line and a cannon fired.

The first people to board were Her Majesty's Customs and Excise officers from Falmouth. As they jumped across the senior officer, trying to keep a straight face, asked the time-honoured question:

'Where from?'

'Falmouth,' I replied.

X

Clare Francis

Clare Francis is that pretty and courageous English girl who once bought a boat, *Gulliver G*, and sailed the Atlantic single-handed – for a bet! Her love of boats and highly developed sense of adventure has since led her to compete in several major sailing competitions – notably *The Observer* Trans-atlantic single-handed race in which, sailing her 38-foot yacht *Robertson's Golly*, she took only 29 days to reach Newport, on the coast of Nova Scotia, to become the women's record holder for the journey (and also the smallest person ever to sail the Atlantic alone!). Television viewers may recall seeing a remarkable amateur ciné film which Clare Francis made of that voyage – in that film, and in her engrossing book, *Come Hell or High Water*, England's premier lady yachtswoman emerges as a most likeable personality, with a delightful sense of humour. These are qualities she no doubt required in full, in her later adventure, skippering one of the British yachts racing in Whitbread's Round the World Race – although with other crew members to share the tensions the ordeal was not so great as a single-handed voyage. Just what trials and tribulations, and stresses, may be encountered on such a voyage is colourfully recounted in the following extract....

COME HELL OR HIGH WATER

Clare Francis

As I awoke I became aware that something was wrong. The boat was moving wildly, rolling from side to side then suddenly lurching over and staying there, shuddering with strain. With a groan I remembered the spinnaker. By the feel of the boat, it should have been down hours ago. Still dazed and heavy-eyed, I could not think how long I had been asleep, but it must have been well over an hour, probably nearer two. I pulled on my boots and oilskins and staggered up on deck, nervous of what I might find.

It could have been worse. The wind was force 5 and still from the east. The seas were not any larger than I would have expected, but they were sufficient to make the boat roll considerably and slew from side to side. It was impossible for the self-steering to anticipate these yaws until too late, and only when the boat was well off track could the wind vane sense it and pull her back. But the pull of the spinnaker was often too powerful and the *Golly* would continue to veer off until the spinnaker held her over on her side, lee rail under and main boom dragging in the water. These broaches were horrible to see. They put a lot of strain on the boat, particularly the mast and rigging, and I hurried to lower the spinnaker before she broached again.

Lowering a spinnaker in a strong breeze when alone at night is a frightening experience. One mistake and the spinnaker can tear and wrap itself round the forestay, making it impossible to raise a foresail again. The spinnaker boom, the guy and sheet are all under enormous strain and one slip can result in serious breakage. I wasn't going to take any chances and approached the task with caution. Better to be slow and sure than make a mistake.

The 'Salami' would not slide down over a full spinnaker, so I had to half-collapse the sail before attempting to pull the sausage down over it. Having eased the sheet, there was a terrible commotion of flapping canvas and rattling gear as I rushed forward to pull the sleeve down. I tugged on the line, but nothing happened. I pulled harder, but the mouth of the 'Salami' stayed obstinately where it was, at the top of the sail. Just then the *Golly* broached and I had to cling on as she dived round on her side. For a moment all was confusion, then she righted herself and thundered off into the night. I yanked on the line again, but I could make no impression on the 'Salami' at all. A fine time to jam itself! I tried collapsing the spinnaker further but after a terrifying broach I decided that, whatever the method, the important thing was to get the spinnaker down quickly.

The traditional method of lowering a spinnaker is most satisfactory if you have a crew of five or ten, but single-handed it requires five arms and, by my method, three feet. Having let one corner of the sail fly, you pull on the other corner, gather in the foot of the sail (quite impossible), then with your arms full of sail you let off the halyard (this was where the feet came in – I wrapped them round the sail in place of arms). The halyard must then be lowered slowly (this was where the third foot was needed – I put the halyard under my foot, let it run out a way, then stopped it by stamping hard. Except I sometimes missed, or found my leg in air with the halyard wrapped round my foot and pulling hard). As the sail comes down, all is meant to be gathered in tidily, and in no time the spinnaker should be lying at one's feet in a neat pile.

This time I dropped half the thing in the water, and twice nearly took off behind the ballooning sail. Still, it was down, and I breathed a sigh of relief. Half an hour later I had sorted out the mess of lines, booms, guys and sheets, and hoisted a jib boomed out to windward.

Sleep. I felt that was all and everything I had ever wanted, and I shot below to fall into a heavy and dreamless slumber.

I heard the pinger an hour later and dutifully crawled out of my bunk. The wind had increased, and the boat was running too fast again so that I lowered the jib and left her under mainsail only. This was lazy of me. I should have reefed the main and put up a smaller jib, but I couldn't face the effort and hurried back to my bunk instead.

At three in the morning (everything at sea happens at three

in the morning), I awoke with that familiar feeling that something was wrong again. I was thick with sleep and longing to snuggle into the depths of my sleeping bag, but I managed to pull myself up and take a look on deck. I was shocked to find it was blowing a gale and the boat was careering downhill, veering from side to side as the large waves caught her from behind. Then I did something extraordinary. I must have been half asleep with my brain even more addled than usual. Nothing else could explain the stupidity of my actions.

I decided I must reef the main immediately. Usually, even in the worst crises, I can astonish myself by taking a calm look at the situation and setting about everything in a careful way. But this time I rushed into action, without thought and without consideration of the consequences. I decided I must get the *Golly* up into the wind to reef the main, and straight away. Mustn't strain the self-steering, I thought; mustn't use it to bring her up ... it'll be too sudden for it.

This was completely backwards thinking. I knew very well that the self-steering was all right as long as it was in use, but that once it was disconnected it was free to swing too far and destroy itself. But somehow my brain had decided that the exact opposite was true and was determined to unlatch the gear.

Perhaps it was also fear from the terrible rushing downhill, that violent swerving from side to side that made me panic. It was unnerving to be rocketing into the darkness, more or less out of control. Anyway, whatever it was, tiredness or fear, I did it. I unlatched the gear and pushed the tiller hard over so that the *Golly* would shoot up into the wind and allow me to reef. As the boat turned, the self-steering was thrust sideways. Then, as she fell back again, the gear was pushed the other way. Instinctively I looked back at the gear and my heart froze. All four of the metal struts were bent out of recognition.

The full idiocy of what I had done dawned on me like a blow from a sledge hammer. It was such an obvious and basic mistake – and so irredeemable. I groaned and muttered 'Oh, you twit!' – which was quite kind under the circumstances – and drew a mental breath.

It was difficult to decide how serious my situation really was. One moment I would look at the twisted arms and despair, and the next I would feel a sudden hope that I could once again repair them. The implications of failure were unpleasant – a long trek up to Nova Scotia without self-steering – so I knew I must at least try to straighten those arms. I lowered the mainsail and had a close look at the gear. It would be impossibly difficult to mend the gear in position, so I decided I would have to bring the lower section of the gear inboard where I could dismantle it with greater ease. The only problem was the weight and size of the gear. Made of a heavy alloy, and over five feet in height, it weighed about ten stone to my seven.

Gathering the necessary tools around me, I started on the long and tedious task. I disconnected the various ropes and lines attached to the gear, leaving one line firmly secured to both the gear and the boat. Even allowing for my depleted brain power, I could see it wouldn't be a good idea to drop the gear over the side. Next I had to slide the main spindle out. The whole of the lower moving section of the gear swung on this main spindle, a stainless steel rod an inch thick. Once it was removed the section would be completely unsupported and would drop into the water, whereupon I would pull it up over the rail, hopefully. But I found the removal of the spindle was not just a matter of sliding it out. The gear had to be held up in position while I worked the spindle out, inch by inch. As before I was leaning over the stern rail, gripping with my feet, and often up to my elbows in water. But now I was trying to hold a weight in a precise position while tugging at a spindle as well.

Finally, after much effort, the spindle came away and I felt the lower section of the gear fall as I tried to take its weight. I held on grimly, resting a moment while I waited for a suitable wave that would help me swing the gear round and up over the rail. Without the buoyancy of the water I could never have swung the gear, let alone held it. At last I felt the stern rising and saw the surface rushing up as a large wave approached. I swung the gear round and heaved.

I didn't quite make it first time and, with a gasp, I had to let the gear fall into the water again. By this time my arms were very tired and I had to take a long rest before attempting the lift again. I hung there over the stern, holding firmly onto that precious metal, and waited for perhaps half a minute. A large wave came, I heaved, and got the gear half-way onto the rail. But the weight was still on the wrong side and I felt it slipping back. Summoning some strength I gave a last pull and managed to slide it over another inch. At last, by swinging my weight on it, the gear pivoted over onto my side of the rail. Then, after a final heave, it fell on top of me. I lay back on the wet deck, exhausted but very relieved.

I lay there for five minutes or so, enjoying the rest. I was not in any hurry to get on with the repairs. They would take a long time at whatever speed I tackled them, so I might as well take them slowly and thoughtfully – unlike my earlier actions. Every moment that the *Golly* lay there drifting, we were forfeiting marvellous mileage. Seven or eight knots was the *Golly*'s speed downwind in a good breeze. It was sad to lose such easy progress, but it was more important to get the gear repaired properly than to rush the job and bend the gear again.

Leaving the *Golly* drifting, I dismantled the bent struts and took them below for that favourite task of mine: weld-bending as I called it. After heating the struts I attempted to bend them. But either the blow lamp and the gas rings never got the struts hot enough or else the metal wasn't heatable anyway, because the heat never seemed to make much difference. So in the end it was always back to plain old bending. The main problem was finding some leverage against which to bend the metal. Most of the interior fittings were wood and too soft to form a good base for the vice, so that the boat echoed to the sound of splintering wood as I tried the vice on bulkheads, bunk ends and shelf edges. By the time I had got the worst bends out, the boat looked like matchwood.

It took me five hours of sweat and toil to straighten the struts and even then they looked like snakes. As before, I hung on them, swung on them, heaved, pushed and yanked. Sometimes I would even make the kinks worse by exerting the pressure in the wrong place but I only did that five times, then I learnt. Quick, I am.

I also discovered that I was brainless, for the tenth time that day. As I grunted and pulled and heaved I suddenly realised that I had wasted five whole hours in useless pursuit, trying to bend metal against wood. There had been the perfect leverage available all the time – I had been so intent on using the vice that I had forgotten it would be completely unnecessary if I levered the metal directly against the most solid and well-bedded metal you could find. The engine. It took me ten minutes to straighten all four struts against the engine, and the thought of five hours' wasted effort almost made me laugh or weep, I wasn't sure which. I knocked my head against a locker a couple of times, but didn't want any more splintered wood around, so I gave up self-reproach and crawled back on deck to reassemble the gear.

It was still blowing a gale from the east, very grey but mercifully warmer than before so that I could work without freezing hands, and after half an hour the gear was ready to put back over the side. But I decided to wait. I was worried about the main casting which had been cracked during the storm (was it months before?). The main casting supported the spindle at either end and would be under severe strain as I slid the spindle back into position. It would only need one wave to twist the lower section round and the casting would surely break.

I decided to wait until the gale abated. But rather than waste more of that marvellous following wind, I set a small jib and steered by hand for a while. But I was dog tired and it was all I could do to keep awake for more than a moment. Technicolour dreams leapt into my head at every opportunity and wild situations rushed through my imagination like a horrendous carnival.

Eventually I decided the wind had abated sufficiently to put the self-steering back on. This was a lot of nonsense. The waves were just as large as before but my judgement had gone and, in my eagerness to get the gear working again so that I could sleep, I was not as cautious as I should have been.

If the effort of taking the gear off was tiring, it was terrible to put it back. Once I had swung it over the rail I had to hold it in a precise position so that I could slide the spindle in through the holes in the casting and the lower section. The gear was turning and twisting with every movement of the boat and the waves and, with only one hand free to hold it, it was a terrible weight to manœuvre. With my other hand, I just managed to get the spindle in through one end of the main casting and part of the lower section when I felt something give. Then the whole of the lower section was swinging sideways, and with a sinking heart I saw why. The main casting had sheered. It hung in two sections, split across the middle and completely unable to do its job of supporting the spindle and the gear. With a last superhuman effort I hoisted the lower section inboard and sat down to rest.

Whichever way I looked at it, I could not go on without self-steering. And without a welding kit complete with masked welder I could see no way of repairing the gear. What an idiot I'd been! So impatient to get going that I'd broken the gear beyond repair. I flung reproaches and recriminations at myself, but it didn't do any good. I was still faced with the problem of what to do next. And it always came back to two alternatives; mend the gear or make for the nearest port.

I looked at the gear from every angle. I wondered how I might support it, but I could think of nothing that would be strong enough to hold the casting solid against the considerable strains it must withstand. There seemed to be no hope and yet I couldn't believe it. There must be a fiendishly clever way of fixing that gear, but my slender knowledge of metallurgy, carpentry, not to mention engineering, did not volunteer a single solution.

I was miserable, but there was nothing for it but to examine the chart and look for a suitable port. And, as I reminded myself, it could be a great deal worse. This might have happened in the middle of the empty stretch between Newfoundland and England and then I would have had a much greater problem. As it was, Newfoundland was 140 miles to the north, while Nova Scotia was over 200 miles to the north-west. Although it was further, I much preferred Nova Scotia because it was closer to my route. With a bit of luck I could get there in two or three days and, allowing a day for repairs, I would lose a total of only three to four days. The rules of the race permitted competitors to stop at any port they wished, so I could continue to race as before.

It was difficult to know which port to make for, though. I had a large chart of Nova Scotia, but there appeared to be no major harbours on the coast until Halifax, which was miles away. The nearest small harbour was Canso, on the eastern tip of the land. It had a radio beacon to guide me in, and a radio station from which I had received weather forecasts. If it was large enough to have a radio station it should be large enough for me, or that's what I thought anyway.

My first instinct was to call England and let them know what had happened. My parents were in the States and Jacques had gone to see his family in Paris, so I tried Jack Hill. But, for all the times I had got through, this was the one occasion when it was impossible. Greeks were exchanging news on everyone in the village, Italians were talking to each one of their fifteen children, and a chap from Liverpool wanted to know why his wife hadn't been in when he phoned last Saturday night (she'd been at her Mum's, she said).

It was frustrating to sit there by the radio, longing to talk to someone, but utterly helpless to get through. I decided to try Canso instead, and was greatly cheered when they answered straightaway. After explaining my problems, I asked for information on Canso Harbour and its suitability for me; whether it was easy to enter, whether it had welding facilities, and so on. The radio operator asked me to wait while he found out. (Didn't he know about the size of the harbour, at least?) He came back and asked me how much my vessel drew. I replied, six feet. Ohhh, he replied, he didn't know about that. (If it didn't have six feet of water, then what did it have? Rocks?) I kept asking for details; was it well buoyed, was there a pilot, did his vessel have radar to find me in the fog? Considering the radio station was also a coastguard station, they were horribly vague. Evidently there was a pilot, but that was about all they could tell me.

I felt more miserable than before. Here I was faced with three days at the tiller, little sleep and at the end of it a harbour that might not turn out to be a harbour at all. And it was bound to be shrouded in fog, whatever it was. Nevertheless I decided to make for Canso and try to get more information as I approached. I calculated my course as 300° and climbed wearily up into the cockpit to start the long and tedious task of hand-steering for over 200 miles.

Tiredness can be a pleasant feeling when sleep is imminent, but I was now exhausted and, if I wanted to reach land in a few days, I would have to cut my sleep down to the very minimum. I had been very tired the day before but now, after a night and morning of heaving the self-steering about, I was in a zombie-like daze. I found myself staring at the compass but not reading it. Then I would fall asleep for seconds at a time, my head on my chest until the boat would slew off course and the motion woke me. The gale had abated, but as there were still big seas running I had to steer carefully. Twice I fell asleep at the wrong moment and awoke to find myself up to my waist in water as a wave swept into the cockpit. The water soon drained away but I was left wet and cold, although I hardly noticed it.

I steered on and on for hours in a nightmare of half-sleep and grim, grey reality. Most of the time I hardly knew what I was doing, yet I was aware of one thing. I must press on; I must get to Newport somehow, or else my family would be gone. That thought drove me on with grim determination through those endless hours.

At last, by the late evening, the sea had dropped to manageable proportions. There was no danger of being pooped again. And, with a bit of luck, there was hope of persuading the *Golly* to steer herself by careful balancing and trimming of the sails. I experimented with different sail areas and finally settled on a reefed main and working jib. Although this left the *Golly* very much underpowered, she did stay more or less on course for up to ten minutes at a time. This gave me a chance to do other things. First I looked at the chart and tried to estimate our position. At the same time I checked the course, 300°. Then I groaned and buried my head in my hands. Just to compound my series of mistakes, I had been steering 330° for the last seven hours, not 300°. In my exhausted state this was almost too much to bear and, after all that I had been through, after the hours of effort and toil, it was the straw that broke my back. I sat down and wept great floods of tears.

After a while I sat back and reached for the bottle of whisky. I don't drink at sea but this didn't count because it was strictly medicinal. After a couple of drams I began to feel better. After three life was just about picking up. And the fourth had me thinking about parties and human company and it being Saturday evening. I wanted to talk to someone more than ever and, knowing that Jacques was away, I tried to call Jack Hill again. This time I got through straightaway. It was midnight in England and Jack had been asleep, though I would never have known it from his cheerful response. But he was very upset at my news, particularly when I told him the gear was unrepairable. He offered to go and fetch Jacques from on board *Gulliver G* to cheer me up, but I pointed out that he wouldn't be there. In fact he was; he had never gone to Paris!

I had good reason to be very grateful to Jack Hill that night. Not only did he insist that I speak to Jacques straightaway but he sprinted across Lymington, picked Jacques up from the boat and had him by the phone in half an hour. Although Jacques was a wizard with mechanical things, I knew he wouldn't be able to sort this one out. Yet he was adamant. 'You can't get to Nova Scotia without some self-steering,' he repeated several times. 'Somehow you *must* find a way of repairing the gear so that you can sleep!' His insistence gave me new determination and, after arranging to call back twelve hours later, I took another, more hopeful, look at the broken gear.

The casting had a jagged break in it and when the two pieces were pressed together, they fitted like a jigsaw. That little ray of hope became brighter; if I could lash the two pieces together firmly enough, the jaggedness would hold the casting in place, preventing sideways movement. But I would have to get the lashing really tight and I could never do that by pulling alone. I considered a kind of tourniquet, but settled on double lashings, one around the casting and another to pull on the first one at right angles, like a bowman pulling on the string of his bow.

I placed lashings at every conceivable angle and tightened them time and time again until the casting was held in a vice-like grip. By this time I was certain it would work – and what a simple solution it had been. If I had thought of it when the casting had only been cracked, it would never have broken. Thanks to Jacques' marvellous encouragement, however, I had the solution before I had lost any more time.

All I had to do now was lift the lower section of the gear into place. It should have been easier in the calmer seas, but I soon found it wasn't. Without the buoyancy of the large waves the gear felt like a ton weight as I lifted it over the side. With the spindle between my teeth, I manœuvred it into position and, holding it there with one hand, grabbed the spindle with the other and tried to slide it in. Twice I had to stop and rest, letting the gear fall into the water until I had the strength to lift it again. But at last I felt the spindle slide in through one hole, another, and finally all four. Another rest, and I was ready to connect the various lines and pulleys.

Not only was the gear back together again, but it worked. And, though I watched the casting like a hawk, it never moved an inch. I felt as though a massive weight had been lifted from my mind. What a marvellous turnabout in my luck! I was on my way under self-steering again, and able to sleep. Leaving the *Golly* on course for Nova Scotia, I fell into my bunk and slept a dreamless sleep.

The next day I awoke a new person, still tired but no longer exhausted. My body felt as if it had been through three rounds with an all-in wrestler, and an angry one at that. I was very stiff and ached all over, so that every movement brought a twang from complaining muscles. Nevertheless, I felt marvellous.

I looked at the self-steering as I had done at intervals through the night. The struts were straight – if you ignored the slight kinks – and the casting was meshed firmly together. A sight for sore eyes. But there was one small thing bothering me. I was still heading for Canso. This was the sensible thing to do, for the gear must be permanently repaired if it was to survive another gale. And yet I longed to turn for Newport. I worked out that a stop in Canso would put my arrival back to the 7th or 8th of July at the very best. I didn't care about the race – I had already lost well over two days and was sure that I must be miles behind everyone else – but I did care about seeing Jacques and my parents for more than just a couple of days.

There was no more doubt in my mind. I turned the *Golly* round and headed for Newport.

After that my spirits soared. I called the two J's in Lymington and they were absolutely delighted to hear that I was heading for Newport. But, in his usual thoughtful way, the wonderful Jack Hill had found charts of Canso and every other harbour along the coast in case I should need information about them. Jack was a marvellous ally. Out of curiosity I asked Jacques what Canso looked like on the large chart. 'Er... interesting,' he said.

'That bad, eh?'

'Er... yes.'

Which meant it must be surrounded by rocks, full of shoals

and exposed to the seas. I was rather glad I wasn't going there.

The next twenty-four hours were blissful. I slept nearly all the time, just pausing to put food in my mouth, check the sails and eye the self-steering. I even found out where I was. My position was disappointing, of course. After struggling to make all that southing, I had rushed north and was just where I had planned not to be. I would now pass to the north of Sable Island where there was more likelihood of being becalmed, and certainly more chance of meeting fishing boats. But it would not be worth working round to the south of the island again, so I pressed on, hoping to gain some southing later.

Sable Island is a graveyard of ships. Long, low and, like everything else in the area, often hidden in fog, it forms a natural trap. I soon picked up its radio beacon, however, and by taking numerous bearings on it, I was confident I was well clear of it. Now all I had to worry about were boats and the self-steering.

After a day of sunshine and breezes, the mist came down and the wind dropped. On went my little black box to listen for fishing boats and up went more sail. As I was still being very careful about straining the self-steering, I was determined not to put up too much canvas, go too fast and ruin the gear yet again. Caution and care were the most important considerations, not speed. With a light easterly wind I would have hoisted a spinnaker under normal circumstances, but it would not be wise now. Anyway I was looking forward to another long, marvellous sleep and a spinnaker would be too much like hard work.

Then I saw it. A yacht clearly visible through the fog. It *had* to be one of us, but who? I got out the binoculars and peered. The boat seemed to be smaller than the *Golly*, white-hulled and, I was somewhat peeved to notice, carrying a spinnaker! I thought I recognised the boat and yet I couldn't quite place her. Nor could I identify her number at first; it was just too far away to see. I kept on peering through the glasses, and finally managed to pick out a number, then another, and hurried below to look her up. It was that new racing stripe down the side that had fooled me. It hadn't been there during the Round Britain Race. But there was no doubt it was Gustaf, the cuddly Belgian, in the *Golly*'s smaller sister, *Tyfoon*. I switched on the VHF, gave him a call and we were soon chattering away like squirrels.

'We haf bottle of champagne in Newport, yes?' said Gustaf.

'Absolutely,' I replied.

'Vot about two?'

'Even better.'

'Last von to arrive gifs first bottle, yes?'

'You drive a hard bargain, Gustaf, but you're on.'

There was not a moment to lose, and, scuttling around like an ant, I had the spinnaker hoisted and pulling within minutes. If the self-steering fell apart it was just too bad. Never mind all this careful and safe progress at the expense of speed. It was Newport or bust!

XI

John Riding

John Riding tried to enter his 12-foot-long egg-shaped boat, *Sjo-Äg*, in the single-handed Atlantic race, but was refused on the grounds that his craft was too small. Undeterred, and perhaps rather cheekily, he set off for America on his own – a voyage described with great good humour in *The Voyage of the Sea Egg*. Despite the enormous difficulties that the boat's design presented to a single-handed sailor some 6 feet 4 inches in height John Riding continued to sail *Sjo-Äg* from Bermuda and along the Western seaboard of the USA. Passing through the Sargasso Sea to Puerto Rico, Panama, Costa Rica and Mexico his 18-month voyage involved him in many alarming incidents, all of which he survived with great courage. In the introduction to *The Sea Egg Again: From Atlantic to Pacific*, in which he describes this latest voyage, John Riding explains, for the benefit of his armchair readers, what he actually is attempting. 'My sailing this vessel has to be more, much more than one man and his bloody boat. It should not appear to be of an individual luckily opting out of the responsibilities inherent in our society . . . for this is not so. It should in part be an expression of the freedom every man wishes to exult in or embrace as his own, perhaps a cry of hope in an increasingly depressing environment.' And he concludes, 'I *am* sailing this vessel for mine own satisfaction, a satisfaction and purpose that may one day become apparent'. In this extract, almost casually, Riding relives some of his most dramatic moments. . . .

THE VIEW FROM SEAWARD WAS UNSETTLING

John Riding

'*13th September:* 92nd day. I was by now pretty weak and gave myself another week of reasonable physical ability.

'*0200:* Ken Ackerman's Music till dawn is sustaining me; good reception.

'*0300:* still flat calm. Think that boil is going to get worse before better. Light still to NE, bow pointing east.

'*0600:* Light breeze. Temperature 64°. Freed weed. Course W magnetic.

'*1145:* So cold I have door shut in flat calm.

'*1200:* Small boat engine out to the west. A pair of oars would be useful here, something else I intended to do in Acapulco. Face looks definitely thinner this a.m. Arm excruciating; put alcohol on and have taken a tetracycline. Oh for coffee and cigarettes. Let's see, 17+62+13 makes 92 days... wouldn't be surprised if parents call out the fire-brigade on the 95th even if against my express wishes. This calm is sheer unadulterated cruelty.

'*1415:* Finally nerved myself to continue letter home (have avoided it since 6th), and will. Tacked to NE in light air.

'*1500:* Land in sight to the NE.

'*1539:* Ex-meridian puts me under Colnett when I expected to be much, much higher... if not Punta Banda, then close. I hope I'm wrong. Tried paddling a little but am too weak. Can't have lost that much ground. Let's face it, a sight on time would have still given me this Colnett. Oh, what cruel fate... was writing home too. Can't see how I've drifted that much. After writing home I'm very near breaking point with this. Land is very flat though....

'*1800:* I am closing with the beach. There are some signs of habitation, but pretty bleak. Breakers... but some bare patches....

'I've got to get word home. I've got to eat and smoke, and if Colnett arrange tow to Ensenada; I'd have said this was more like Sto Thomás, San Jose....

'There are people... vacationers with trucks, etc. Maybe a hippie group.

'Don't know whether I'll make it in by nightfall. Coastline goes North. Hope it's beach 'twixt Jose and Thomás.

'Hell, breakers all over in front of beaches and heavy cloud from SW following me in! Will get anchor ready ... had tiny shot [of] brandy....

'*1930:* This is crazy!'

The view from seaward through binoculars was an unsettling one. The huge green backs of curling surf intermittently blotted out the two people walking along the beach. I angled out in the failing breeze at the first sign of being caught by the sucking power of the initial swells destined to spend their enormous energy in furious explosions of surf. The noise was terrific. A dune-buggy careered along the beach as I gesticulated for the two passengers to stop. I saw the woman on the beach break away and race to intercept it, she being very quick to comprehend my wild wavings. I had a fast decision to make... to risk my boat and everything it meant to me and stood for; to see the very definite possibility of it being smashed, torn and split asunder in this spuming cauldron of Mexican coastline surf... or to head out to sea for another long, foodless, heart-breaking crawl up the coast with the necessary further delay and my family's ignorance of my lot. I was weak and would grow weaker, lose essential efficiency and heighten the risk. Here the problem, or dilemma, was resolved into a yes or no, now or never decision. I went into the cabin and took off my watch, got out my bayonet knife and put shorts on... sweater off. One way or the other I knew I'd end up in the sea with clothing a soggy hindrance. I then jerked a shell into the chamber of the Savage and after a quick look around saw the buggy climb a hill ... indecision (for I was hoping the buggy would be the ideal vehicle to pull *Äg* in as far as possible and stop the keels jouncing on the beach), then it came down again and parked next to the two people. Two or three guys jumped down from the vehicle with surf boards and I saw one enter the water. Good... I fired the shot, the typically flat sharp crack stunning the turbulent seas into a momentary pause in their thunder, a hiccup in the middle of their puking. I threw the rifle inside, grabbed my logbook and made the 1930 entry. Knocked back the last tiny shot of booze saved for 'landfall' and put the logbook in the stern locker for easy access in case of a break-up. Closed the hatch and door and pointed the bow in....

'It was Friday the 13th, an ominous day in any sailor's log, and we were walking on the beach when I and my wife caught sight of a tiny object on the horizon. Slowly, but methodically, it came closer and closer to the beach. Becoming concerned we peered through the binoculars to discover it was a small boat with a man wildly waving his arms. He had very long hair and a full beard and was on the bow. Suddenly he went below deck, returned with a gun, and fired it in the air ... obviously for assistance. The boat continued to approach and when it was approximately two to three hundred yards away my fifteen-year-old son Frank began paddling out to the craft being tossed violently in the swells. Getting to the boat was a bigger task than he expected because the surf was extremely rough, and rip-tides and undertows were a constant danger....'

I was over the first two or three big swells and angling over to this guy on the surfboard, who was by now close by. There was a lull and I shouted to him, asking rather belatedly what he thought my chances were, and whether it was sand all the way. To the latter all was well... to the former he shouted that my chances were very poor, virtually impossible. 'Are you with me if I try?'... 'Sure!' says this young fellow. It was too late to turn back now in any case. The first breaking swell swung at me as I presented a square stern to it. A terrific wall of water rushed at the boat, hitting Frank first; for the surfboard it was insurmountable and the surfboard spun out of the top of the wave minus its owner. Now I had two things on my mind and yelled for him to make for the boat. This was after the vertical wall hit my stern, most of it sweeping over the boat (and me, jammed tight in the cockpit with only my head showing) with stunning force. Smothered, *Äg* thundered before – and as a part of – this onslaught, half out of control. I then threw over an already prepared 75 lb piece of lead attached to about 150 feet of one-inch diameter synthetic line, keeping about fifty feet inboard. The idea was to keep my stern to the seas and if possible, time the passage of unbroken swell under me... for the breakers were worse some way ahead before quieting down nearer the beach.

I successfully negotiated the next two swells before they

broke in this manner, but the following one was not to be cheated. Both from ashore and my own observation it was approximately ten or more feet to the crest looming over my stern. Knowing it would break before I could slide up its face I let out all the line and gripped the tiller. I can only try to describe what it was like. . . .

What remaining light there was to the day was blotted out completely – I could see the top of the wave above my head and at the same time sense the tautening of my drag-line behind. There was a momentary silence as the sea enveloped me in a greenish bubble extending almost half-way up the mast and sail. This sea struck the sail first before the explosion of the collapse of the wave; a stupendous punch in my back, a roar, then water over my head . . . solid water that taxed to the limit my last huge lungful of air. Through the contact of my straining fingers and back, and my feet jammed against the door, I could feel her tremendous racking struggle to survive in this wild express-train surge *through* the water, on-on-on until I felt with bursting lungs that I ought to allow the clutching ocean to pluck me from the cockpit. Like a periscope my head was suddenly thrust above the water in time to witness and hear the furious seething back of the boiling wavetop rushing backward . . . there was a curious patch close to my bow – did I come through *that*? Already the ocean had drawn another sucking breath to heave itself aloft as the line slackened (but not enough for me to free it). The steep forward slope of this eight-foot curler spun the boat on a now taut line, pivoting it about the port quarter cleat so that in that position 'another huge wave that sprang up without warning smacked the side of the vessel and flipped it on its side, sending the mast crashing to the water. The boat disappeared. Then sure enough, up it popped and promptly righted itself . . . Frank's friends, Jim Isler and Jack Grey, then started paddling out to the boat again.

The unexpected thing was that the mast and boat had flipped to seaward, but if one thinks about it, that was understandable. Because of this contrariness the wave thumped me tighter into the cockpit instead of exerting a sucking influence in passing. The line had got to go; the thirteen-inch blade flashed and it was gone in time for a six-foot wave already poised for a strike. Tiller gone, I went over the side and grabbed the stern to keep it into the wave – flattening myself as tightly as possible against the stern with one arm about the rudder as protection against being splattered. The feeling was indescribable in the smash, all I recall is wedging my chest in the angle between the stern and the rudder so that I wouldn't have the air punched out, and the surge had me wildly grasping for a more certain hold on the stern.

I was through the worst but now my concern, and another reason why I was still hanging onto the stern, was that the keels weren't punched through the bottom of the hull in the troughs before final grounding. Frank was not too far away and I yelled that my feet had touched bottom (at arm's length with head underwater). In the 'draw' before the next four-foot wave *Äg* lightly tapped both keels on the bottom with me streamed out behind. Then she swerved with a gust of wind in the mainsail and touched her starb'd keel gently on the beach. I was at right-angles to the boat with my feet pointing out to sea, so when the breaker struck her side it was too much for me and we parted company. Spluttering, I surfaced to see that brave little boat unconcernedly sailing away parallel to the beach in the direction of San Diego! Swearing mightily I started to swim as fast as I could after the truant, yelling at the top of my lungs for Frank (who was out to seaward but nearer) to make for the boat and grab a line. I knew we'd get her eventually so my main concern now was sharks in the surf! My treasured knife was slipping down my waistband because with the exertion of swimming I couldn't keep my belly tight, so it was not an amusing picture to me seeing myself after 92 days at sea swimming along after my boat with this huge knife clutched in my teeth; my nose wasn't getting enough air into my lungs either, so I was gulping water with my mouth in an effort to breathe. Giving up on that idea I stuck it back in my trousers and nearly castrated myself when the sheath slipped. Frank just beat me to the boat and together we hung on and guided her in while I clarified for him what the hell I was doing out there in the first place. His friends were there and we got *Äg* into the shallows in, hell forbid, a rising tide. Other people were streaming into the water fully clothed and a line was passed to them, everyone hauling mightily to get her keels grounded firmly ... she touched once, then twice and no more in the gentlest of groundings on what I learned was Playa San Antonio del Mar. Espying a man in khakis with a breast pocket bulging with cigarettes I lunged towards him (he said later that he wasn't so sure whether I was going to attack him or not. I presented a wild appearance staggering out of the sea half alive). 'Have you a cigarette,' I asked, already reaching for them. 'Here,' says he, grabbing them out and holding them at arm's length, 'have 'em all, have 'em all.'

The same gentleman, at whose encampment I stayed for several days, sent me up a steep bluff for a shot of brandy. I stumbled in on his poor wife, and after apologising for what I'd come for she filled a half-pint beer glass with this beautiful amber liquid. I downed it in such speedy fashion that I'm surprised I didn't drop dead. Fortified, I descended the dusty hill to discover that a man named Mike Groza had arrived with a heavy-duty truck, ropes, tackles and an army of Mexican friends, chief among whom was a Chinese Mexican called Toni. Immediately they had things organised. A post-hole was dug after futile attempts to pull *Äg* much further up the beach, and a tight line taken and made fast from the bow of *Äg* to its base. All was well for the night when the tide started to gradually fall. The Whipples and others came to the campfire that night loaded down with fish caught fresh from the surf. Grilled over the fire and eaten with our hands it was a symbolic statement of where I'd been and where I was. We talked on into the early hours of the next morning until the finally unreplenished fire had no more heat to give. . . .

XII
Dougal Robertson

Dougal Robertson sold up all his possessions and bought the 50-year-old, 19-ton, 43-foot-long schooner, *Lucette*, in which with his wife and three children he planned to circumnavigate the world. They had crossed the Atlantic and were into the Pacific and had left the Marquesas Islands, sailing along quite happily, when 'sledgehammer blows of incredible force struck the hull beneath my feet hurling me against the bunk, the noise of the impact almost deafening my ears to the roar of inrushing water'. A killer whale had holed *Lucette*, which sank in minutes. During that brief time Robertson and his family managed to launch a small dinghy and an inflatable raft, and to grab a few essential items of equipment, notably a knife, before jumping aboard their last chance of survival. For the next 38 days the Robertsons, and a young student friend who was accompanying them, managed to survive all the sea's hazards cramped together under appalling conditions. They fed themselves on turtle meat and drank turtle blood, they caught other fish by ingeniously devised means – and water they gathered, whenever it rained, in canvas bags. Throughout all this period the family spirits kept up miraculously. All this (and much more too) Dougal Robertson managed to convey most vividly in what has rightly become a classic among sea rescue stories, *Survive the Savage Sea*. In this, our last episode in this anthology about survival at sea, we are fortunate to be able to print a moving personal account of just what it can mean, after facing death and disaster and terrible discomforts, at last to be RESCUED!

RESCUED!

Dougal Robertson

Noon position 8°21′ North and 85 miles west of Espinosa, twelve miles nearer land, was not a great boost to our morale but I pointed out that throughout all the time we had been adrift we had either been becalmed or the wind had been favourable. There hadn't been a day yet when I had had to record an adverse run. The calming seas also indicated that we might soon be able to row although the heavy cross swell would have to diminish a little too before that would be possible.

Lyn bathed the twins that afternoon and after their daily exercises and a half-hour apiece on the centre thwart to move around a bit, they retreated under the canopy again as a heavy shower threatened. The dorado, caught in the morning, now hung in wet strips from the forestay while the drying turtle meat festooned the stays and cross lines which had been rigged to carry the extra load of meat from two turtles. We worked a little on the thole pins binding canvas on them to save wear on the rope, then realising that we were neglecting the most important job of making a flotation piece, took the unused piece of sleeve and started to bind one end with fishing line. The clouds grew thicker as the afternoon advanced; it was going to be a wet night again and perhaps we would be able to fill the water sleeve. Seven gallons of water seemed like wealth beyond measure in our altered sense of values.

I chopped up some dried turtle meat for tea, and Lyn put it with a little wet fish to soak in meat juice. She spread the dry sheets for the twins under the canopy, then prepared their little supper as we started to talk of Dougal's Kitchen and if it should have a wine licence. As we pondered the delights of Gaelic coffee, my eye, looking past the sail, caught sight of something that wasn't sea. I stopped talking and stared; the others all looked at me. 'A ship,' I said. 'There's a ship and it's coming towards us!' I could hardly believe it but it seemed solid enough. 'Keep still now!' In the sudden surge of excitement, everyone wanted to see. 'Trim her! We mustn't capsize now!' All sank back to their places.

I felt my voice tremble as I told them that I was going to stand on the thwart and hold a flare above the sail. They trimmed the dinghy as I stood on the thwart. 'Right, hand me a flare, and remember what happened with the last ship we saw!' They suddenly fell silent in memory of that terrible despondency when our signals had been unnoticed. 'Oh God!' prayed Lyn, 'please let them see us.' I could see the ship quite clearly now, a Japanese tunny fisher. Her grey and white paint stood out clearly against the dark cross swell. 'Like a great white bird,' Lyn said to the twins, and she would pass within about a mile of us at her nearest approach. I relayed the information as they listened excitedly, the tension of not knowing, of imminent rescue, building like a tangible, touchable, unbearable unreality around me. My eye caught the outlines of two large sharks, a hundred yards to starboard. 'Watch the trim,' I warned. 'We have two man-eating sharks waiting if we capsize!' Then, 'I'm going to light the flare now, have the torch ready in case it doesn't work.'

I ripped the caps off, pulled out the striker and struck the primer. The flare smoked then sparked into life, the red glare illuminating *Ednamair* and the sea around us in the twilight. I could feel my index finger roasting under the heat of the flare and waved it to and fro to escape the searing heat radiating outwards in the calm air, then unable to bear the heat any longer, I dropped my arm, nearly scorching Lyn's face, and threw the flare high in the air. It curved in a brilliant arc and dropped into the sea. 'Hand me another, I think she's altered course!' My voice was hoarse with pain and excitement and I felt sick with apprehension that it might only be the ship cork-screwing in the swell, for she had made no signal that she had seen us. The second flare didn't work. I cursed it in frustrated anguish as the priming substance chipped off instead of lighting. 'The torch!' I shouted, but it wasn't needed, she had seen us, and was coming towards us.

I flopped down on the thwart. 'Our ordeal is over,' I said quietly. Lyn and the twins were crying with happiness; Douglas, with tears of joy in his eyes, hugged his mother.

Robin laughed and cried at the same time, slapped me on the back and shouted 'Wonderful! We've done it. Oh! Wonderful!' I put my arms about Lyn feeling the tears stinging my own eyes: 'We'll get these boys to land after all.' As we shared our happiness and watched the fishing boat close with us, death could have taken me quite easily just then, for I knew that I would never experience another such pinnacle of contentment.

The high flared bows of *Tokamaru I* towered over us as she closed in, pitching and rolling in the uneasy swell. We emptied turtle oil on the sea to try to smooth it as the dinghy rocked violently in the cross chop of waves deflected from the steel wall of the ship's side; then, as they drew near enough, the Japanese seamen lining the bulwarks threw heaving lines, snaking through the air to land in the water beside us. The rise and fall of the dinghy was too great to make the line fast so I held it as we were pulled alongside the bulwark door. Willing hands reached down and we were hauled bodily through the bulwark door, Neil first, then Sandy. 'Come on Douglas, you next,' I said, as Douglas hesitated, waiting for his mother to go first, but to do so would have resulted in too much weight on one side and the sharks were still waiting. *Ednamair* bumped heavily as the swell flung her against the side of the ship; with aching arms I wound the line round my wrist and 'Right Lyn, on you go,' Lyn's legs kicked as she was hoisted aboard, 'Come on Robin, lad.' I looked at the empty *Ednamair* with sudden desolation in my heart, we must have her too! I threw the polythene bag containing the dried turtle and my log book, and one or two of the little trinkets from the sewing basket, on to the deck of the fishing vessel, then passed the line round the mast and brought the end with me as I was lifted to the deck.

Lyn, Douglas, Robin and the twins lay in a line along the deck and I wondered what was wrong with them, until I tried to walk and my legs wouldn't work. I clutched at the bulwark for support, then, to my dismay, saw the Japanese sailor cast off the *Ednamair* – they were going to leave her. I gestured wildly, for no one spoke our language, that we must have the boat as well but they shook their heads and held their noses. (I couldn't smell the fish and turtle drying on the rigging but to them it must have been overpowering!) I leaned out trying to catch the rigging and something in my appeal must have reached them, for at a word of command from the bridge, they brought boat hooks and lifted *Ednamair*'s stern up to the deck. I grasped at the handles to help them but they motioned me away, then they cut all the lashings to the mast, canopy, oars and sea anchor, tipped *Ednamair* upside down and emptied everything into the sea; with a heave *Ednamair* was brought on deck. The sucker fish which we had thrown over from the turtles were still clinging to the fibreglass bottom and were knocked off as the hosepipe and brushes got to work in the capable hands of the Japanese seamen. We smiled and said 'Thank you'. They smiled back and nodded, unable to communicate their understanding.

My blistered finger smarted painfully from the burn of the flare as I staggered to the companionway leading to the bridge. Pulling myself up with my arms I greeted the Captain of the *Tokamaru* at the top and thanked him warmly in sign language for the efficiency of his crew in spotting us. We could only gesture for I had no Japanese and he no English, but gestures were adequate. I produced my log book and we went into the chartroom to check positions and to give details of who we were and where we had come from, for as far as I knew we had not yet been reported missing!

My estimated latitude at 8°20′ North was good, only five miles wrong, but my estimated longitude, though a hundred miles wrong, was better, for we were a hundred miles nearer land than I had estimated and would have reached it five days sooner than I had said! We were rescued in position 8°15′ North, 90°55′ West. My estimate of 8°20′ North, 92°45′ West, without sextant, chart or compass, wasn't a bad guess after thirty-seven days adrift in the cross currents and trade drifts which complicate that particular part of the Pacific Ocean. We had travelled over seven hundred and fifty miles by raft and dinghy and had about two hundred and ninety to go. We would have reached the American Coastal shipping lanes in ten more days and the coast in fifteen. Laboriously, I drew in on the chart the position of our sinking, and pointed out on the calendar the date we had been sunk. I drew a small picture of *Lucette* and the killer whales, then wrote a list of our names and nationality so that our worried relatives would know we were safe. The Captain nodded his understanding and shaking hands once more he wrinkled his nose and pointing at my tattered underclothing said 'Showa! Showa!' I could well imagine the powerful odours emanating from my blood and grease soaked rags though I could smell nothing. (I remembered how during my days in the Mercantile Marine, we had picked up some survivors in the Karimata Straits near Indonesia after they had been adrift for ten days, and they had smelled with a pretty powerful odour then.) The only part of our bodies that seemed to be in no need of cleaning was our teeth! They were unfurred and felt smooth and polished to the feel of our tongues.

I staggered back to the foredeck where the family and Robin were seated with their backs against the hatch coaming, in their hands tins of cool orange juice, and a look of blissful content on their faces. I picked up the tin that was left for me, smiled my thanks to the Japanese who grinned broadly back at me, then lifting my arm said 'Cheers'. I shall remember the taste of that beautiful liquid to the end of my days. I looked at the twins, the juice seemed to be reflected in their bright eyes and their smiling lips, and suddenly my legs gave way and I flopped on the deck, holding my can of juice from spilling. We all laughed at my awkwardness and I crawled beside Lyn, sat down with the can to my lips and sucked like a child at the breast; mother's milk must taste like this to a hungry child, and I thought how lucky I was; an hour ago I had been ready to accept death and here I was, being re-born!

The Japanese crew carried the twins to the large four-feet deep, hot sea water bath, Robin and Douglas tottering along behind on uncertain legs. There in the fresh water shower (we had to readjust our ideas to the notion that fresh water could be used for other things besides drinking!) they soaped and lathered and wallowed in luxury, scrubbing at the brown scurf which our skins had developed, but this took many days to disappear. Then Lyn and I luxuriated in the warmth of the deep tub. The ecstasy of not having to protect boil covered parts of our anatomies from solid contacts had to be experienced to be believed, and the simple joy of soap lathering in fresh water is surely one of the greatest luxuries of civilised mankind.

New clothes had been laid out for us from the ship's stores

and the kind concern shown us by these smiling warm-hearted seamen was almost too much for our shattered emotions. How cosy to have garments that were soft and dry. With the tingling sensation of cleanliness came awareness of the rags we had taken off, poor worn done things, they had kept the sun off and had held the moisture next to our skins to keep us cool; they had even, on occasion, helped to keep us warm when the night winds blew on our rain-soaked bodies; now destined for the broad reaches of the Pacific, I felt thankful that my bones were not inside them.

On our return to the foredeck, there on the hatch stood a huge tray of bread and butter and a strange brown sweet liquid called coffee. Our eyes gleamed as our teeth bit into these strange luxuries and in a very short space of time the tray was empty, the coffee pot was empty and our stomachs were so full that we couldn't squeeze in another drop. It felt rather like having swallowed a football. We tried to settle down to sleep on the tarpaulins and flags spread out on the deck inside the fo'c'stle for us, but the unaccustomed warmth became a stifling heat; the vibration of the engines, the whole attitude of relaxation and freedom to move around was so strange that sleep would not come, exhausted as we were. I lay thinking strange thoughts of the life in the sea, like a merman suddenly abstracted from an environment which has become his own and returned to a forgotten way of life amongst strangers. I felt lonely for the sea and for the uncomplicated issues there at stake, until I realised that my thoughts had for so long been centred on devising ways to reach land that this unexpected interruption of our plans, the destruction of our painfully acquired stores of food and water, the sudden abrogation of the survival laws, the tyranny of which still dominated our minds, was all rather overwhelming and we would need a few days to readjust to civilised channels of thought.

At about midnight, we could stand it no longer and staggered out on deck to seek the cool night air, the starlit skies, and the swell of the ocean. Robin, lucky man, was asleep. The junior watchkeeper, Hidemi Saito, a personable young Japanese who could speak one or two words in English, and had a phrase book with the usual inappropriate situations, came up the foredeck and after enquiring the cause of our unease, brought us our second meal, a noodle congė with small pieces of beef. The flavour was enchanting! He then plied us with sleeping pills which didn't make the slightest difference to our mental turmoil. Robin appeared just in time to finish off the remainder of the congė and we brought our pieces of bedding out on deck and rested under the stars.

In the days that followed we indulged in the luxury of eating and drinking wonderful food, the meals growing in quantity and sophistication. The familiar figure of the cook, Sakae Sasaki, became the symbol around which our whole existence revolved as he bore tray after tray up the foredeck to us. Spinach soup, prawns, fruit juices, fried chicken, roast pork, tinned fruit, fermented rice water, coffee and, a special treat, lemon-flavoured tea; and always in the background of our diet, like the foundation stones of a building, bread and butter. The assault upon our stomachs seemed unending and even when they were full, we still felt hungry – a most frustrating sensation! Our bones and bodies ached in contact with the unyielding deck, luxuriated in the deep hot sea water bath, groaned under the burden of indigestion, relaxed in the cool of the tropical night, and each day we gently exercised our swollen ankles and weakly legs, learning to walk again.

The Japanese crew took the twins to their hearts and showered them with kindness. They had already made gifts of clothing to us all, soap and toilet requisites, towels, notebooks and pens. They delighted in watching the twins draw, write and play together.

It took four days for *Tokamaru* to reach Balboa, by which time we had to some extent learned to use our legs again; in four days Captain Kiyato Suzuki and his wonderful crew brought the milk of human kindness to our tortured spirits and peace to our savage minds. They also removed the bitter canker of revenge from my character for when I had been a young man, my ship had been bombed and sunk by the Japanese war machine, and the memory of the screams of the trapped firemen in the stokehold and the flesh hanging in strips from the bodies of my friends had lived with me in bitterness through the years, through my later visits to Japan, and even through the rescue of my family and myself. These kindly fishermen were a new generation of men whose character bore no resemblance to the ogres in my memory, for they not only bore friendship to us, but also to each other. Their humanity regained my respect for their nation.

If for no other reason than this one, the voyage of *Lucette* had been worth my while, but as we watched Douglas and the twins talking and drawing pictures with their new-found Japanese friends Lyn and I felt that they too had become citizens of the world, learning to communicate without the help of language, knowing that men and women of other nations and races had hopes, fears and ambitions which were not so different from our own.

We arrived in Panama at four o'clock in the morning and as *Tokamaru I* eased her way under the Bridge of the Americas and entered her berth in Balboa, the popping of flashbulbs from the cameras of the press, the shouted questions, and the rush and bustle of television and radio reporters thrusting microphones under our noses, made us wonder if the broad silent reaches of the Pacific Ocean were not to be preferred! An oasis of peace was imparted to us by the able management of the situation by Mr Daly, the British Consul in Panama City, and in his care and protection we were conducted through a short press conference and had photographs taken with our Japanese friends. Lyn and the children wept as they said 'Goodbye' in new-learned Japanese: 'Me-na-san, ka-za-ku, sy-an-ara.' (Thank you, we shall not forget, farewell!) The news fraternity, delighted to have this demonstration of emotion on our return to civilisation, allowed us to go in peace and we were whisked off to the large American-style Hotel Executive where we immediately resumed our pursuit of allaying the insatiable hunger of our bodies by the consumption of large quantities of steak and eggs, with pancakes and waffles on the side, and ice cream to follow. (Douglas and Robin had three breakfasts each that morning, only one of which was supposed to satisfy a rancher!)

Our medical examination, conducted with care by the staff of Santo Tomas Hospital, Panama City, found us to be anaemic (in spite of our bloodthirsty practices) but already recovering from the after-effects of severe dehydration (one of which is an inability to walk). Sandy had a slight bronchial pneumonia which was treated with antibiotics without requiring his admittance to hospital, and Neil had suffered more generally from the effects of dehydration than the rest of us. Our legs were subject to swelling if exercised too much and we were told to resume normal activity slowly. Blood pressures were not exceptional and pulse rates although high (90 to 120) were attributed to the strain and the overloading of our digestive systems, also to our continuing sleeplessness. (I could still only manage two hours a night.) We had all lost weight, between twenty and thirty pounds each, from bodies that weren't fat to start with, but this and subsequent examinations have disclosed no lasting ill-effects either external or internal.

During the ensuing days in Panama City we received cables and telephone calls from our friends and relatives from all parts of the world, offering and giving help to us in our time of need. It was an experience in friendship which completed the good work already started by our Japanese friends, and made our rehabilitation so much easier. Robin flew back to England ten days later and we boarded the MV *Port Auckland* in Colon the following day to return at a more leisurely pace. As we waved goodbye to the Jansen family, our good friends in Colon, we felt that a new world had opened before us, and that though *Lucette* was gone and our small savings with her, the wealth and depth of the experience we had gained could not be measured in terms of money.